W W Bates

2020

Casting into Mystery

ROBERT REID

with engravings by

WESLEY W. BATES

Published by The Porcupine's Quill, 68 Main Street, PO Box 160, Erin, Ontario NOB 1TO. http://porcupinesquill.ca

Edited by Stephanie Small.

Represented in Canada by Canadian Manda.
Trade orders are available from University of Toronto Press.

Library and Archives Canada Cataloguing in Publication

Title: Casting into mystery / Robert Reid ; engravings by Wesley W. Bates.
Names: Reid, Robert Frederick, 1951– author. | Bates, Wesley W., illustrator.
Identifiers: Canadiana 20190177845 | ISBN 9780889844285 (softcover)
Subjects: LCSH: Fly fishing. | LCSH: Fly fishing—Anecdotes.
Classification: LCC SH456 .R45 2019 | DDC 799.12/4—dc23

We acknowledge the support of the Ontario Arts Council and the Canada Council for the Arts for our publishing program. The financial support of the Government of Canada is also gratefully acknowledged.

For Dylan Thomas and Robertson Taylor.
Cast straight and true, my sons.

—Robert Reid

To the memory of my parents
Ann and Stuart Bates
and to Juanita for her continuing encouragement.

—Wesley Bates

Table of Contents

———

Wild Speck 9

Wild Speck

Fish hits,
            shattering a
     sleepless stupor.

           Living bamboo wand lifts,
        spontaneous reflex
                setting hook.

Conversation begins.

Line tightens, slicing water,
          audible as a guitar string.

Rod bends
           in sweetly singing arc,
        shivering, quivering
             roused from slumber.

Throbbing vibration, electric current
            sliver of reflected, refracted light,
       fleeting and evanescent.

             Time contracts—
      past and future
        frozen in Now.

Heart races erratically
         as fish torpedoes,
       conspiring with roiling current.

Shout of 'fish on'
interrupts eventide silence.

Primeval battle anew.

Fish and angler connect,
        a tenuous, tenacious thread woven
    into the brocade of life—
            until victory is declared.

Elation or dumb regret
            disproportionate to size,
        savage beauty
            beyond description, beyond translation.

Ferocious life fighting
            on lip of presumed death.

Wild speck answering
                mad mystic Willie Blake:
            eternity in palm of hand,
                world where *every* thing is Holy.

The Calling

The Mystery of Fly Fishing

———————

The book you are holding is a creative partnership between a writer and an engraver, both of whom cast in awe of the mystery of fly fishing. It therefore embodies and reflects two currents in the river of art: word and image.

I am excited by this creative fusion. I believe engraving is the ideal visual companion to prose narrative. Norman Maclean apparently agrees. In his masterwork, *A River Runs Through It*, he describes a river's anatomy in terms that an engraver would recognize. Maclean connects patterns to rivers to books, which makes it possible for word and image to merge.

The creative partnership on which our book is built evolved from friendship. I started writing a blog after retiring from newspaper journalism in 2015. It featured postings on fly fishing among other passions. I soon began dreaming about publishing a collection of essays. I had a specific book in mind—one that would blend text and image in an organic way, like complementary current seams in a river. I dreamed of collaborating with Wesley, whom I had met in 2001 when he was artist-in-residence at Kitchener's historic Joseph Schneider Haus.

Our paths crossed a few times over the years. We discovered we admired many of the same writers and artists, including American agrarian writer Wendell Berry, with whom Wesley continues to collaborate, as well as American artists Winslow Homer and Rockwell Kent. Wesley was commissioned to do engravings for books written by Canadian authors I respect, including W. O. Mitchell (who taught his sons to fly fish), Timothy Findley and James Reaney. I was pleased to learn that Wesley enjoyed fly fishing. He also did a lot of canoeing while living on the West Coast.

I suggested to John Tutt, co-owner of Waterloo's Princess Cinemas, that he invite Wesley to the screening of *Look & See*, a poetic film on the life, writing and influence of Berry, in which the engraver appears. Wesley lives in Clifford, an hour's drive north of Waterloo, so there is a connective thread between rural southwestern Ontario and Berry's rural Kentucky in which I take deep delight.

After the screening we adjourned to a brewery pub and I hoisted a pint with Wesley and his wife, Juanita, a singer/songwriter. Between sips he asked if I would consider working together on a book devoted to fly fishing. I could not believe my ears. He had suggested the *exact* creative collaboration I had been contemplating.

Wesley's engravings are not conventional illustrations. Rather they comprise a graphic narrative that enhances and enriches the prose narrative. Think of two fly anglers sharing a stretch of river or casting from the bow and stern of a canoe on a lake.

Working—and playing—with Wesley has been great fun. Joining him on photographing and sketching trips on my home water (the Grand River) and fishing with him on his home water (the Saugeen River) have been deeply satisfying. Discussions regarding our book's nature confirmed that we continued to read the water from complementary perspectives. Watching his engravings evolve from ideas through sketches and watercolours has been revelatory.

I associate engraving with fly fishing. I find it interesting that the golden age of fly fishing at the turn of the last century coincided with the golden age of wood engraving as a graphic art form. An accident? I think not. When it comes to engraving and fly fishing, less is more. Both are introverted activities, contemplative and meditative in approach and execution. Recalling Henry David Thoreau, engravers

and fly anglers march to a different drummer, which puts them out of step in the cacophonous parade of modernity.

Wesley carving the end grain of a hard-maple wood block reminds me of a fly tier over a vise. These are meeting places where nature and science, tradition and innovation, organic and industrial, art and craft, merge. Engraving is a communion of wood and metal (burin); fly tying is a communion of fur and feather, fabric and metal. Both are acts of transformation that require faith in the process as much as skill with tools of the trade. Both are philosophical, as well as aesthetic, enterprises.

The process of carving a wood block reminds me of casting a fly rod. Both are unforgiving. Precision is everything. Nothing is random. There is no room for error. A bad cut cannot be saved any more than a bad cast can be redeemed.

Wesley and I settled on our title, *Casting into Mystery*, because it encompasses a variety of considerations bridging fly fishing and art. Like art, water, fish and angling lend themselves to symbolic meaning beyond the literal and commonplace. They bridge the profane and the sacred. They are archetypal in thrust.

The word *casting* carries multiple meanings as both verb and noun, subject and object. In application it is both literal and figurative.

In its verb form *casting* refers to placing a fly attached to the tippet at the end of a leader onto the water. This is called presentation. Anglers cast the fly purposely at specific spots where fish are seen rising or are believed to be holding. Conversely, they cast to spread the fly over a wide area when they are uncertain where fish are holding. This down-and-across swing cast is used with wet flies, nymphs and streamers.

Anglers avoid casting shadows on water that spook skittish fish who survive by protecting themselves from predators. Only the most literal of fly anglers reject the notion that, at least poetically, fly fishing casts an ineffable spell best described as magical.

In its noun form *casting* commonly refers to an object made by pouring molten metal into a mold and, in the process, changing a liquid into a solid. This describes Wesley and me in our efforts to transform our experiences on the water into images and words that transcend the practice of fishing and dip into deeper metaphysical currents.

Some of the essays that became chapters in *Casting into Mystery* had their genesis on the water, the result of casting my mind at fleeting thoughts that subsequently acquired shape as observations or ideas. Other essays originated at my writing desk as I cast my thoughts back to earlier experiences on the water. Casting is both imagination (William Blake) and memory (William Wordsworth), both of which are necessary to the poetry of fly angling.

Although we do not include the word *line* in the title, it is implied. All manner of lines give shape to our book. They draw together many of its themes, preoccupations and concerns. Lines connect substance and structure, content and form. They connect vocation with avocation. The difference between fly fishing and other types of angling entails the line propelling an artificial fly rather than a lure or hook and sinker propelling the line. When anglers cast, they 'inscribe' lines on water, as artists draw lines on paper. I have heard it said of fly casters that they 'paint' the water with lines. I can only imagine what it would have been like to witness Tom Thomson or Winslow Homer brushing the water with the strokes of a fly rod.

Poetry and prose, music and visual art wade through these pages. Writing is an art of lines, whether made by discursive writing with a fountain pen, by typewriter keys onto bonded paper or by keyboard onto computer screen. Likewise line is the foundational element of visual art. Engraving is an art of lines in relief, carved with a burin on a block of wood cut across the end grain.

We customarily refer to lines of poetry, as we do to lines of melody. Music compositions are notated on lined paper. Richard Hugo hears music when he casts a fly line. In 'Langaig', collected in *The Right Madness of Skye*, the Seattle-born poet and fly angler tells anglers to hum a tune while fishing hard. This is good advice.

Fly fishing is synonymous with mystery. It is the central concept underlying and informing our book. I am not the first writer to make this observation. In his introduction to the Modern Library edition of *The Compleat Angler*, Howell Raines, an American newspaperman and avid angler, equates fish with truth, and contends that Izaak Walton's book endures because mystery lies at the heart of fishing.

The mystery begins with water, the source of life—and home to fish. My Scottish ancestors believed that water is holy, that water is alive with mystery. It is also a repository for stories, which Linda

Hogan, in *Dwellings: A Spiritual History of the Living World*, places at the centre of healing, ceremony and ritual. Prayer is the language of water, as water is the language of prayer.

Water is a living symbol of cleansing, purification, healing, fertility, regeneration, restoration and renewal. It is the archetypal source of being since *all* life issues from, and returns to, water. There is no life without water. It is home to the Great Goddess found in many of the world's enduring mythologies.

Water is a meeting place. The preeminent element of spirit, it is associated with memory and remembrance, dream and vision. Anglers recognize the mystery in the surface film of water between the seen and unseen, visible and invisible, known and unknown, actual and abstract—representing the line between consciousness and the unconscious. Sounding like Blake transplanted to New England, Thoreau touches on the metaphysics of water in *Walden* when he observes: 'Time is but the stream I go a-fishing in. I drink at it; but while I drink I see the sandy bottom and detect how shallow it is. Its thin current slides away, but eternity remains.'

Jerry Kustich evokes the sacred mystery of rivers in his angling memoir, *Holy Water*, when he contemplates the nature of rivers in evocative, generous, open-ended language: 'One leads to another, and then another. They flow on forever, and forever connected, they enrich our souls and touch our spirits with mysteries that none of us can fully comprehend.'

Like rivers, fish are emblems of mystery. They swim through the currents of myth, legend, literature, art, music, religion, ritual and ceremony. Chad Wriglesworth, who read a draft of my manuscript with an eye to correspondences, reminded me of the last paragraph of Cormac McCarthy's futuristic elegy *The Road*, which draws a line between brook trout in mountain streams and the hum of mystery.

Spanning the primordial past and the anxious present, the practice of fishing abounds in mystery. In *A Week on the Concord and Merrimack Rivers*, Thoreau describes a fisherman as a religious sage: 'Human life is to him very much like a river.... His fishing was not a sport, nor solely a means of subsistence, but a sort of solemn sacrament and withdrawal from the world, just as the aged read their bibles.' I am grateful to have met a couple such anglers, especially in my youth when experience shapes an enquiring heart.

In *Walden* Thoreau recognizes the mystery of fishing as a 'higher law' connecting primitivism with adventure, and wildness with spirituality:

I found in myself, and still find, an instinct toward a higher, or, as it is named, spiritual life, as most men do, and another toward a primitive rank and savage one, and I reverence them both. I love the wild not less than the good. The wildness and adventure that are in fishing still recommended it to me.

Fly fishing is mystery made tangible. As American author and fly angler Maximilian Werner observes in *The Bone Pile: Essays on Nature & Culture*: 'To fish is to wonder, and wondering is a kind of fishing.' As such it provides framework by which anglers direct their sense of wonder into a purposeful and meaningful worldview.

In her poem 'The Fish' from *American Primitive*, Mary Oliver celebrates the mystery of fishing, from catching and gutting to cooking and eating. As the poem unfolds the narrator becomes water, becomes fish, finally recognizing that humans are sustained by the mystery with which fishing is imbued.

More than any other sport or recreation, let alone other forms of angling, fly fishing welcomes simile and metaphor, symbol and allegory. It occupies a room with a view of a cascading river in the home of literature.

No element of fly fishing embodies and enacts mystery as much as casting. It is choreographed ballet on water, grace in motion, both sensual and sensuous. Presenting the right fly, the right way, to the right place, at the right time, does not guarantee a hit or a strike. Setting the hook and landing a fish is never a certainty. The process is wrapped in chance, tied with luck and knotted with fortune. Fishing is not necessarily catching. If it were, its mystery would vanish, like a magician's cheap parlour trick.

The insects fish eat—including caddis and stoneflies, but especially mayflies—embody mystery which they enact through stages of metamorphosis. They play out the cycle of life in a drama unfolding over as short a period as twenty-four hours. The cycle of one species is replaced by the cycle of another species.

Insect hatches and spinner falls possess mystery because they connect the element of air to the element of water. These transformative processes, which revolve around procreation, arise as suddenly as snow squalls. Engaged in the dance of life in death, they rouse fish from slumber and stimulate insatiable appetite.

I know of no better description of rises than that of British politician and angler John Waller Hills, who writes eloquently of the natural phenomenon in *A Summer on the Test*:

There is a quality of magic about these early spring rises. The river looks dead and lifeless.... The stream runs with a dull, lead-like surface, which nothing disturbs and apparently nothing will disturb. You expect a rise and it does not come, and then suddenly, when you have given up expecting, trout start moving simultaneously.... At one moment you see fly after fly sailing down untaken, and you think nothing will ever break the unbroken surface: at the next the river is alive with rings of rising fish. It has come to life, and the sturdy vital trout, which a moment ago were hidden so completely that you doubted their existence, have mysteriously appeared.

The mystery of hatches and spinner falls cannot be explained in polite company if the topic of sex is off limits. The long and short of it is, mayflies fornicate themselves to death. I will leave it to others to decide whether this makes the bugs the envy of Creation. Still when a fly angler muses, 'I wish I were a mayfly,' it is not simple whimsy.

Similarly, there is mystery in riseforms, sometimes called dimple rings. Watch closely the endlessly expanding concentric circles caused by fish rising to eat insects off the surface film of water. It is impossible to tell when they dissipate—like a trout shadow darting for cover or the dreams of childhood that are no more, like slipping into slumber or closing your eyes for the last time. Vanishing is a process forever eluding our grasp.

Sometimes fish quietly sip infinitesimal bugs like grandams relishing orange pekoe from china cups; other times they loudly slurp huge bugs like ravenous adolescent boys after football practice. The eating habits of fish defy digestive logic. Anglers often catch fish with flies that are as big as the fish eating them.

In *A River Runs Through It* Maclean describes riseforms poetically when he recalls his father thinking of the timelessness of raindrops. These are as rich in mystery as the daily cycle embedded in the seasonal cycle, which comprise the fly anglers' calendar. They are as potent with mystery to me as the standing stones were to the ancient Celts. Rivers are sites of ceremony and ritual.

Watching a dry fly approach and penetrate a riseform is an electrifying moment to which all fly anglers are drawn. For some reason it reminds me of magnified images of male sperm penetrating the female ovum at the moment of fertilization, thus initiating the eternal cycle of life and death. Harry Plunket Greene celebrates this occurrence in *Where the Bright Waters Meet*:

I love looking into the light on the water, watching for the rise, and seeing my fly float down into the ring, and never knowing till it comes to him whether he will rise or not.... The tense excitement of watching it enter the circle and waiting for the strike is, for me, far greater than that of seeing any fish, however big, come to your fly.

Tying artificial flies is not only emblematic of mystery, it is an active agent of mystery. If imitation is the highest form of flattery, then nothing compliments nature more elegantly than inert natural and synthetic materials transformed into 'living' aquatic insects and critters, terrestrial bugs and fish to entice other fish to eat. This legerdemain is never less than craft. At its highest level, it is art.

I know of no angling author who writes more eloquently of fly tying than Ted Leeson in *The Habit of Rivers*, where he links 'things with feathers' to hope, which beats at the heart of angling. The difference between fly fishing and other forms of the sport is that the pleasure lies primarily in *participation* rather than in achievement, which is to say, catching fish. I concede this assertion might not apply to all fly anglers, but it does to both Leeson and me. I agree when he asserts that lovers, poets and religious fanatics share much in common.

All of which leads inevitably and inexorably to the mystery of art. I have spent half a century trying to solve this mystery through study, contemplation and commentary—and failed. In essence making art defies explication. Despite interpretation and analysis, creativity remains an alchemical process. How a blank page becomes a story or a block of wood becomes an image are enigmas that transcend concept and technique, material and execution.

The mystery of fly fishing unfolds in the space between creation and recreation. It is in this shadowy space where art resides. This is what the protagonist Norman refers to in *A River Runs Through It* when he describes his brother Paul shadow-casting—a cast the author invents to serve the needs of his art, and which he explains as a fancy stunt. Paul's fly rod becomes a magic wand which enables him to become one with the river. By endowing fly fishing with beauty through perfection, he transforms craft into art.

Shadow-casting is a figure of speech that applies to many things and many situations. Although it has a basis in the poetics of fly fishing, it transcends the recreational sport. Montana poet James Galvin takes up Maclean's notion in 'Shadow-Casting', collected in *Resurrection Update*. The poem is an account of a boy in the aftermath of his father's death. The boy goes to a stretch of river he always fished with his father. His grief is too painful for words. It can be expressed only through the grace of muscle memory. Shadow-casting becomes a metaphor for mourning, the personification of grief.

The mystery of friendship suffuses this book. I have long been fascinated by creative friendships including those of Coleridge and Wordsworth, of Emerson and Thoreau. The same goes for the friendship of Tom Thomson and the artists who became the Group of Seven, not to mention songwriters Bill Morrissey, Greg Brown and Garnet Rogers.

Then there are the fellowships forged by a shared dedication to fishing. Izaak Walton and Charles Cotton comprise the most famous friendship in angling history. Fellow Michigan-born writers Jim Harrison and Thomas McGuane shared angling adventures for years, sometimes in the company of such merry pranksters as Richard Brautigan, Russell Chatham, Dan Gerber, Guy de la Valdene and Jimmy Buffett.

My friendships with Gary Bowen and Dan Kennaley extend beyond fly fishing. Still, this book would not have been written had I not befriended both men, many years apart.

Long before I returned to fishing at mid-life and subsequently picked up a fly rod, I enjoyed an extended dialogue with angling. That dialogue shapes this book. In addition to recording personal experiences on the water, the essays are conversations with writers, musicians and visual artists who share my passion. Wesley's engravings are another voice in this cordial exchange. I have not met Jerry Kustich, except through a bamboo fly rod I cherish, email exchanges and his quartet of angling memoirs. Yet I converse with him throughout these pages. His generosity and fidelity represent fly fishing at its most collegial. Even if I did not write about fly fishing, I would still enjoy the recreational sport. But it would be with less devotion, less passion, with less heart, less soul. The writers, musicians and visual artists who wade through these pages accompany me on the streams, rivers and lakes I fish. They are welcome companions when I relax in my armchair over an evening of reflection at home. Their words, melodies and images deepen and broaden my contemplation of life both on and off the water.

The above paragraph should be taken literally. Readers expecting something like a *Diary of Pastoral Rambles on Gentle Streams*, with a morsel of homespun philosophy to aid digestion, are sure to suffer heartburn—even though I tip my oilskin fedora to this literary tradition, which I very much admire. Rather, *Casting into Mystery* is a trout of different spots. My approach is encapsulated in an observation Mark Browning makes in *Haunted by Waters: Fly Fishing in North American Literature*—that mystery is at the heart of angling and writing, as it is at the heart of reader and author.

My intention is to place fly angling in a cultural context—albeit a highly personal, maybe even eccentric, context. I think of our book as a streamside cultural companion, an anatomy or miscellany of the literature, visual art, music, film and spirituality that enrich and enlarge the recreational sport. With this in mind, I encourage readers to study Wesley's engravings closely. They are more complex than they might at first appear. Remember they are not illustrations, but windows opening onto the river of mystery.

Like most fly anglers, I fish for different species, on different rivers or different stretches of the same river, at different times of the day and of the year, even if trout remain my species of choice at dusk on home water. This habit of angling is replicated in the structure of *Casting into Mystery*, making it a literary fusion of styles and approaches. While most of the chapters are memoir, they also adapt other narrative forms spanning essay and critical commentary, travelogue and eulogy, appreciation and profile.

Some of the chapters are journalistic in approach. It is hard for me to abandon a habit of writing developed with so much sweat and more than a little blood. Others are personal, a new habit of writing that I am trying to polish as I muddle through my allotted four score and ten with fly rod firmly in hand.

I agree that fly anglers need to be methodical if they want to be successful; however, spontaneous joy evaporates when order becomes systematized. I prefer following the contours of a river, going where it takes me—organically, if you will. Casting should not always be predictable. Surprise is a vital element of fly angling. It is part of the fun. I apply this principle to reading and writing. As a reader I prefer not knowing where the writer is taking me. As a writer I enjoy meandering occasionally. Prospecting down a tributary provides its own rewards.

I take pleasure in Thoreau referring to walking as sauntering, which he viewed as *purposeful* wandering. As a result of how I like to fish, read and write, the chapters comprising *Casting into Mystery* are sometimes discursive. Still I hope they never lose sight of themselves and become tiresome. Time is precious and should not be squandered, especially when it cuts into angling.

I have come to believe that there are essentially two kinds of fly anglers: poets and pragmatists. I have encountered the latter who have jokingly queried whether the title of this book is *Casting into Misery*. I confess I wrote this book for the poets among fly anglers and non-anglers alike, whether or not they have ever written a line of verse.

As humans we strive to find answers to the fundamental questions that existence asks. Some seek answers in various wisdom traditions, in literature, music and art. Others seek answers in religion,

mind-expanding drugs and at the bottom of a bottle. Fly fishing has taught me that answers are not as important as asking the right questions. When I stand knee deep in a river, casting my bamboo fly rod, I am held in the embrace of mystery. I am one precious note in a cosmic symphony, a whisper on the wind.

So it remains for readers to cast their imaginations into mystery while savouring a pint of local craft beer or a dram of *usage beatha*, distilled from the pure, clear waters of trout and salmon in the country of my ancestors.

Tight lines and *Sláinte*!

The Idea of North

I am a fly fisherman because of an idea with tendrils in childhood and friendship. It involves my closest childhood friend, Bill Everett, and his parents, Len and Selina. Like my dad, Len was a firefighter. Unlike my working mom, Selina was a homemaker.

Billy, an only child, lived around the corner. We went to the same elementary school until my family moved across town before I started grade five. He was like a brother. One of the joys of friendship was travelling with him and his parents. They introduced me to camping and fishing. When I was ten years old I joined them on a six-week road trip 'out West' to British Columbia. It was the great summer adventure of my youth.

It was through them that I was introduced to the 'Idea of North'. The phrase comes from the title of one of three one-hour documentaries Glenn Gould produced for CBC Radio under the title of *Solitude Trilogy*. Canada's legendary pianist and composer, who spent considerable time at his family cottage on Lake Muskoka, developed an intimate relationship with the Canadian North. It formed the basis of his trilogy which he started in 1967 and completed in 1977. I am still debating with myself whether he heard the music of J.S. Bach in northern winds or heard northern winds in the music of J.S. Bach.

The Idea of North has always suggested to me that North is more than a cardinal point on the compass, a geographical region, a geological formation or a degree of latitude. North is a frame of mind, an interior geography, a metaphysical construct. It is a country of the imagination, a frontier where old spirits dwell, a shifting, wavering borderline reflecting the aurora borealis. This is the true north, strong and free; the Great White North of literature, music and visual art; the mythology of the country's natural character, a meeting place of mind, heart and soul. It offers a solution to the riddle celebrated literary critic Northrop Frye posed in *The Bush Garden*, which he held as central to Canadian sensibility: Where is here?

My love of rivers and passion for fly fishing are offshoots of the Idea of North, which I first experienced when I started going 'Up North' with Billy to visit his uncle Fred and aunt Pat. Technically they lived in southern Ontario, but my introduction to the Canadian Shield was all the North my youthful imagination required. These trips were a litmus experience that shaped many of my ideas about life and living far beyond the outdoors.

Uncle Fred and Aunt Pat lived the life envisioned by Thoreau in his essay 'Walking' where he refers to 'man' as 'an inhabitant, or a part and parcel of Nature'. They embodied the process whereby people who inhabit the land become an integral part of the landscape, forming a blood bond of heart, body and soul—a process Harry Middleton describes poetically in *The Earth is Enough*.

Middleton was a nature writer in the Southern 'poetic' tradition who died much too young, at the age of forty-three, from a suspected brain aneurysm. He wrote about fly fishing with a biblical passion, equal parts prayer and hymn. He recognized that there is no separation between matter and spirit, earth and soul. Despite hardship, our Good Earth provides generously and abundantly. It is all we need, according this great undervalued writer.

Uncle Fred and Aunt Pat lived on a marginal farm outside of South River, a village in the foothills of the Laurentian Mountains, fifty-two kilometres south of North Bay. Talk about excitement. We left school at noon on the Friday morning of a long weekend, whether Easter, Victoria Day or Thanksgiving. We spent longer periods visiting over Christmas or March Break and during the summer.

The six-hour drive in hospitable weather grew more thrilling when we left the four lanes of the 401 and 400 and travelled the two lanes of Highway 11. The towns we passed had the allure of *X*s marked on a treasure map: Orillia, Gravenhurst, Bracebridge, Huntsville, Burk's Falls, Sundridge. Despite what official maps indicated, these were *northern* towns—at least to my mind at that time, half a century ago—in a *northern* land that embodied and enacted a *northern* spirit.

We always stopped for a late supper at the Girls' Truck Diner, a truckstop festooned with stuffed animals from the Canadian wilds. Outside there were a couple of forlorn bears in a cage salivating over whatever scraps were tossed their way—a sad, cruel thought today, but exciting as hell for a boy who slept with his BB gun beside his bed and thought fishing was surpassed only by hockey.

Best of all were Uncle Fred and Aunt Pat. They were figures cut from wilderness romance who followed the needle of their own compass—which always pointed True North. Although it was the 1960s, visiting was akin to folding back the blankets of time and crawling under the sheets of pioneer days. They subsisted on four hundred acres of hardscrabble, Precambrian scrubland—most of which was bush—not far from the southwest boundary of Algonquin Park. They had neither electricity nor indoor plumbing. They cooked and heated by hardwood cut with chainsaw and split with axe by Uncle Fred. The kitchen was always the coziest room in the house, its heart and its soul.

Aunt Pat was a robust redhead, freckled, with a smile as bright as the ivory keys on the piano she played with graceful enthusiasm. She had a temper, but it burned out quicker than it ignited. She augmented Uncle Fred's meagre disability pension by driving a school bus. Every Christmas she made Billy and me flannel pyjamas, stitched on a treadle Singer sewing machine.

Uncle Fred was a small man, sinewy as binder twine. His eyebrows resembled fat caterpillars perched above eyes of robin's-egg blue—one of which was glass. He had a high forehead, but his snowy hair was thick and tightly spun. He had lost his left leg at the knee to an errant forty-tonne log and wore a prosthetic brace. Despite his physical blemishes, he was a curiously handsome man, with a gentle disposition as durable as hickory. Despite his natural temperament, he had a wasplike stubborn streak when his ire was aroused. When I first read J.R.R. Tolkien's *The Hobbit* I immediately thought of Uncle Fred.

The index finger on his right hand being severed at the second knuckle did not prevent him from rolling his own cigarettes from Players rough-cut tobacco that came in a can (perfect for storing marbles, old coins, fishing lures, leather shoelaces, rocks, rodent skulls, snake skins, stones, fossils and shells). One, not always lit, was glued to the side of his toothless mouth from sunrise to bedtime. In the summer he wore hand-me-down white shirts—rolled up to the elbows—to discourage bloodthirsty blackflies.

Uncle Fred had names for each of the dozen head of beef cattle he raised and identified by their bells. Every morning at daybreak he retrieved buckets of cold water from a nearby creek. Every evening he would go searching for them. They treated fences as obstacles to freedom that were built for the sole purpose of being defied. He would scour the bush. *Ke-bosh, ke-bo-o-sh, ke-bosh*, he would call repeatedly: *Here me Maudie, me Maudie, me Maudie. Here me Susie, me Susie, me Susie.* Eventually the herd would come ambling homeward to stalls of hay in sheds hewn from Precambrian stone and timber beams as old as Confederation.

He bled Maple Leaf blue, shamelessly praising Keon and Armstrong, Kelly and the Big M, Horton and Stanley, Brewer and Baun. Conversely he spit raw contempt at the Canadiens. He did not have much to say about the other four teams comprising the Original Six. His devotion to the federal Conservatives, historic enemies of the dastardly Liberals, was steadfast. John Diefenbaker, whom he always referred to as Dief, was his man on The Hill.

Uncle Fred's eyes would moisten whenever he recalled having to put down his pair of border collies following a misunderstanding with a porcupine years earlier. He put down King with one merciful shot. The subsequent bullet grazed Queenie and his tender heart prevented him from putting another cartridge in the chamber. She lived a long life, despite quills lodged deep in her throat.

Meals were an occasion. We ate homemade bread baked in an antique wood-burning stove. (Uncle Fred continued baking bread well into his eighties, long after Aunt Pat died.) We enjoyed pan-fried brook trout and breaded partridge, roast venison and moose, even bear steaks. We also had such domesticated fare as roast beef with Yorkshire pudding; eggs collected daily from range-fed chickens; fresh vegetables from the garden or put up for winter; wild blueberries for mouthwatering pancakes and pies and preserves. We drank throat-numbing hard water from a hand pump.

I recall with mixed emotion the outhouse. In winter we negotiated a narrow path Uncle Fred packed down by snowshoe because of snow that exceeded six feet. The two-holer would be rimmed with thick, hoary frost. During the long, cold winter nights, which could plunge as low as forty degrees below zero, we used what we euphemistically called a thunder jug, tucked beneath queen-sized beds made cozy with layers of heavy quilt blankets.

I remember going outside for a pee with Billy and Uncle Fred at night. Once during a frosty Thanksgiving Uncle Fred observed: 'Boys, look at that sky. You don't see stars like that in the city.' He was right. Another time he described the call of a whippoorwill as 'lonesome'—a more poetic word than *lonely*, as Hank Williams well knew. Uncle Fred called the stream where we fished for brook trout 'the crick' and he referred to 'the bush' rather than to woods or forest.

Best of all was spending evenings around the big kitchen table, bathed in the warm patina of Coleman lanterns and coal oil lamps. The adults retold stories from the past while sipping bottles of Cinci beer (Len and Selina) or a glass of Canadian rye and cola (Uncle Fred). Aunt Pat was a teetotaller. Some of the stories involved Uncle Fred and Aunt Pat eloping, the young couple heading West so he could operate a bulldozer on the Al-Can Highway, along the British Columbia interior into Alaska during the Second World War. She once shooed away a grizzly by wielding a frenzied broom when their sons were babies.

I learned years later that they did not exchange vows until Aunt Pat was on her deathbed. They shared a full, rich life; however, they suffered more than their share of piercing sadness including the loss of their sons, Freddy and Tucky, to muscular dystrophy.

My recollections remain fresh today, six decades later: Walks in search of beaver ponds or abandoned shacks with forgotten stories of unknown people … hunting partridge after we obtained licences. One of my prized possessions was a twelve-gauge Winchester pump shotgun, purchased with savings from my first job as a bellhop at the Hotel London.… Dapping (also known as dappling) for brookies with long bamboo poles purchased for a couple of dollars at a hardware store in South River.… Helping Uncle Fred 'bring in' cords of winter wood which he spent weeks cutting throughout the fall, all the while cussing his temperamental chainsaw.… Taking in the crisp rustling of fall foliage or the thick snowfall of winter with a silence so intense you could hear your heartbeat pulsing against your eardrums.… Skating on frozen ponds in frozen fields, oblivious to penetrating winds and numbing sub-zero temperatures.… Playing as boys do: cowboys in the high country, explorers in uncharted territory, pioneers carving out a home in the New World or soldiers in harm's way behind enemy lines.

The Idea of North has stuck to the ribs of my imagination throughout my life. My first wife, Jude, and I honeymooned in Muskoka because we both had fond childhood memories of the area.

Although we were happy to be married, there was something out of joint. I sensed that a visit to Uncle Fred's would remedy our newlywed disenchantment.

It had been more than a decade since I had last seen Uncle Fred and Aunt Pat, who had passed in the intervening years. Uncle Fred, who had moved into town after selling the farm, was delighted to see me and my new bride. He served us tea with thick slices of homemade bread smothered in butter. We reminisced for a couple of hours. The visit changed the mood of our honeymoon and Jude and I returned home to London bathed in infectious delight.

The Idea of North was the driving force behind a vacation I took at age seventeen to the French and Ottawa rivers in my first car, a British-built Envoy Epic, with one of my dearest friends, Dave Salhani. Dave and I met in grade 10, after which I got him a job with me as a bellhop. He was best man at my first wedding and later became godfather to my sons, to whom my second wife, Lydia, gave birth. We remain dear friends more than fifty years later.

I remembered the Idea of North whenever Lydia, our sons, Dylan and Robertson (Robin), and I spent a week's vacation in the Kawartha Lakes not far from Bancroft. The rustic cottage, festooned with outdoor memorabilia, was on a private island in a lake boiling with large-mouth and smallmouth bass.

I carried the Idea of North with me whenever we travelled to Parry Sound to visit another dear friend, Steve Leslie and his family. Steve was best man when Lydia and I married. He died too young, a little more than a year into early retirement after he and his wife had built their dream home in Lake of Bays township.

I have fond memories of Steve inviting me to a fishing camp for a week in Temagami with eight other teachers. I caught bass and walleye for the freezer, in addition to my first Northern pike. Although I did not catch the forty-four-inch leviathan on the fly, I landed it on eight-pound monofilament rigged with bass tackle. I was so excited when we returned to camp that I polished off most of a bottle of single malt.

And I refresh and reset the Idea of North whenever I visit Dan Kennaley and his wife, Jan, at their island cottage on a small lake in Muskoka. Or visit Gary Bowen at the hunting camp he shares with his brothers, John and Rob, outside of Havelock, in Eastern Ontario.

The Idea of North defines much of who I am and determines

many of the beliefs I hold closest to my heart. Now that I read and write in response to choice and inclination rather than obligation and necessity, it shapes my creative life. It is reflected in the literature, visual art and music I most cherish. The Idea of North answers the question of why I fly fish after turning the page on the final chapter. It permeates this book as I remember those I love as family.

The Company of Rivers

I am a fly angler in no small measure because of my passion for rivers. Few writers knew rivers better and fewer still wrote about them more eloquently than the revered West Coast author Roderick Haig-Brown. I have taken to heart his observation in *A River Never Sleeps* that knowing a river thoroughly contributes significantly to the joy of fly fishing. And I share with him the pleasure of stepping into a river he so eloquently describes in *The Master and His Fish*, when he not only becomes one with the river, but one with the landscape. The immediate sensations of the river frees his mind, as he contemplates vast distances of time and space.

I have taken joy from the company of rivers all my life. The companionship began with the Thames River in my hometown of London, Ontario. I lived within walking distance of the river until I left for university at twenty-one years of age.

For the first decade, I lived four blocks from the river's south branch. I recall being eight or nine years old and making rafts out of pallets salvaged from General Steel Wares, located along the river for four or five city blocks. (I would be the fourth generation to work at the appliance manufacturer.) Accompanied by a couple of school chums, we were untamed Huck Finns ready to light out on *our* river.

Later I lived a block from its 'forks', where the north and south branches converge in the shadow of Museum London, the historic County Court House and Labatt Park, the oldest continuously operating baseball park in the world. The area was once known as Skunk's Hollow and it is where my dad was born and raised. I crossed the Dundas Street Bridge for the four years I attended H.B. Beal Secondary School and worked as a bellhop at the Hotel London, located 'in the heart of downtown London'.

Recalling those days I am reminded of Willie P. Bennett's song 'Music in Your Eyes' from his debut album *Trying to Start Out Clean*. The song's narrator looks back on his youth, when he sat on the riverbank and watched the river flowing by, dreaming about things that cannot be recovered once they are lost. Bennett lived in London when he wrote this bittersweet love song of longing, which more than any other evokes for me a green world turned to rust.

When I reflect on the river of my youth I think of the American poet James Wright. He grew up along the Ohio River in Martins Ferry, on the border of Ohio and West Virginia. Although he left the Ohio, the river never left him. It flows through his poetry. In 'Two Moments in Venice', he contends that, in contrast to what Thomas Wolfe claimed, people can find their way home again—by following the sound of water.

Then there was the Otonabee River in Peterborough, where I earned an honours bachelor's degree from Trent University. Margaret Laurence refers to it in *The Diviners* as 'the River of Now and Then' that flows both ways. One of my English professors, Barbara Rooke, told me she read one of my essays to Laurence over afternoon tea in nearby Lakefield, where the writer lived in a converted funeral home. In the essay I compared the notion of a river flowing both ways to Coleridge's 'Frost at Midnight', a poem I love dearly.

I befriended the St. John River for the eighteen months I lived in Fredericton earning a master's degree in English from the University of New Brunswick while working construction with a group of men on day parole after being convicted of sundry misdemeanours.

I spent nine months in Timmins, located on the banks of the Mattagami River, which was frozen for much of the time I was city editor at *The Daily Press*—Lord Thompson of Fleet's Art Deco dream crumbling in the cold heart of mining country.

I was introduced to the Grand River in 1984 when I joined the *Brantford Expositor*. One of my beat responsibilities was covering the Six Nations Reserve, so I came to learn that in 1784 the Haldimand Proclamation awarded the Haudenosaunee (Iroquois), also known as Six Nations Confederacy, a tract of land spanning ten kilometres on either side of the Grand, totalling 3,800 square kilometres. The decree was signed by Sir Frederick Haldimand, governor of Québec, in acknowledgement of the support the British received from their indigenous allies in the American Revolutionary War.

As my former newspaper colleague Bob Burtt records in his book *rare Moments in Time*—a history of the *rare* Charitable Research

Reserve in Cambridge, Ontario—the Grand's series of name changes reflects its history. Those who travelled its route for two millennia called it Tintaatuoa, French fur traders named it La rivière Rapide as early as 1669. It was later known as the River Urse. By the mid-1770s it was La Grande Rivière, and finally the Grand River.

I moved upriver two years later when I landed at the *Waterloo Region Record*. I have lived in Waterloo Region ever since, longer than anywhere else. It is where Dylan and Robertson were born. I know the Grand best for the simple reason that it is where I learned to fly fish. Fly rods are instruments of knowledge. The best way of learning about a city or forest is on foot. Likewise the best way of learning about a river is on foot, in chest waders and wading boots. Wading a river is travelling a living past, traversing the currents of history and geography.

The second-best way of learning about a river is by canoe. I have paddled the Grand from Inverhaugh, near Elora, to Paris. When I wound my way through Waterloo, Kitchener and Cambridge, I was amazed how different each city looks from the river. It was often difficult to identify locations familiar from streetscapes and bridges.

Rivers are vessels of time, both linear, which is to say chronological, and spatial, which is to say geological. When I stand in the Grand casting a fly rod I am in awe of the condensed layers of time of which

I am a part: prehistoric, indigenous and post–European contact. I am humbled by the limestone cliffs that guard so much of the river I most often fish. I love the fact that they are composed of the shells and skeletons of aquatic life compressed and compacted over millennia into hard sedimentary rock. Here is a synopsis of the river's evolution as outlined by Bob in *rare Moments in Time*:

• A river produced by retreating glaciers and climate change shapes the evolution of its landscape, along with its flora and fauna, while woolly mammoths and mastodons roam the watershed with elk, caribou and Arctic hare.

• A landscape resembling tundra gives way to a spruce/pine forest 10,500 years ago before subsequently giving way to an oak/pine forest between 8,000 and 10,000 years ago. About 4,000 years ago the landscape begins changing into a predominantly deciduous forest comprising the northern limits of the Carolinian Zone.

• Archeological findings confirm continuous habitation beginning in the Paleo Period (13,000 years ago). Iroquois arrive after the Woodland Period (3,000 to 10,000 years ago) and remain the primary occupants until the arrival of United Empire Loyalists from the American colonies, Mennonites from central Europe via Pennsylvania and dispossessed immigrants from the British Isles and Europe.

Rivers have distinct voices. Despite my fondness for the Grand, the headwaters of the Saugeen River, both the Rocky and the Beatty, speak to me most intimately of trout—native brookies, wild brown and rainbow. I also enjoy fishing for steelhead near the mouth of the Bighead River, which flows down from the Niagara escarpment into Georgian Bay.

I wish I had known better the rivers that coursed through my life. Still I am grateful the Grand has proven the exception. Thanks to fly fishing, I have become a student of rivers and, by extension, a student of cultures. My bamboo fly rods bridge East and West, connecting me to the wisdom traditions of an ancient culture.

Through contemplative recreation I study the nature of rivers. They are unique, idiosyncratic, fickle, constantly and continuously changing in character and mood, even appearance. They are seductive, cunning and shy, placid one minute, angry the next. Every time I wade into a river it is different from when I last waded it. And the next time will be different again. Rivers are not static. They are 'living, sentient creature[s]', as acknowledged by American literary critic and indefatigable fly fisherman Bliss Perry in *Pools and Ripples: Fishing Essays*. They are shaped constantly and continuously by the passage of time, which alters everything. Nothing remains the same.

Of course, this is not an original idea. Insisting that change is the most dependable constant in the universe, Heraclitus famously observed more than 2,500 years ago: 'No man ever steps in the same river twice, for it's not the same river and he's not the same man.' The Greek philosopher acknowledges that rivers and humanity are active agents in the same natural cycle. The concept encompasses geography and history, psychology and spirituality. Amerindian cultures refer to the Medicine Wheel. Buddhists refer to the Wheel of Life or Wheel of Becoming, a mandala that takes in the universe.

Every river has a story to tell, evoking memory, recollection and reminiscence. No wonder anglers are such irrepressible storytellers, tale-spinners who cast fact and fiction, wish and dream, not to mention exaggeration and hyperbole, into the current of narrative. I have come to associate rivers with personal narratives. Nothing would please me more than readers interpreting *Casting into Mystery* as a river flowing between covers.

When I cast a line on a river I invite conversation and dialogue. As Walton writes in *The Compleat Angler*, 'I love any discourse of rivers, and fish and fishing.' An angler asks and a river answers in a call and response, like an old folk song accompanying fieldwork or a hymn in a austere country church.

When wading a river I am accompanied by the friendly spirits of all who have cast an artificial fly before me. I anticipate all who will cast a fly after me, whether actual people, fictional characters of prose, poetry and song, or figures memorialized in drawings, paintings, prints and sculpture. I understand Edward Abbey, in *Down the River*, when he acknowledges ghosts who dip their toes in the moving waters.

Although fly fishing is a solitary act, I am never lonely on the water. This is no small matter in our manufactured world where loneliness is epidemic and where humankind is alienated from all the other species inhabiting the natural world. When I cast my fly rod the line extends backward to my origins and forward to my destiny. Casting is breathing in time to the heartbeat of the cosmos, as my Celtic ancestors believed. Rivers possess secrets, which they reveal slowly to patient anglers who answer the call—those who see and hear, smell and taste through senses, while processing thoughts through intellect, intuition and imagination. Coaxing a river to reveal what it keeps hidden beckons me to return again and again and again. Those confidences I carry with me, always.

LITERARY RIVERS

I relish the language and lexicon of rivers. I get almost as much pleasure from reading books about rivers as I do from wading in, or paddling on, rivers. A river does not have to be legendary, prominent or even well-known to hold my attention. Its mysteries are enough.

Many of the river books I love most share common themes and moods. While celebratory, they tend to be elegiac because they lament loss. In his essay 'History, Myth and the Western Writer', collected in *The Sound of Mountain Water*, Wallace Stegner mourns what civilization has done to destroy the wild and the beautiful, the dignified and the valiant.

Stegner did not write exclusively about rivers. But he wrote passionately, knowledgeably and eloquently about them. In addition to being one of the enduring writers of the American West, he was an influential literary conservationist in a line connecting Thoreau, John Burroughs and John Muir, through Ansel Adams, Aldo Leopold and Sigurd Olson, to Rick Bass, Gary Snyder, Barry Lopez, Annie Dillard and Abbey. His love of wilderness and his pioneering commitment to conservation is reflected in his prose, including a lyrical 'Overture' interlude in *The Sound of Mountain Water*. His writing awakens the senses before meditating on philosophical matters. His example informs the fly angling literature I love most. He is in tune with the symphony of life, given voice through the harmony of rivers.

My love of literary rivers began with *The Adventures of Huckleberry Finn*, which I read as an undergraduate. I remember being blown away by the novel. I concurred with Ernest Hemingway's assertion in *The Green Hills of Africa* that, 'All modern American literature comes from one book by Mark Twain called *Huckleberry Finn*.'

The language of Twain's masterwork is as green as the country that gave rise to it. It is the language of the American heartland before the infestation of industrial profit. To say it is vernacular would be accurate, but it would not capture its essence, which has the rigour, rhythm and syntax of poetry. Children do not actually speak like Huck. Yet the words strike a reader's ear as language spoken through the consciousness of childhood on the threshold between innocence and experience.

So I took my paddle and slid out from shore just a step or two, and then let the canoe drop along down amongst the shadows. The moon was shining, and outside of the shadows it made it most as light as day. I poked along well on to an hour, everything still as rocks and sound asleep. Well, by this time I was most down to the foot of the island. A little ripply, cool breeze begun to blow, and that was as good as saying the night was about done. I give her a turn with the paddle and brung her nose to shore; then I got my gun and slipped out and into the edge of the woods. I sat down there on a log, and looked out through the leaves. I see the moon go off watch, and the darkness begin to blanket the river. But in a little while I see a pale streak over the treetops, and knowed the day was coming.

I doubt there is in all of literature a fresher description of the moment when the darkness of night gives way to the light of day. A reader can smell its rich pungency. I cannot imagine Hemingway, not to mention Stegner or Cormac McCarthy, without Twain.

The second river book I came to admire was *A Week on the Concord and Merrimack Rivers*, which I first read in graduate school. Thoreau wrote the book while learning the right way to live at Walden Pond. Although he barely mentions his brother, John, the book eulogizes his death, which haunted Thoreau throughout his own short life.

I regret that *A Week* is so overshadowed by *Walden* (admittedly a much better book). Based on a trip the brothers made in 1839 from Concord, Massachusetts, to Concord, New Hampshire, Thoreau's first published work assembles essays, passages from his *Journal* and some of his best poetry, a literary form he never mastered. It reflects the enthusiasms of the Transcendental mystic who was on his way to becoming America's first literary naturalist. The book was not only a precursor to all of Thoreau's published work, but also provided the template for the tradition of river books it inspired. Early on the writer implies that it is more than a journal of a journey on local rivers:

Gradually the village murmur subsided, and we seemed to be embarked on the placid current of our dreams, floating from past to future as silently as one wakes to fresh morning or evening thoughts.

Like Thoreau, Edward Abbey was an American original, a thorny contrarian who had no truck with fools or fakes. The tradition of intellectual orneriness and moral disobedience unites the two writers. Thoreau brought wildness to cultivated Concord; Abbey brought cultivation to the wildness of the southwest desert.

Of all Abbey's writing, my favourite involves river trips, including the 'Down the River' chapter in *Desert Solitaire* and the chapters in his essay collection *Down the River*, especially 'Down the River with Henry Thoreau'. Abbey concludes the latter—which records a trip down Utah's Green River he made in the fall of 1980 armed with a dog-eared paperback copy of *Walden*—with incantatory words resembling a prayer as the New England mystic accompanies the modern iconoclast on a river which is America itself, past, present and future.

Rivers are living elegies. Many of the books I most cherish are written in homage to rivers that are about to change or even disappear through human intervention. Consequently they are books of memory—what was and is no more—preserved against the erosion of time.

Goodbye to a River is John Graves's account of his farewell to Texas's Brazos River in anticipation of a series of proposed dams expected to alter not only the river and its watershed, but the lives of people whose ancestors persevered in a beautiful yet unforgivably harsh environment. As Graves journeys by canoe with his beloved dachshund, Blue, in the fall of 1957, he respects what McCarthy referred to in *Blood Meridian* as the bloodlands while celebrating a river he knows intimately and loves unreservedly.

John Nichols's *The Annual Big Arsenic Fishing Contest* is also set in Texas. It is a ribald fish tale featuring three longtime buddies who gather every autumn over twenty years to compete in an angling contest, washed down with copious amounts of alcohol, sex and tomfoolery. The novel's fourth character is the Big Arsenic Springs on the Wild River section of the Rio Grande. Nichols's passion for the dramatic riverscape brings to mind Ansel Adams's majestic photographs. The juxtaposition of desert and river forms the basis of Barry Lopez's *Desert Notes/River Notes*, which brings together two visionary essays/narrative dream poems. Subtitled 'The Dance of Herons', the latter is a hymn to a mountain river in which the writer dreams of being a salmon. Although he does not mention fly fishing, Lopez knows instinctively that rivers are imprinted with the dreams of anglers who fish them.

Annie Dillard's *Pilgrim at Tinker Creek* is an account of a year spent in Virginia's Roanoke Valley, where the creek named in the title is located. Although her spiritual memoir is not specifically a river book, it is a meditation on the nature of *seeing*. Its theological frame is built on a foundation of close observation of the natural world, which reflects what Thoreau refers to in his *Journal* as 'a meteorological journal of the mind'.

Dillard's philosophical flights often elude my intellectual grasp. However, I gain hold when she focuses on the particulars of nature. Fly anglers can learn from her description of stalking a muskrat as an absolute form of skill. Change the word *muskrat* to *trout* and you have sage angling advice. Fishing is a form of hunting that predates ancient cave paintings, even if many fly anglers are reluctant to acknowledge this elemental fact.

I have fished the Blue Ridge Mountains of North Carolina only once. It is a region to which I intend to return. Meanwhile, I retain deep respect for a couple of books devoted to the region's rivers.

It would be difficult to find an angler more intimately connected to rivers than Christopher Camuto. *A Fly Fisherman's Blue Ridge* is an affectionate anatomy of the region's small, freestone, headwater trout rivers. Tracing the cycle of one season, he presents fly angling as a living tradition rather than a sport. Camuto is as interested in the flora and fauna, the climate and weather, the history and geography, as he is in native brook trout, wild brownies and rainbows. He casts a mournful eye on the ecological degradation caused by destructive land-use practices condoned by governments pandering to the interests of big business rather than to environmental protection. Sadly his dire warning continues to be ignored by the twin engines of aggressive capitalism and passive government.

Noah Adams's *Far Appalachia* pays tribute to a river in the aftermath of human intervention including mining, logging, railway development and dam construction. A native of eastern Kentucky, Adams returns to Appalachia in 1997 to travel the New River from its source on North Carolina's Snake Mountain, through Virginia, to its mouth in West Virginia. Travelling by canoe and raft, with intervals on foot and bicycle, he distills the region's history and natural beauty with the lives of people he meets along the way.

James Dickey's *Deliverance* is a river novel with a dark, sinister current. Equal parts Southern gothic, hillbilly noir, pastoral satire, wilderness thriller and eco-dystopia, it traces four suburbanites as they canoe the fictional Cahulawassee River, in the southern most reaches of Appalachia, days before the river valley is flooded by a dam to create a reservoir. The river's nascent violence eventually impinges on the narrator's consciousness, an intimation of the peril that stalks the quartet of unsuspecting canoeists.

Dickey's 1970 novel—which, like *A River Runs Through It,* was adapted into a popular feature film—has proven disturbingly prescient in light of the urgent warnings that have become commonplace regarding a planet in crisis.

Like Camuto, Steven J. Meyers explores rivers through the practice of fly angling. Based in the San Juan Mountains of southwestern Colorado, Meyers was a professional guide and photographer before he turned to teaching. In *Notes from the San Juans* he guides readers on one of America's premiere trout waters. He offers advice on fishing a river that supports considerable angling pressure, but takes time off to paint a portrait in word and image of a landscape he loves. In *San Juan River Chronicle* the river becomes a path through which Meyers finds a home, even if his absent father remains lost.

A River Runs Through It is celebrated for many reasons, not the least of which is Norman Maclean's depiction of fly fishing. But its title acknowledges that it is also a book about a river, which runs through the narrative as it runs through the body, heart and soul of the aspiring writer Norman, his doomed brother, Paul, and their Scots Presbyterian preacher father. The tragic story ends with the murder of Norman's brother many years earlier and after their beloved Big Blackfoot has succumbed to irreparable degradation caused by pollution. Both eventualities weigh on the writer's heart, as they direct his pen. Maclean acknowledges that he, his brother and his father regarded their bond to the Big Blackfoot as familial. Seldom has the notion of home water been more eloquently expressed. There are certain requirements before any watercourse is endowed with this stature: intimate knowledge, sympathetic observation, personal history and pride leavened by humility.

Over time a sense of belonging matures into propriety stewardship born of love. This inhabiting of a specific place is not a contract of ownership, with its sundry deeds and leases, but an obligation of caretaking, if not caregiving. Thomas McGuane recognizes this moral imperative in *The Longest Silence* when he asserts that it is time fishermen became riverkeepers. A river becomes home water when an angler absorbs it into his fibre, sinews, organs; when he is as inseparable from the river as the river is inseparable from him or her. It shapes an angler's sense of place. Consequently it is as much *mind*scape, *emotion*scape or *soul*scape as landscape.

The novella closes with one of the most beloved prose passages in the history of fly fishing. I hear biblical rhythms in these final words: Genesis, Ecclesiastes and the Gospel of John. I never tire of their elegance and depth which express reverence for a sacred landscape.

Maclean sees Creation in a drop of water. These are not only the words he heard from his father's Presbyterian pulpit, but remnants of an oral tradition passed down through generations by his Scots ancestors (on his mother's side) who immigrated to Cape Breton before making their way to the American heartland. To my ear *A River Runs Through It* echoes the Gaelic cadences of Alistair MacLeod's short stories, not to mention his novel *No Great Mischief.*

RIVERS OF DREAM

I dream of rivers. I was compelled to write this chapter after waking from a river dream. I was reminded of James Wright's 'On a Phrase from Southern Ohio' wherein he compares dreams to shimmering spiderwebs above the river of youth. When viewed from a high altitude rivers resemble webs woven on the earth's surface. It is the river of my youth, the Thames, that shimmers in memory.

Bliss Perry writes evocatively of rivers and recurring dreams in *Pools and Ripples:*

To revisit a river is like trying to redream a dream. You are aware, of course, that you have changed and that the river must have changed and that no two dreams are precisely alike. Yet the identities are more profound than the differences, and the moment you are on the stream you have the old illusion of timelessness. This mortal has put on immortality.

When the time comes, it is my wish that my ashes float down a river, like lines from one of my favourite river poems. James Reaney knew a number of rivers, including the Thames; however, it is the river that courses through South Easthope Township, where he was born and raised, that he celebrates in 'To the Avon River, Above Stratford, Canada'. I cannot imagine a more mundane stretch of river anywhere. Yet he sees wonder and mystery through the eyes of imagination. The lines drift with the tenderness of a lullaby, ending with a young man's wish preserved in lines of poetry:

> What did the Indians call you?
> For you do not flow
> With English accents …
>   before
> I drank coffee or tea
>   I drank you
>   With my cupped hands …
> You are the first river
>   I crossed
> And like the first whirlwind
>   The first rainbow
>   First snow, first
>   Falling star I saw.…
>   you shall
>   Always flow
>   Through my heart.
> The rain and the snow of my mind
> Shall supply the spring of that river
>   Forever …
> And printed above this shield
> One of my earliest wishes
> 'To flow like you.'

Reaney was not a fly angler. There is nothing about fly fishing in his poem. Still he understood that poems are rivers, as rivers are poems. Like a fly angler, he wades into the river by casting his imagination on the waters of inspiration. In so doing he inhabits a river world, if only momentarily. It is this understanding that speaks to the fly angler in me with such deep emotional resonance.

Writers and fly anglers share a common sensibility when it comes to rivers. Both identify or are identified with rivers: Reaney with the Avon, Haig-Brown with the Campbell, Hemingway with the Two Hearted, Maclean with the Big Blackfoot, Twain with the Mississippi, Wright with the Ohio, Thoreau with the Concord and Merrimack, Dillard with Tinker Creek, David Adams Richards with the Miramichi, to name a few. Who knows, perhaps someday I will be identified with the Grand River.

Following the example of poets, mystics and spiritual pilgrims, fly anglers habitually *re*-name sites on rivers with localized names to make them their own, not for proprietary reasons but to mark particular places as significant. It is a ritualistic practice in which all pagan peoples engaged, including the Celts.

Poetry is a language of particularization, which anglers adopt when they re-name places on rivers. For example, stretches on the Grand River tailwater have either been christened by anglers or local names have been applied by anglers not only as referents, but as designators that connect anglers to place. The re-named stretches are a consubstantial blend of imagination, geography, biology and history. Some of these include Second Line Flats, Can Roberts (roadways), Trestle Pool (railways), Caddis Run, Hendrickson Pool (entomology), Cedar Run (botany), Tombstone, Frustration Flats (poetry), Centennial Park, Iron Bridge (landmarks), Carrol Creek, Swan Creek (waterways) and Blondies, Wilson's Flats, Musselman's (history). (For a poetic exploration of place-names and landscape I highly recommend Robert Macfarlane's *The Wild Places*, *The Old Ways* and *Landmarks*.)

The pace and rhythm of Reaney's poem unfolds like a graceful cast, long and true. It symbolically replicates the process whereby the language of fly fishing, based on English grammar, migrated to North America and adopted its own native syntax.

The relationship between fly angler and river is intimate, even sensuous. Equal parts reality and dream, memory and imagination, it is the river an angler knows first that flows through his heart. Every time I catch a fish I hold the river's holy water in cupped hands—an offering of gratitude, an act of communion, a ritualistic cleansing.

Although it was not his intention, James Reaney has written the most beautiful poem devoted to home waters I know of. I pray fly anglers get to know it, and love it, as I do. For I am not the first, nor will I be the last, to wish to flow like a river.

Spring

Give Us This Day

When I waded into the Credit River on the opening weekend of trout season, I was not the angler that had stepped out of the Bighead River after a day of steelheading the previous fall. In the intervening months I had suffered a heart attack and, for the first time, looked down the barrel of mortality—not without more than a little trepidation.

It had been a good night six weeks before the season opener. I had accepted an invitation to attend a folk concert in Toronto. Dante Pocrnich, an eye surgeon from my hometown of London, who conducted cataract surgery on my left eye the previous summer, and his wife, Erminie, are not only friends. They are fellow acoustic music buffs.

We spent the evening enjoying veteran American songwriter Richard Shindell at Hugh's Room. After they dropped me off at my apartment I watched the London Knights win their major junior hockey game. Robertson arrived home from work, I poured a nightcap and we began discussing the game. We were in high spirits.

Before the dram of malt whisky touched my lips, I began feeling lousy. Nauseous, clammy, with an uneasy heaviness in my chest and a dull ache along my left arm. After an hour I told my son that I thought I had better go to the hospital. I phoned a cab.

After nine hours of tests, blood work and monitoring I was discharged with a requisition for a stress test. Before I left the hospital, however, I received an anxious call on my cellphone from an emergency nurse instructing me to return immediately. Apparently the doctor who read the results of my blood work initially failed to notice that I had suffered a heart attack. I remained in hospital for observation and tests for five days. An angioplasty showed I had a blocked artery requiring a stent. The cardiologist also discovered an abdominal aortic aneurysm that might need to be addressed at some point. During the angioplasty I chatted with a nurse about fly fishing. Not only is her brother an avid angler, it so happens his fly-tying mentor lives amidst the headwaters of the Saugeen River, one of my favoured areas to pursue trout. The world of fly fishing might encompass the planet, but it remains a local, intimate affair.

It was during the procedure that I realized how much I define myself as a fly angler. As usual fly fishing was on my mind. I seldom go anywhere without a book, a habit developed over four decades of newspaper reporting which was often punctuated with periods of waiting while on assignment. When the cab arrived I grabbed *Holy Water*, Jerry Kustich's most recent of four collections of personal fly fishing essays. The volume proved the perfect bedside companion while recovering in hospital.

Given the vicissitudes that accompany unexpected illness, I was especially sensitive to the connection Kustich observes between fly fishing and spirituality. I took solace and comfort in his description of home waters—places where anglers feel the deepest connection to the natural world. For Kustich home water is holy water:

… these familiar places forever meander through our minds with the timeless capacity of transporting our spirit to another dimension that can be just as comforting as home itself. It really doesn't matter where you are on the journey of life either. Home water is as much a state of mind as it is a state of being, and in one's heart it is always close at hand. Just close your eyes.

Kustich is well read and I am sure he is familiar with the writings of D.H. Lawrence. In 'The Spirit of Place', the opening chapter of *Studies in Classic American Literature*, Lawrence uses the term, not to describe a particular place, but to evoke its soul which sets it apart from all other places and which influences the behaviour and values, beliefs and practices of the people who inhabit it. This is powerful stuff because it shapes customs, traditions and identity. The spirit of place is not confined to metaphor or symbol; it is reality. Fly fishing is an emanation of the spirit of place.

I share Kustich's assertion that fly angling is 'a meaningful way to pray in the grand cathedral of nature'. Moreover, I do not believe it was a random accident when I grabbed *Holy Water* off the bookshelf. It had been waiting patiently for me as a source of solace and sanctuary at a time of uncertainty and worry.

* * *

Like the book of Ecclesiastes says: *To every thing there is a season.* The return of the opening day of trout season reaffirmed the cycle of life, forever turning. I was reminded of the first day of school when I was a kid. Hitting a river I had never fished before, as the Credit was, was like starting a new grade with a new teacher.

It was a beautiful Sunday, boasting deep blue skies and smiling sun when Dan Kennaley and I hiked into Forks of the Credit Provincial Park through the tiny hamlet of Brimstone (I kid you not). Bisected by the Bruce Trail, this is a lovely area of the Caledon Hills, with its undulating hills, soft contoured valleys and long, winding roads.

High, fast water and cool temperatures—patches of stubborn snow still clung in damp, low-lying areas in the woods—conspired to keep native speckled and brown trout hunkered down. None of the fly anglers I met reported so much as a nibble, let alone a bite, save for an angler with spin-casting gear. 'I had one hit on my trout magnet,' he confided, referring to a popular spinning lure. Neither Dan nor I fared as well.

We separated before hitting the cascading water. After making my way along the north branch of the river, casting where the rushing, tumbling current seemed slower, I eventually returned to the path. I sat on a bench and soaked in the day's solitude. My thoughts wandered without destination. It was more a matter of prospecting than casting to rising fish.

Dry, brittle leaves seemed to defy gravity by ascending the lee of a nearby hill, fluttering in the chilly breeze like yellow butterflies. A reconnoitring rough-legged hawk breasted the wind on an updraft high above the treetops.

One of the things I relish about fly fishing is the opportunity it affords of slowing down and allowing my life to catch up through reflection and recollection. As Socrates is supposed to have said at his trial: 'An unexamined life is not worth living.' He must have been a fly angler. I cannot explain why—perhaps the absence of trout, my recent brush with mortality or my growing awareness of the transience of things—but I started thinking about fly fishing and religion which, in turn, led to thoughts about Wendell Berry.

* * *

Throughout my life I have been a capricious churchgoer. Baptized Anglican, confirmed United Church of Canada and married in Presbyterian and United churches, I am a spiritual mongrel tonguing a scent I cannot locate. I have attended Anglican and United Church services, as well as other denominations, for short periods—which is to say a year or two or three. Conversely, for the last four decades Celtic spirituality, both pagan and early Christian, has spoken to me with persuasive eloquence.

When I took up fly fishing I began feeling on the water as I wish I had felt in a church. I did not know what to make of my feelings until I read *This Day*, by Wendell Berry. The volume contains poems he composed over more than thirty-five years on Sunday walks around his hillside farm in rural Kentucky. These solitary walks took him to meadow and field, pasture and woodland, as well as stream.

By turns contemplative and meditative, these poems of strength, doubt and moral affirmation bridge past and present while anticipating the future as Berry pays homage to family, friends, community, ideas, nature and God. The poems of love and devotion, gratitude and grace—which I read as pastoral pensées—are balanced with occasional rants directed at the pernicious forces of a mechanized industrial economy inimical to this Good Earth. Berry's Sabbath poems have a syntax and diction that are clear, precise and pure, resembling prayers more than academic poetry that celebrates obtuseness, obfuscation and obscurity. They possess a quiet luminosity. Berry says his poems were written slowly and patiently, mainly out of doors. And this is how they should be read—like a field turned with horse and plough, a walk in the woods or a cast of a dry fly at rising trout. I can think of no better literary companion to take to a river.

In the preface Berry says he often accompanies his family to church, where his wife plays the piano. But, just as often, he heads to the woods, following in the footsteps of Thoreau and others, including literary friends Wallace Stegner, Edward Abbey, John Haines, Hayden Carruth, Donald Hall and Gary Snyder, to find spiritual sustenance in a cathedral of grass, trees, water, rocks, sky, fish, birds and animals.

Berry's Sunday walks put me in mind of when I cast my thoughts on the waters of reflection. Every time I leave the world of work, family and community to wade into a river with fly rod in hand, I enter a sacred space that sometimes finds expression in the written word.

Berry talks about writing his Sabbath poems in silence and solitude. They speak most eloquently to readers who embrace the deep solitude out of which art rises like a mayfly hatch at dusk. When I enter a river, even when accompanied by an angling companion, there is a part of me that finds solace in the stillness of solitude. Similarly, despite the riverscape's constant music, I cast into the silence beneath the rushing current with my heart and my mind open and unfettered.

In the introduction Berry expands on the nature of his Sabbath poems which, to my mind, applies to fly fishing—at least as I approach the contemplative recreation. He begins by pointing out the biblical roots of honouring the Sabbath as a day of rest. Freedom from the expectations of work is one of the rewards of a day on the water. Fly anglers undoubtedly intend to catch fish, but lack of success does not constitute failure in the same way it does in the workaday world.

Unencumbered by the duties and responsibilities of work, Berry opens himself to inspiration. His Sunday walks give rise to his most intimate and revealing poetry. They enable him to map out the geography of his mind, heart and soul. This is the equivalent of what fly anglers recognize as home waters.

Berry's invocation of the muse as she relates to poetry echoes how my thoughts have evolved concerning the muse as she relates to angling. Fly anglers routinely refer to 'fishing gods' when things go well or, alternatively, when things go poorly. However, I have come to believe that anglers should think in terms of a muse instead of gods.

Writers, artists and musicians often talk of muses in terms of inspiration. Muses can be literal or they can be figurative. Angling historians and commentators—including Paul Schullery, Glenn Law, Arnold Gingrich, Mark Browning, John Randolph and Leonard M. Wright Jr.—agree that fly fishing has inspired more enduring literature over its long history than any other recreation or sport. Moreover, the practice is craft that approaches art when executed at the highest level. Like a pen, burin or guitar, a fly rod is a creative tool, an instrument of imagination. It is clear from reading his Sabbath poems that Sunday walks around his farm in rural Kentucky bring Berry into intimate contact with Creation. Similarly fly fishing on the Grand River in southwestern Ontario brings me closest to Creation. For Berry the meaning of the Sabbath deepens in the context of nature's abundant health. I can say the same of fly fishing.

When I asked Wesley Bates whether I was casting on barren water by comparing Berry's Sabbath poems to fly fishing, he confirmed, 'It's appropriate.' This pleased me, as Wesley knows Berry personally and is steeped in his work. He added that, while 'Wendell has connections to a church and has written about religion and God, he strikes me as a person for whom religion is neither a program nor attached to an organization. It is very personal and, as the Sabbath poems show, attached to place. So, it is place that is the muse, and its expression is, well, a poetic pursuit.' This intimate knowledge of, and communion with, *place* is what connects Berry to my experience of fly fishing. Place and home waters are synonymous, two sides of the same philosophical, artistic and spiritual coin.

The antithesis of wholeness and health is brokenness and sickness. Humanity's mechanized assault on the planet worries Berry, which he addresses in his poems, some of which are elegies. Fly anglers across North America, not to mention throughout the planet, are becoming increasingly aware of the destructive impact of pollution and overpopulation as accelerators of climate change. Consequently loss and sorrow find refuge between the lines of Berry's Sabbath poems. They are the shadows of the lines I cast on troubled water.

Berry's Sunday walks make him an integral part of the turning cycle, wherein every thing has its season: birth, growth, death; hunger and fulfillment; decay and regeneration; time and eternity. Fly fishing leads me to the same point on the revolving wheel.

Berry acknowledges that his work as a writer—encompassing poems, novels, short stories, essays, literary criticism and memoir—is inextricably related to his work as a farmer. As writer and farmer, Berry does not view nature as something to be exploited, but as a husbandry relationship which is also aesthetic and spiritual. Whether at the typewriter, at the plough or enjoying a Sunday walk, he is a philosopher of living things, driven by a moral imperative that speaks to matters that extend beyond time and place.

Since retiring from newspaper journalism, my writing is inextricably related to fly fishing. Berry's vocation is my avocation. Writing is the line—a gift of grace, elegant in its beauty, like a cast into mystery—that connects us most intimately to the rhythms of place, of home.

Lessons Rivers Teach

My devotion to literature expresses itself in various ways: as a reader, a student, a collector and donor of books, former arts journalist and non-fiction writer. After losing my personal library to fire at the midpoint of life, I have spent the subsequent years reclaiming books I hold to be essential. I named my two sons after writers I admire: my eldest Dylan Thomas, after the Welsh poet rather than the American songwriter; my youngest Robertson Taylor, after Robertson Davies and Samuel Taylor Coleridge.

Literature has been a constant lover; in contrast, fly fishing is a new mistress with promises to keep. So it gave me intense pleasure to move to the Neighbourhood of Poets. Or rather, to a street that carries the surname of the greatest writer in the English language in an area whose streets honour Browning, Coleridge, Tennyson, Keats, Marlowe and Longfellow.

Seated at the computer in my kitchen office, I can look out on a knoll bordered by a line of conifers. Just out of sight is a gully that protects a copse where I routinely watch a leash of foxes cavorting at dawn. I see cottontails, skunks, raccoons, groundhogs and squirrels. I can turn in my chair during wintertide and watch birds at the feeder—chickadees and nuthatches, juncos and cardinals, blue jays and grosbeaks.

When I raise my eyes from the keyboard, I can gaze at a print of a painting of a fly fisherman at eventide by Russell Chatham; a print of a fly fisherman casting from an Adirondack guide boat by Winslow Homer; a quartet of salmon flies inspired by patterns designed by Carrie Stevens; an engraving by Wesley Bates of a fly fisherman in a pastoral stream accompanied by a silhouette of a dry fly; and, most special of all, a photo of Dylan and Robertson in a boat at dusk, proudly showing off their catch of smallmouth bass. This gallery of angling art and artifact is a source of deep delight when, like an evening hatch, I wait on that elusive *right* word.

Within reach is my library of well-thumbed books devoted to nature, ecology, nature, wildlife art, hunting, fishing and critical commentary. Most special of all are the books—poetry, novels, short stories, memoirs and biographies, even a few classic instructional manuals—about fly fishing, spanning its history, heritage and legacy. These are not material objects, but cherished companions that provide refuge and solace. They teach, instruct and entertain. Over the past couple of years, I have culled my library, resulting in a higher proportion of fly angling literature to provide comfort in my declining years. The currents of literature and fly fishing merge in the river of imagination. When I am casting a line on the water reality takes a back seat to fantasy and projection. This makes catching fish somewhat incidental, another element of narrative in a life story. Putting my angling experiences down on paper has become the poetry of my life.

For me, fly fishing and poetry are the forward and backward motions of the same cast—equal parts empirical and transcendent, existential and metaphysical. Both are acts of faith that require confidence. Over many years as a journalist I found that my abilities improved with confidence. Conversely my confidence improved with my abilities. This forward and backward motion repeated itself when I took up fly fishing. And repeated itself again when I began writing about fly fishing.

I found myself brooding over the creative sympathy between poetry and fly fishing when I opened the inland trout season on the Grand River with Dan Kennaley and his longtime angling pal, Craig Wardlaw. It had been a long, if not particularly harsh, winter. And while we enjoyed intermittent spells of warm weather, it remained belligerently cool through mid-May. Despite the inhospitable weather, neither Dan nor I were dissuaded from getting out. After all, an evening on the river is better than an evening not on the river. Weather be damned.

The inclement weather turned for the better, making this particular evening spring-perfect. We tasted the sweetness of spring as we fished a stretch of river bounded by high banks, boasting sedimentary bands of limestone comprising layers of compressed time and history. We were three among eight fishermen spread out like sentinels, knee-deep along a kilometre of river. There was plenty of room for each of us; we were solitary in the fellowship of anglers.

Moreover, the Hendricksons, the Grand tailwater's first major hatch, was reportedly on. After an interminably long winter, these eagerly anticipated aquatic insects turn anglers into rowdy schoolboys at recess. Not only does this mayfly species mark the real beginning of trout season (as opposed to the date specified in provincial regulations), it is a direct link to the Catskills, the cradle of fly fishing in North America. This makes the hatch, which generally spans the last couple of weeks in May throughout the Grand's trout water, especially significant for anglers who respect the recreational sport's history, heritage and legacy.

Despite my enthusiasm for the Hendricksons we saw nary an insect. Not to be discouraged, we started with dry flies. Then we changed it up. It was nymphs or small streamers—or go home.

Craig did well with his ever-reliable black Woolly Worm with red tail. I watched as he landed a nice two-year-old brown trout exceeding nine inches. I thought back a few years and recalled Craig out-fishing me one spring day on the Conestogo River. His fly of choice: a black Woolly Worm with red tail. With fly fishing, patterns often apply more to anglers than to dressings. Dan was less successful than Craig, but more successful than I was, landing a single recently stocked brownie.

As much as I learn from the literature of angling, there is no substitute to being on the water. Even though I failed to land a fish, I was schooled once again in the classroom of rivers. I seldom spend time on the water without taking away a lesson or two—provided I am an attentive student. On this evening it was about confidence. Or said another way, the power of faith.

Two weeks previously Grand River Troutfitters founder Ken Collins reminded members at the monthly meeting of KW Flyfishers to try yellow nymphs for spring trout. After striking out with a couple of Hendrickson patterns, I rummaged through my nymph box and found, to my surprise, a bright yellow fly I had never used before. It reminded me of a black and yellow #2 Mepps from my days as a spin fisherman. Remembering the advice of a fly angler who has forgotten more than I will ever know, I tied it on. But without confidence. I cast without expecting to catch anything. Yet within a couple of tosses I got a strike from a substantial fish. I was not prepared. I failed to set the hook. I continued casting, still without conviction, and within minutes I got two more hits. I failed to set the hook yet again.

You could say I was distracted, but more accurately I lacked confidence in the fly pattern. The fly did not let me down; I let the fly down. Faith came calling and I lacked ears to hear.

A few days after suffering from the crisis in confidence I was reassured to read another angler who puts stock in faith as it concerns fishing generally, and flies specifically. In *Trout from the Hills*, Scottish-born angling writer Ian Niall talks of faith as an integral part of an angler's constitution. He points out, quite rightly, that an angler's most successful fly is the one he or she most believes in.

I accept Niall's affirmation of faith as something in which to believe—with one caveat. When I talk of faith I am not referring to the dogma of religion, but to hope as preferable to uncertainty, belief as preferable to doubt. This lesson is more important than catching fish. It is something I need to heed, take to heart, incorporate in my world view. This was the lesson the river taught on that golden spring evening.

Teachers on the Fly

Annie Dillard cautions in *The Writing Life* that hoarding knowledge is not only disgraceful, it does irreparable harm. I have deep respect for teachers who give generously and wholly of what they themselves have learned. That is why I believe students get over bad teachers, but carry good teachers with them, always. Teachers are the alchemical agents that fashion the gold of success from the base metals of potential.

I owe my love of literature, which led to a fulfilling career as an arts journalist, to a devoted grade 10 English teacher. Larry McGuire taught under frustrating conditions in a high school that trained aspiring plumbers, electricians, printers, auto mechanics, carpenters, cabinetmakers, sheet-metal workers and machinists, as well as draftsmen (we were all male) like myself. His dedication to literature set me on a course for which I remain grateful.

I came to fly fishing late, in my fifties, after years as an armchair angler. When I finally mustered the courage to take fly rod in hand, I had two teachers—both of whom happen to be good friends as well as expert fly anglers—who generously passed along their knowledge. I met Steve May for a newspaper story. I met Ken Collins in night-school at Conestoga College where he was teaching an introductory course on fly fishing. In hindsight it seems I was destined to take up an activity I had been reading—and dreaming—about for years. Lydia, my wife at the time, had registered for a course, but low enrolment forced its cancellation. Rather than apply for a refund she asked if I was interested in anything. When I checked the prospectus I found Ken's six-week course. And dream became reality. I felt like the narrator in Thoreau's dream as recounted in *The Maine Woods*:

In the night I dreamed of trout-fishing and, when at length I awoke, it seemed a fable that this painted fish swam there so near my couch, and rose to our hooks the last evening, and I doubted if I had not dreamed it all.

I have been fly fishing for more than a decade now. The contemplative recreation has been the still point in a hectic world of relationship dissolutions, relocation, retirement, passing of friends and family and chronic ailments that are reminders of mutability and mortality. Casting an artificial fly at gamefish might seem a frivolous waste of time. For the dedicated, however, it is a meditative activity that can grow into an obsession. I prefer to use the term *calling*, which Jim Harrison and Thomas McGuane favour. For me fly angling is a river where the currents of passion and imagination meet with the currents of reflection and devotion.

* * *

A fly rod is equal parts compass and passport. Fly anglers circumnavigate the globe in pursuit of prized gamefish on legendary rivers. In *Becoming a Fly Fisher* John Randolph suggests that fly anglers, like early Celtic monks, travel to make connections which are mystical in nature. Thus, fly fishing is paradigm of form, meaning and purpose.

Those with deep pockets can cast to the untamed traditions of Highland and Speyside salmon or 'educated' English chalkstream trout. Or try their luck along Ireland's wild and woolly west coast or Wales's myth-haunted mountain lakes. They can head north to Alaska's Bristol Bay on the west coast or Labrador on the east coast. Siberia and Iceland beckon for those who want to travel farther afield. Those seeking adventure south can head to Central America and the Caribbean including Cuba, not to mention Amazonia, Patagonia and Tierra del Fuego in South America or even far-off Christmas Island and New Zealand. A fly angler can cast to the ends of the earth.

Of course there are holy places throughout the continental United States. These are places 'dreams are made on'—to quote one of literature's great fisher of words. Their names cause anglers' hearts to dance like trout: Beaverkill, Battenkill and Neversink; LeTort, Ausable (New York) and Au Sable (Michigan); Henry's Fork and Big Hole; Deschutes and North Umpqua. Canada's storied Miramichi, Restigouche, Bow and Campbell rivers should not be forgotten.

Fortunately there is good news for fly anglers who reside in Waterloo Region and do not want to break piggy banks or cash in frequent-flyer points to travel vast distances. We are blessed with a world-class fishery on our local riverbank. The lower Grand has a flourishing smallmouth bass and steelhead fishery. There are also pike and walleye, mooneye and perch.

But it is the Grand's tailwater that attracts fly anglers. For twenty-eight kilometres of scenic river between the Shand Dam at the bottom of Belwood Lake and the historic covered bridge at West Montrose, the Canadian Heritage River supports one of the premium tailwater fisheries for brown trout in eastern North America. Annual economic benefits associated with the fishery are estimated to exceed a million dollars. Ironically, as Waterloo Region gained an international reputation as a hub of high-tech research and innovation, a low-tech form of fishing—with roots extending back to Macedonia in AD 200—garnered acclaim. The Grand's tailwater has become such a desirable destination that the area hosted the Canadian Fly Fishing Championship in 2006 and again in 2018. Anglers and the writers covering the initial event were so impressed that the Outdoor Writers of Canada held its annual conference in Elora and Fergus two years later. Split-cane is not forgotten, thanks to the Canadian Cane Gathering, a celebration of making bamboo rods that attracts artisans from throughout North America.

For anglers who want a change of scenery there are numerous rivers brimming with trout, bass, steelhead, walleye, panfish, pike, even muskie, within a couple hours' drive of the region, including the Credit, Thames, Maitland, Bighead and Saugeen rivers. There are also fly shops, outfitters, custom canoe manufacturers and clubs. Waterloo's Princess Cinemas has been hosting the annual International Fly Fishing Film Festival (IF4) since 2012.

* * *

This was not always so, Steve told me, when we first met through a contact at the Grand River Conservation Authority. A former professional guide, commercial fly tier and angling writer, Steve is a fellow member of KW Flyfishers, a club founded in the 1970s and still going strong.

For a number of years Steve produced Bob Izumi's *Real Fishing Show*, Canada's longest-running angling TV show. He continues to write for Canadian and International fly fishing publications. He has been a contract fly tier with Orvis for more than a decade.

Formerly project co-ordinator for the Grand River Fisheries

Management Plan, Steve is a fine writer. In one of his essays, 'Prom Night from Hell', he compares fishing a mayfly hatch at dusk to 'a teenage prom night slasher movie'. He edited the second edition of *Fishing Ontario's Grand River Country*, published by the Grand River Conservation Authority.

The book is an indispensable companion for anyone who wants to fish the Grand, along with *Fly Fishing the Grand River*, a vest-pocket guide co-written by KW Flyfishers founding member Ian D. Martin and his wife, Jane E. Rutherford. Ian is an environmental biology and statistical consultant, while Jane is a retired biology professor who taught at Wilfred Laurier University. They live in a home overlooking the Grand and spent five years researching insects and other invertebrates in its trout waters.

The Grand was once home to native brook trout, Steve recalled. But mechanized farming, industrialization and urbanization, with its accompanying population growth and concentration, reduced the river to a sewer. Things got better when filtration technology improved water quality and a working partnership formed among the Ministry of Natural Resources, local Conservation Authority, Trout Unlimited, Friends of the Grand River and the local fly fishing club.

The partners began rehabilitating habitat to sustain a stocking program. Steve recalls 1989 as an important year because it marked the beginning of hatchery-raised browns being stocked below Shand dam. Designated a Canadian Heritage River in 1994, the Grand became a magnet for fly anglers. Success soon exceeded expectation. 'We knew we were on the right track.' In 2003 stocking was expanded to the Conestogo River.

Including the Grand's major tributaries with brown, brook or rainbow trout—Conestogo, Speed, Nith and Eramosa rivers—the watershed becomes an even more desirable destination for anglers who call themselves Trout Bums. Steve has spotted vehicles with Montana plates parked on the banks of the Grand. He has guided anglers from such distances as Scotland, Argentina, Japan and California. Born and raised on the Oak Ridges Moraine, north of Toronto, Steve got hooked on fishing at a young age. He started fly fishing while attending Lakehead University in Thunder Bay and carried the passion with him when he moved to Waterloo in 1992 to study environmental planning at the University of Waterloo.

Like many fly anglers, Steve ties his own flies, some of which are original designs. However, few tiers achieve the skill and expertise he has. Some of his flies, including Full-Motion Hex, bass and articulated muskie streamer flies (including the Half Chicken and Chicken Combo) have garnered international renown.

'Fly tying is an obvious transition from fishing,' Steve said. 'There's something about fooling a fish with a bait you've created yourself.' In 2000 he started guiding for Grand River Troutfitters, owned and operated by his longtime angling buddy Ken Collins.

Steve does not have much truck with the perceived mystique—some might call it snobbery—that surrounds fly fishing. He bristles when he hears it referred to as a fraternity. In contrast to its elitist image, fly fishing is neither difficult nor intimidating, he insists. 'The physical action of casting a fly rod requires the same skills as drinking a glass of water.' Or a frosty pint of local-brewed draft, I might add.

Although learning the intricacies of the recreational sport is a life-long process, neophytes can enjoy it without becoming experts. 'All you need is a basic level of confidence,' he said, adding that he can have aspiring anglers 'on the water after fifteen minutes of casting instruction'. I'm living proof of Steve's claim. He had me—an enthusiastic, but awkward, apprentice—on the river in a jiffy.

It was a sunny morning in early June when Steve showed me the basics. We went to the Conestogo River, where both expert and beginner were skunked. However, the newbie was able to report he caught three trout on his first outing on the Grand, two 'dinks' (guide talk for tiny fish) and one that measured a respectable sixteen inches. After more than a decade of fly fishing, I can verify that I have caught few trout—and landed even fewer—to equal that beauty in length and girth.

Steve guided me through what I needed to know. Here is the checklist (think of it as *Fly Fishing 101*):

• Rigging the rod with reel, line, tapered leader and tippet. Anglers need to know a couple of knots to do this properly. The best way of becoming adept at tying knots is doing it repeatedly while watching a hockey or baseball game on television. Practice might not make perfect, but mastering a few knots is essential. An angler NEVER wants to lose a fish of a lifetime because of a bad knot—believe me!

• Casting, which differs from casting a spinning rod or bait-casting rod because the line propels the fly rather than the lure propelling the line. While casting comes easier for some anglers than others (think of learning to ride a bike), the fact remains: casting proficiency (accuracy as much as distance) is proportional to success on the water.

• Matching the fly pattern to the aquatic insects and critters your targeted species are eating. Fish also eat terrestrials and other fish. Matching the hatch is one of the mantras of modern fly fishing. However, eighty per cent of what fish eat are subaquatic rather than floating on the surface of the water.

• Reading the water to determine where fish are located. Fish are happiest where they breathe (they need oxygen), can easily get food and are protected from strong current and prey. They don't burn more calories than they get from their food source—I call this survival of the hungriest.

• Presenting the dry or wet fly, nymph or streamer, which involves placing the fly where the fish are without spooking them. To paraphrase UCLA Bruins football coach Henry Russell 'Red' Sanders, presentation isn't everything; it's the only thing.

There are many worthwhile instructional books on the sport. As a place to start, Steve suggests *Fly Fishing for Dummies*. For anglers who have progressed beyond the entry level, I recommend the various instructional books written by Tom Rosenbauer, as well as the series of videos he produced for Orvis.

✳ ✳ ✳

Casting is the first thing aspiring fly anglers have to learn. It's the most intimidating—and the most graceful—element of the recreational sport. More than anything else, it defines fly fishing. It is easy to do, but difficult to master. It takes time and timing. And more time.

Ken Collins is one of the best fly casters I know. I recall one occasion at Grand Opportunities, the annual outdoor fly fishing symposium sponsored by Friends of the Grand River, when he conducted a casting seminar from a lawn chair. He had ripped a tendon or ligament in his leg and was encased in a cast from ankle to hip. But that did not prevent him from casting a fly (actually a piece of yarn) into a circle no larger than a frisbee from a distance of more than twenty-seven metres (ninety feet). In contrast, I am comfortable casting between twelve and fifteen metres (forty to fifty feet).

Ken has been a passionate fly angler since he was introduced to the recreational sport when a gym teacher took a group of grade 7 students fishing in Algonquin Park. The teacher demonstrated how to tie Woolly Buggers around the campfire and the students caught fish the next day on flies tied the night before. 'I was hooked,' he said. 'Catching a fish on a fly you have tied yourself is the pinnacle of angling.'

Ken studied forestry technology at Algonquin College in Pembroke. After graduating in 1984 he landed contract work related to forestry. But more significantly, he started working part-time at Kitchener's Natural Sports, a general-purpose fishing store. He was hired full-time in 1993. Although his interests encompassed all types of angling, he was 'drawn back to fly fishing because of its simplicity and its intimate connection to nature'.

While at Natural Sports he developed the fly fishing department. He also became Ontario's first Fly Fishing Federation–certified teacher and began instructing. Ken's growth as a fly fishing specialist coincided with the development of the Grand tailwater as a brown trout fishery. He described the stocking program—including the introduction of mandatory catch-and-release regulations in designated zones in 1993—as 'a flagship model'.

Like most fly anglers, Ken is a committed conservationist. He was founding president of Friends of the Grand River, a not-for-profit organization of volunteers incorporated in 1995 to develop, promote and implement projects to preserve, conserve and enhance the Grand's watershed. The brown trout fishery came of age the same year *Canadian Fly Fisher*, Canada's premier fly fishing magazine at the time, published its first story on the tailwater.

Confident that the tailwater was becoming a world-class fishery, Ken opened Grand River Troutfitters in Fergus in 1984—the same year the river received its heritage designation. By following his passion he transformed avocation into vocation when he opened the full-service fly shop, the first in this part of southwestern Ontario. 'The writing was on the wall,' he said. 'I knew the area was going to go crazy wild.'

Troutfitters prospered as an authorized dealer for an assortment of prestigious product lines. It also provided professional guiding and outfitting services that extended beyond the Grand to seventeen of the province's most productive angling waters for trout, steelhead, salmon, bass, pike and muskie, even carp. It also hosted excursions to some of the world's hottest fly fishing destinations including the Bahamas, Cuba and Newfoundland. In 2012 Ken closed the doors of his handsome batten-and-timber store, located in the historic lime-stone Market on the banks of the Grand. He reset and refreshed his business model to an online guiding and instructional service. Ken has developed three Golden Rules of Casting to make the practice easier and more efficient. I can personally attest to their effectiveness:

• *Rule No. 1*: It is not about heroes, which translates to 'don't go beyond your capabilities.' Casting a fly rod doesn't require muscle. This is why women learn to cast quicker than men. Women are also better listeners, most experienced instructors agree.

• *Rule No. 2*: The line always follows the tip of the rod, which translates to 'never place the tip of your rod over your head' unless you want to catch an ear. Always wear glasses (prescription or polarized sunglasses) when casting a fly rod to protect your eyes from errant flies with nasty hooks. Although Ken suggests that the rod move through an arc from ten (forward) to two o'clock (backward), I personally prefer a shorter arc of eleven and one o'clock which produces a tighter loop.

• *Rule No. 3*: Get rhythm, which translates to 'counting to three on both back and forward casts to propel the line.' This is where the graceful elegance of casting comes into play. Ken's timing varies slightly from Norman Maclean in *A River Runs Through It* when he describes his father's classic 'four-count rhythm' approach to casting. Whereas Maclean's father favours a Presbyterian-approved metronome, Ken prefers a more relaxed country waltz count.

As far as gear goes, an angler can spend hundreds of dollars on rods made from graphite, the most popular material. Traditionalists might prefer fibreglass or bamboo. Rods can be expensive because the best are either custom-made or handmade by skilled craftsmen to demanding specifications. Quality matters.

Anglers with deep pockets can purchase vintage bamboo rods

made by legendary masters with names that are mythic in fly fishing circles: Leonard, Payne, Edwards, Carlson, Thomas, Garrison, Carmichael, et al. My love of the meditative recreation grew from an affair to marriage vows when I acquired my first bamboo rod. My Sweetgrass rod, which I fish with at every opportunity, is a cherished heirloom I intend to pass down to my sons. I hope my passion for fly fishing is passed down as well.

Reels can also be expensive. They house dacron backing and tapered synthetic line. The line's core is braided nylon or dacron coated with PVC, which has been treated with various substances such as microscopic glass spheres for 'floatability'—or other additives that cause the line to sink at desired rates. Many fly anglers view reels as jewelry that need not be costly to function efficiently. The exceptions are reels for either big fish (steelhead, salmon, pike, muskie) or saltwater species that require quality disc-drag systems.

Buying the best fly line an angler can afford—ranging from one-weight (lightest) to fourteen-weight (heaviest)—is recommended because quality line casts better. Think of it as a wise investment. The most important line types are floating and sinking tip or full sinking.

Breathable waders, wading boots, vests and polarized sunglasses vary in price. In the height of summer when water temperatures rise, wet wading (with shorts or light long pants and an old pair of running shoes) is the way to go. This is guaranteed to arouse one's inner child—at least in men.

Commercial flies cost between $2 and $5 each, depending on type (dry and wet flies are cheapest; streamers, bass bugs and large flies cost more). It is important to have enough types and sizes to cover a variety of conditions; however, most anglers carry more flies than they need. As with lottery tickets, one will catch fish—provided it is the *right* one.

Although fly fishing gear and tackle can cost thousands, they do not have to. Science and technology provide anglers with *quality* gear at *cheaper* prices than ever before. Good quality equipment that will last years can be purchased for between $800 and $1,500. When compared with the price of green fees for a summer of golf, the cost-effectiveness of fly fishing is clear. The cost of a provincial fishing licence is nominal and not required by resident anglers sixty-five years of age and older. It is one of the few perks of growing old.

A cautionary note: fly fishing has myriad seductions and

temptations. Gear, clothing, paraphernalia, memorabilia and memberships, not to mention trips to exotic locations, can add up. There is always something an angler *thinks* he needs, and therefore, *must* have, irrespective of cost, whether rods, reels, tackle, books or art. Of course there are those expensive trips of a lifetime an angler cannot pass up. The list goes on.

My fly angling library has expanded exponentially, while just about every square inch of available wall space has become home to a painting, engraving or print featuring a river, fish or angler. A hand-painted brook trout adorns my chosen coffee mug, my go-to beer glasses sport fly patterns and my salt and pepper shakers are housed in a replica of a fly reel. I have drink coasters featuring bass caught on the fly and my summer clothing consists primarily of T-shirts in a variety of colours boasting a variety of fly angling themes. Need I confess more?

I am reminded of Noah Adams's *Saint Croix Notes*, a collection of essays written when he lived in the Saint Croix River Valley of Wisconsin and Minnesota. Adams opines, with tongue firmly in cheek, that it was Thoreau who first asserted that nothing was worth undertaking unless it involved buying lots of stuff. I am proof of Adams's observation—as are many of my fly angling companions.

Whether expensive or economical, the relative cost of fly fishing is irrelevant unless it answers the elemental question: why fly fish in the first place?

'It's a good stress reliever,' Steve said, adding he has known strong personalities 'who were so relaxed after leaving the water they talked slower.' While it is not uncommon for a golfer to break a club in frustration, seldom, if ever, will a fly angler toss a rod in anger. Fly fishing does not always go as planned, but even days when you don't catch fish are better than days not spent on the water.

Fly fishing provides un-regimented, low-impact exercise. Wading along the riverbed, standing in the current and casting burn calories without taxing joints and muscles. 'It's not a muscle sport,' Steve said. I can attest to the therapeutic benefits of the activity. I have arthritis in my left knee and wading amidst a gentle current in cold water is very soothing.

Then there is the natural beauty of the landscape. Most gamefish inhabit beautiful places. The countryside close to home is a case in point—whether the limestone cliffs of the Elora Gorge or the pastoral serenity of farm country. Anglers can fish the Grand coursing through cities—whether Kitchener, Waterloo, Cambridge or Brantford—and imagine themselves in the heart of rural Ontario, far away from urban distraction. 'There's something restorative about standing in a flow of water in beautiful surroundings,' Steve said.

Most fly anglers follow such ecologically responsible practices as fishing with single, barbless hooks and catch-and-release, an ethic that returns fish as unharmed as possible to the waters they inhabit. Many fly anglers follow the eco-aesthetic of leaving as faint a footprint on the planet as possible. This varies from picking up garbage and planting trees, to improving watershed habitat and stocking hatchery fish. In order to be successful, Ken said, 'anglers have to be observant and attentive. They have to be in tune with natural surroundings.' This includes respect and stewardship.

Fly fishing builds relationships. It has no age, gender, status, class or experience barriers. Young and mature, men and women, working folk and the rich and famous join the ranks of novices mentored by seasoned experts. Some of my closest friendships have developed through the contemplative sport.

Steve and Ken have fly fished throughout North America—and many places beyond. However, both are big on the Grand. They even co-authored a chapter, 'Exceptional Waters', about the Grand (between Paris and Brantford), in American bass legend Bob Clouser's *Fly-Fishing for Smallmouth in Rivers and Streams*.

Jim Harrison once observed that 'good art smells like life'. For me fly fishing smells like life. And I thank Steve and Ken for clearing my nasal passages so I might breathe in its sweet aroma.

Women on the Water

In *Little Rivers* Margot Page observes that women anglers identify with their own rivers, in which they stand in wonder of the mysteries of their lives.

For much of fly fishing's long history, women did not have rivers of their own. With few exceptions, fly fishing was an old boys' club. This historical reality has been reflected in such commercial hook and bullet press as *Field & Stream*, not to mention most of the exemplary writing about the recreational sport. Think of the modern writers whose narratives are overtly masculine: Ernest Hemingway, Jim Harrison, Thomas McGuane, Norman Maclean, et al. The same goes for Canada's Roderick Haig-Brown and Paul Quarrington. (David Adams Richards proves the exception in *Lines on the Water*.)

Increasingly women are discovering the joys of what is referred to variously as a sport, pastime, hobby, passion, obsession or contemplation. I prefer the term *calling*. For the first time in its long history women comprise the fastest growing demographic in fly fishing. Robert Traver's declaration in *Trout Magic*, that fishing recognizes no gender, seems to be coming true. At long last. A *New York Times* story published in the fall of 2017 cited a study by the *Recreational Boating & Fishing Foundation* that estimated women make up thirty-one per cent of the 6.5 million Americans who cast fur and feather. In 2016 more than two million women participated in the sport, representing an increase of 142,000 from the previous year. I was unable to find figures for Canada—Fisheries & Oceans Canada was in the midst of working with Statistics Canada to compile results from a 2015 survey—but one assumes proportional numbers of women have taken up the sport across the Great White North.

* * *

Before women were bitten by the mayfly bug in record numbers there were a few notable exceptions to overwhelming male domination.

However, like so much in the history of fly angling, the role women have played is not without controversy, intrigue and mystery, not to mention irony.

While records of fly fishing date back to the Roman Empire, one of the foundational works in the Western tradition devoted to the subject dates from the fifteenth century. And it was for many years purported to have been written by a woman. The *Boke of Seynt Albans* (now known as *Book of Saint Albans*) was printed in 1496, a full 157 years before *The Compleat Angler*, published in 1653 by Richard Marriot. Walton's famous celebration of the piscatorial arts is the most frequently reprinted English-language book of all time, save for the *Bible* and *Pilgrim's Progress*. No wonder fly fishing is so often packed in quasi-religious luggage.

I do not know how many people still read John Bunyan's moral allegory—not many I suspect—and I would be hard pressed to name a book so often misinterpreted by so many in support of so much dangerous dogma as the Bible. As for Walton's Holy Grail of Angling, few popular books are so seldom read, whether in its original text or in modern translation. I think of it as the *Finnegans Wake* of fly fishing.

This is in contrast to the work of his fishing companion who, when not tossing a line, was vicar of London's St. Dunstan's Church, where Walton served as churchwarden. Those who love literature will recognize the angling vicar as the great Metaphysical poet John Donne. Walton includes 'The Bait'—a poem Donne wrote in response to Christopher Marlowe's pastoral verse 'The Passionate Shepherd'—in *The Compleat Angler*. The poem, which brilliantly blends aquatic and piscine imagery, refers to fly fishing in the lines: 'Let curious traitors sleave silk flies'/To witch poor wandering fishes' eyes....' The fact that Walton was a bait fisherman has done little to unseat his piscatorial tome from the high shelf of fly angling literature. In a letter to Samuel Taylor Coleridge, the essayist Charles Lamb described the discourse on angling as breathing 'the very spirit of innocence, purity and simplicity of heart.'

Sir Izaak's fishing companion Charles Cotton, however, was a fly fisherman and his contribution was incorporated into the fifth printing of *The Compleat Angler* in 1676. The book remains the most celebrated angling book in the world despite wading in a cesspool of scandal. In 1954 an American book collector discovered that Walton had plagiarized extensively from the obscure *The Arte of Angling*, published in 1577 by, you guessed it, an unknown author.

I have not read *The Arte of Angling*, nor do I expect to—ever. So I cannot say how much Walton cribbed from the earlier volume. While plagiarism is a serious academic felony today, such intellectual larceny in the age of Walton was a more loosey-goosey affair. We need look no further than Shakespeare who stole whatever intellectual morsels he needed to serve a meal on the table of art. Fact is, *The Compleat Angler* has stood the test of time—leaving aside the question of whether anyone reads it anymore. In contrast *The Arte of the Angling* has been dutifully forgotten by time. I leave it to scholars to decide whether an injustice has been committed.

The *Book of Saint Albans* is not without its own current of irony. An essay in the volume, 'Treatyse of Fysshynge wyth an Angle', has been historically attributed to Dame Juliana Berners, a woman of means who, for some mysterious reason, decided to become a nun. I say attributed because the author remains lost in the spinner fall of time. Nobody has ever found proof or evidence that she ever lived, let alone wrote the 'Treatyse'.

Recent scholarship has reached consensus that the writer was actually Wynkyn de Worde, an Alsatian-born printer and publisher in London who worked with William Caxton. It should not be surprisingly that de Worde is suspected of plagiarizing an unknown text written by, you guessed it again, an unknown author.

The 'Treatyse' was long acknowledged as the first writing of consequence in Western literature devoted to fly fishing; however, this claim has been invalidated by recent scholarship. Richard Hoffman, professor emeritus in the history department at York University and author of *The Catch: Medieval European Fisheries and the Antecedents of Today's World Fisheries Crisis*, has shown that other European countries, including Germany, France and Spain, had their own longstanding angling traditions alongside that of Merrie Olde England.

Readers can be forgiven for dismissing the history of fly angling as a parody written by a sporting satirist who had a beef to pick with fishing. Still, despite historical intrigue and literary skullduggery, myth and romance demand the acknowledgement of Dame Juliana as the Materfamilias of Fly Fishing. And I am enough of a layman devotee of Swiss psychologist Carl Jung to see value in fly angling's intriguing *anima* figure. The contemplative sport is richer for recognizing its feminine side. Others concur.

∗ ∗ ∗

Fast forward to the turn of the twentieth century.

The first female angler of note was Cornelia Thurza Crosby. She lobbied through the Maine Sportsmen's Fish and Game Association for many years to licence guides as a means of generating funds for fish and game protection. In appreciation of her efforts, and despite never having been a registered guide, her home state ceremonially awarded 'Fly Rod' Crosby with Licence No. 1 in 1898. Fly Rod's most famous utterance echoes the sentiments of many a fly angler, then as now: 'I would rather fish any day than go to heaven.'

And then there is what many angling historians refer to as the golden age of fly fishing in the Catskills. According to Austin M. Francis in *Catskill Rivers*, his history of the so-called birthplace of fly fishing in America, women fly anglers began frequenting trout streams in greater numbers after the First World War.

Francis lists the prominent female fly anglers of the day including: Theodore Gordon's unnamed companion on the Neversink River; Louise Miller, celebrated in her husband Sparse Grey Hackles's *Fishless Days, Angling Nights* as Lady Beaverkill; Maxine Atherton, whose husband, John, wrote *The Fly and the Fish*; and Joan Salvato Wulff, a master fly caster who continues operating a fly fishing school in the Catskills after the death of her husband, legendary sportsman Lee Wulff. As well, Francis pays homage to legendary fly dressers Winnie Dette, daughter Mary, and Elsie Darbee.

Fly fishing is celebrated for the tradition of quality writing that has been devoted to it since Dame Juliana. While men have most often picked up quill or pen, or sat down at the typewriter or keyboard, more women than ever are writing about the sport from a female perspective. Three books I happen to have in my library include:

• *Little Rivers: Tales of a Woman Angler* by Margot Page, who from 1990 through 1996 was editor of *American Fly Fisher*, the quarterly journal of The American Museum of Fly Fishing in Manchester, Vermont;

- *Green River Virgins and Other Passionate Anglers*, a collection of short stories by Mallory Burton, an American-born teacher, linguist and fly angler who at the time of publication lived in Prince Rupert, BC; and

- *Moose in the Water, Bamboo on the Bench: A Journal and a Journey*, by Michigan-raised Kathy Scott, examines the subculture of split-cane rod makers and the anglers who cast bamboo as their rod of choice.

Tales of fly fishermen who were introduced to the sport by fathers, grandfathers, older brothers, uncles or other male mentors are as abundant as mayfly hatches under ideal conditions. Stories of how women came to fly fishing, while fewer and less familiar, are no less compelling.

* * *

When I first met sisters Sherri Steele and Heather Jones there were no more prominent women fly anglers in southwestern Ontario. Born and raised in Stratford, and known as the Robins Twins from before

they married, the sisters started fishing young and became known in fly fishing circles by introducing the sport to other women. They learned much from their mother, Sue, whose legacy they continued to play forward through their love of the activity that brought their parents together in the first place.

Marriage and childbirth customarily draw mothers and daughters closer together. Sherri and Heather maintained a strong bond with their mom; however, they were denied the opportunity of connecting on a deeper level when they married. And neither had her mom at her side when she gave birth. All of which makes the identical twins deeply grateful for fly fishing. 'Fly fishing gave us what we wouldn't have had otherwise,' Sherri said.

The cold, bright stars seemed in alignment on 22 February, 2007. Six weeks earlier, Sue, an elementary school teacher, had joined her husband, Ken, in retirement. Just three days previously, the couple had celebrated their thirty-seventh anniversary. And they were packed to leave for Florida, eagerly anticipating their favourite pastime.

The night before heading south, Sue visited her mother in a nursing home outside Stratford. She would never go away without dropping in, even though her mom was suffering from dementia and would not recognize her daughter. Upon leaving the nursing home, Sue was engulfed in a harsh snowstorm. As she was leaving the parking lot, her car was hit by an oncoming vehicle. Her death at age fifty-five was not only devastating for family and friends, it plunged Ontario's fly fishing community into a state of mourning. *Canadian Fly Fisher*, at the time Canada's leading magazine devoted to the sport, honoured her life with a moving memorial tribute.

Sue led a vanguard of women discovering the pleasures of fly fishing. Not only was it integral to her life, she was a popular instructor committed to introducing women to the sport she loved. Her daughters have carried on the tradition by conducting workshops, seminars and clinics.

Sue and Ken Robins went fishing on their first date in 1970. They honeymooned in Northern Ontario while pursuing brook trout, before teaching one another the fundamentals of fly fishing by sharing a library copy of Joe Brook's seminal book *Trout Fishing*. 'When Mom met Dad, she quickly realized she would have to learn to fly fish if they were going to spend time together,' Heather said.

Ken, a high school science teacher, eventually acquired the knowledge and skills of an expert fly angler. He wrote a chapter on brook trout in *The Fishing Book*, a chronicle of sportfishing in Ontario and remains a knowledgeable and engaging speaker whenever he gives a talk to fellow members of KW Flyfishers. Sue held her ground alongside her husband and, in the process, developed instructional programs.

The Robins Twins—as they are still known among fly anglers—fished for perch with spinning rods soon after they started walking. Their dad insisted that 'the family that fishes together, stays together', Sherri said. They switched to fly fishing when their dad built them custom rods when they were seven.

They shared smiles when they recalled their parents packing them into the car and heading out to Montana when they were thirteen. Although their parents said it would be hot and dry, Sherri remembers the trip differently. 'When we got there, the weather was awful, it was the coldest, wettest summer in memory. The fishing wasn't great, but we still had a wonderful time.'

Although Sue could have taught her daughters the basics of fly fishing, she deferred to her husband. Initially the instructive sessions allowed Ken to bond with his daughters, but as they grew older, they turned to their mother. 'We really became friends with Mom through fly fishing,' Heather said.

Not only did the twins fish with their mom, they joined her in teaching the recreational sport. They assisted in clinics and workshops, including the *Ontario Out of Doors'* Spring Fishing Show, the Ontario Federation of Anglers & Hunters Women's Outdoor Weekend and Izaak Walton Fly Fishing Club's Canadian Fly Fishing Forum, in addition to Grand Opportunities, organized annually at Belwood Lake Conservation Area by Friends of the Grand River (where I first met them). They also joined their mother by participating in Casting for Recovery, founded in the US by a female oncologist as a therapeutic program for women recovering from breast cancer. 'Our relationship deepened when we began teaching with Mom,' Heather said.

The twins have continued to honour their mother's memory by adopting her teaching methods. 'People always say how much we look like our Mom, but it's more than a physical resemblance,' Sherri said.

'We teach fly fishing the same way Mom taught it. She wanted women to experience the joy and wonder and delight of fly fishing.' Sue always insisted fly fishing should not be limited to men. 'It's not about skill sets or technicalities, but love of the sport,' Heather added.

Sue taught through the art of narrative. She was an irrepressible storyteller, which her daughters have inherited. 'Since Mom passed away women have been returning to our workshops two or three times because they want to hear the stories. Women love hearing the stories of other women,' Sherri said. 'Mom's stories live on through us,' Heather added.

When asked about the joy of fly fishing, the twins reeled off qualities and elements. 'It's something you can do cheaply,' Sherri said. 'Mom and Dad didn't have a lot of money. It was something we could do inexpensively as a family.' Fly fishing is an active, rather than a passive recreation, even though it is low impact in terms of stress on the body. 'It's not a boring sport because you're always doing something,' Sherri said. 'It's not like sitting on a riverbank and staring at a worm and bobber or sitting in a boat with an outboard motor and trolling.'

Heather is drawn to the sport's mystique. 'We felt special because it wasn't something a lot of people did. We were proud to tell people we enjoyed it.' She appreciates the peacefulness and serenity of fly angling. 'It puts you in intimate contact with nature.' Sherri and Heather agree that women approach fly fishing differently than men. They also insist it is easier to teach women. (Interestingly, all of the male fly fishing instructors and guides I've talked to concur.) Sue wanted women to get over the intimidation factor. 'But it wasn't political,' Sherri said, adding that, 'Women have fewer preconceptions than men. Men see fly fishing as a power thing. Size is everything.'

The twins do not fish together as much as they used to. 'It's been placed on the back burner with the birth of our kids,' Sherri said. Instructing has also been put on hold 'for the time being.' They acknowledge it took their dad a while before he returned to the passion he shared so long with his wife. He now fly fishes with his partner, Lilianna, including a memorable angling adventure to Poland.

Their husbands do not fly fish. However, the twin's eyes sparkled when they talked about fly fishing together more regularly again—when it is time to teach their children the graceful art of casting an artificial fly. They did not waste any time introducing their children to fishing with spin-casting gear.

When the twins were young, their parents purchased a trailer on the Saugeen River to accommodate the family devotion to fly fishing. Appropriately their home water was chosen as their mother's final resting place. 'Mom's ashes were dispersed on the river,' Heather said. 'When light dances on the water and gives it a twinkle, we think of her,' Sherri added. 'We feel her presence on the water.'

Allure of Bamboo

I was not interested in reading about bamboo fly rods until I purchased one. I soon had three, then four. My first two rods were commercially made in America more than half a century ago by the Montague and Granger companies. The other was made by an unknown rod builder from, I assume, southwestern Ontario. Then I purchased a lovingly cared for Sweetgrass.

Catching my first trout on a bamboo rod was deeply satisfying—especially for an angler who does not tie his own flies. I would rather spend time in an armchair reading about my passion than sitting at a vise transforming bits of fuzz, feather and yarn into artful imitations of insects and aquatic critters.

I baptized my first cane rod during an end-of-September visit to the Catskills with Lois Hayward, my partner at the time. The fishing was challenging because of late-season low water, so I failed to net any trout. No matter. Casting bamboo made me feel closer to the tradition and heritage of the contemplative sport I had grown to love.

There is something unique about holding a bamboo rod and casting on peaceful waters. Technology has made graphite rods—even less expensive models—efficient and effective instruments to cast. But a special joy, even bliss, accompanies casting a rod born of nature and handmade by dedicated artisans rather than mass-produced on an assembly line.

Like fibreglass—which superseded bamboo as commercial rods of choice from the 1950s through 1970s—graphite rods are machined from manufactured materials. They are evaluated by performance specifications that are measured, calibrated and quantified in industrial quality control laboratories. Conversely bamboo rods are made by skilled artisans with hand tools. They have a personality that eludes synthetic rods and are judged by how they perform on the water.

The beloved Michigan-based writer Robert Traver—a kind of fly angling Will Rogers—revered split-cane rods. In *Trout Madness* he confides that not only did he have a thing for his bamboo rods, they had a thing for him. It was love at first cast.

Bamboo is a living plant that comes from one specific area in China. Of the more than a thousand different bamboo species, the preferred choice of fly rod builders is Tonkin cane, which grows in a small area of about 190 square kilometres up the Sui River, in the Tonkin Gulf region of Guangdong Province. Tonkin replaced Calcutta cane because of the high density of its fibres which gives the material maximum strength, straightness and flexibility. It also has well-spaced nodes which enhances aesthetic appeal.

It gives me pleasure to know that the cane used to make fly rods comes from the same country that not only invented landscape art—as we recognize it today—in the tenth century, but was the first to interpret the landscape symbolically. Landscape and fly angling are inextricably woven together, both literally and figuratively. Mind and eye coalesce in an elegant symbiosis.

Casting a split-cane rod is both an intimate act and an aesthetic practice. It is as if the rod comes *alive* in my hands. I feel the transference of energy, of spirit, of soul from rod to body. It slows me down, increases my attentiveness to the sensual grace of casting. It connects me intimately to fish through the terminal end of my rod. It is meditative physics in motion—a ballet between angler and rod choreographed to the melody of rivers.

Jerry Kustich, an eloquent angling writer and bamboo rod maker, expresses what I feel about split-cane in *Wisp in the Wind*, one of his four memoirs:

It is curious how much I rely upon walking next to a stream to seek comfort, consolation and meaning. I once thought it was pure escapism, but now I am not so sure. For me, taking along a bamboo rod not only heightens the significance of the experience, but somehow the soul of the universe seems a bit closer with a wisp of cane in my hand.

Kustich puts his finger on a significant element of escapism. When we dislike or fear something, we want to escape *from* it as an act of self-preservation. Conversely, when we like or enjoy something we want to escape *to* it. Escaping *to* is the thrust of adventure, of the imagination, in pursuit of something worthwhile—fly fishing for instance.

I eventually sold my Montague and Granger rods to help finance my first trip to the West Branch of the Ausable River in the Adirondacks. I am pleased that a young fly angler—he would have been in his early thirties—purchased them. He was buying as many bamboo rods as he could afford as models for a rod he intended to make by hand. At the time he was teaching his four-year-old son to fish. My vintage rods could not have found a better home.

Since I am an obsessive armchair fly angler, the acquisition of split-cane rods sent me on the intellectual adventure of prospecting the literature devoted to bamboo. I discovered a charming tributary that feeds into the mainstream of fly angling literature. There are many books about fly fishing with bamboo, some of which are classics. These are simply the titles I stumbled across and enjoyed, all written by contemporary fly anglers. They have a hallowed place in my library.

John Gierach is well known to fly anglers who enjoy reading about the sport. His *Fishing Bamboo* is as good a place to start as any, especially with the recent hardcover reprint of the original, published in 1997. I prize my signed copy, which comes with a new introduction in which Gierach confesses he does not fish with bamboo as much as he once did. The book has the sardonic, no-nonsense, everyman approach that has made him undoubtedly the most popular fly angling writer of his generation.

Gierach suggests bamboo appeals to fishermen who value tradition and nostalgia, who appreciate handmade objects of wood rather than plastics or synthetics, who describe rods in organic rather than mechanistic terms. He prefers tradition over new technology. I relate to these words.

That is why I write with a gold-nibbed Parker fountain pen (a gift from Lydia our first Christmas together) and drive a Jeep with standard transmission and roll-down windows. That is why I would rather fish from a canoe than an outboard-powered boat. That is why I read books rather than eBooks. Forget about audio books. That is why I listen to CDs and watch cable TV instead of downloading and live-streaming. That is why my cellphone (which I refer as a dumb-phone) has no data. That is why I prefer acoustic music to electronic music and why engraving remains my preferred art form. For me, being old-fashioned is an affirmation of self-respect.

Gierach's angling buddy and fellow bamboo aficionado Ed Engle celebrates split-cane fly rods not as works of art or as elements of a living tradition, but as effective, practical tools to catch fish. *Splitting Cane* is a collection of conversations between Engle and sixteen celebrated contemporary rod makers, including the late Ted Knott, the Hamilton-area rod builder whose reputation endures.

George Black's *Casting a Spell* offers a comprehensive social history of bamboo rods. He argues that hand-crafted, split-cane rods are a quintessentially American innovation. He traces the evolution of the bamboo rod through the lives of masters who crafted these works of functional art with minimal financial reward. Black examines the history of bamboo rods in the context of larger cultural trends spanning politics, recreation, economics, environmentalism, industrialization and conspicuous consumption. It is a sad, though ultimately uplifting story, of rise and fall and rise again.

Frank Soo's *Bamboo Fly Rod Suite* was inspired after he found and restored an old, beat-up bamboo rod. In contrast to Black's focus on the pursuit of perfection, Soo argues in his novella-length meditation that fly fishing is worthwhile because it teaches how to cope with failure. It is the mistakes people make that matter—a condition fly anglers know well. He also advocates a slower pace in an age of acceleration, balancing a life of work with play so as to make time for wonder.

Kustich left Winston Rods to set up Sweetgrass Rods with Glenn Brackett. I first saw one of his memoirs in a fly shop in Asheville, North Carolina. On a visit to Hunter Banks I perused *Around the Next Bend.* I thought about buying the book, but passed. A few days later I saw the book in Livingston Manor, New York, at the Catskill Fly Fishing Centre and Museum. I read the coincidence as a fortuitous omen and picked up a signed copy.

Although he lived in Montana at the time (he has since relocated to Maryland after stepping back from rod-building), Kustich was born and raised in Buffalo. His passion for fly fishing was triggered by steelhead in the tributaries flowing into the Niagara River, Lake Erie and Lake Ontario. He returns regularly to western New York to fish with his brother Rick, who operated a fly shop in western New York for a decade and, like his brother, is an angling author (I have their co-authored *Fly Fishing for Great Lakes Steelhead*).

Kustich knows Canada well, especially southwestern Ontario. Not many American fly fishing writers recognize the late Red Fisher, proprietor of television's Scuttlebutt Lodge. (I remember watching Red's weekly show with deep fondness.) In an essay about fishing for walleye in *Around the Next Bend*, Kustich recalls:

This plaid-clad guru of Canadian backwoods outdoor shows would take eager TV fans on adventures to magnificent places so full of Northern pike and walleye that it was impossible not to be swayed into the walleye way of thought. Other than *Hockey Night in Canada*, his was the only show worth watching on the Canadian television network in the fifties.

He recounts learning to write about his passion, and examines river etiquette and angling ethics. He strikes cautionary notes about environmental degradation and he champions ecological responsibility. But his deepest passion is fishing for wild trout with a bamboo rod handmade by gifted artisans. I respect his priorities.

Fly fishing would be different today were it not for the 1960s. Like Gierach and a number of other prominent fly anglers including Thomas McGuane and Jim Harrison, Kustich is a product of the decade's rebellious, anti-establishment, conscious/conscience-raising counterculture and back-to-the-land movement. Ted Leeson, an English professor who views fly fishing through the lens of literature, gives expression to this historical and social influence in *The Habit of Rivers* when he asserts that fishing is a form of subversion. If this is not a hippie call to arms—a counterculture mantra of recreational disobedience worthy of Henry David Thoreau—I do not know what is. But I digress.

As in *Around the Next Bend*, Kustich reveals his familiarity with southwestern Ontario in *A Wisp in the Wind*. In addition to steelheading with Rick numerous times, he attended a number of Grand River fly fishing gatherings. He speaks glowingly of the development of the tailwater in the book's title chapter:

The Grand River ... is distinct because it has been resurrected from the trash heap of degraded rivers common to areas of heavy population inspired by the united vision as to what a revitalized river could mean to the health and psyche of a community.... [It] has become a model for reclaimed rivers that could be used throughout North America.

I take pride in the fact that an angler who travels so far to get here understands and appreciates the Grand River's transformation from sewer to trout fishery. That the angler is an esteemed writer is even better. As a fly angler who has taken part in conservation efforts on local rivers, I am glad to have played a tiny role in this ecological metamorphosis. This is not hubris, but an expression of respect and gratitude to the individuals, conservation organizations and government departments that recognize the benefits of clean, if not pure, water. An abundant population of trout is a barometer of a healthy hydrological habitat. We are all better off—fly angler, hard lure and bait fisherman and non-angler alike.

The Grand is the artery that pumps lifeblood into the land, it sustains the spirit of *place* where I live. This environmental ethic is reflected in the bamboo rod tradition I cherish. Consequently Kustich's words are especially resonant when he praises my *home* water.

CODA: FELLOWSHIP OF THE ANGLE

Three of Jerry Kustich's four memoirs, including *At the River's Edge*, are illustrated by Al Hassall, who lived for many years in the southwestern Ontario village of Arthur before moving North of Superior. I tip my oilskin fedora to him whenever I drive through the village en route to the Saugeen headwaters in pursuit of trout and to the Bighead in pursuit of steelhead.

I was pleased to learn that Hassall often dropped by Wesley Bates's studio in Clifford. Wesley, who was unfamiliar with Kustich's writing, was delighted when I told him that Hassall illustrated Kustich's memoirs. I am constantly amazed by fly fishing's six degrees of separation. Fly anglers really do comprise a fellowship. It would not surprise me were Tolkien a fly fisherman.

Sweetgrass Synchronicity

For most people retirement is a significant signpost along the road of life. In the spring of 2015 I marked half a century in the workforce and was eager to celebrate the milestone. One afternoon I was ruminating with Lois Hayward that, as a retirement gift to myself, I would like to order a Sweetgrass fly rod.

I explained that the custom fly rod company was founded in Twin Bridges, Montana, by Glenn Brackett after he resigned from the R.L. Winston Rod Company. Before resigning from Winston, he and Tom Morgan moved the bamboo operation to Montana from San Francisco to enjoy better fishing.

Jerry Kustich also moved to Montana for the fishing. He joined Winston and subsequently co-founded Sweetgrass Rods with Brackett. If you want to read what led to Sweetgrass and the devotion to craftsmanship that shapes the company, I recommend Kustich's quartet of memoirs: *At the River's Edge*, *A Wisp in the Wind*, *Around the Next Bend* and *Holy Water*. The respect with which he describes his fellow Booboys makes me fantasize about hoisting a pint in their honour or, better yet, spending an afternoon in their company on one of Montana's famous trout rivers.

The next best thing to an actual meeting is checking out the Sweetgrass website, which offers a glimpse into the spirit that defines the company. Taking a pattern from the fly box of Patagonia founder Yvon Chouinard, Morgan and Brackett adopted a business philosophy of blurring 'the line between work and play fostering creativity, loyalty and a sense of belonging....'

If these are not words to work by, I do not know what are. I had a yearning to pay tribute to my years of wage labour. I landed my first job at fifteen years of age as an elevator operator and bellhop at an elegantly fading hotel that is long gone. I worked as a factory assembler, mechanical draftsman, courier driver, construction labourer and shipper-receiver in a bookstore before landing a reporting job on the first of six newspapers I worked on across Ontario spanning four decades. I paid my way through university working summer vacations in a factory. While attending graduate school I worked on construction. And I was a union activist for more than a quarter century.

Purchasing a Sweetgrass rod would be an extravagance that cost more than I had ever spent on any other single item, with the exception of cars, houses and orthodontics for my sons. But I knew the rod would be worth every penny—and more.

When this dream first took shape, I had no immediate prospects of retirement. In fact, I was anticipating working for at least another three years, taking me beyond 'normal' retirement at age sixty-five. Moreover, I knew it would take eighteen months to receive the rod after placing an order. Such is the length of Sweetgrass's waiting list.

But fate had other plans. A couple of months later, the newspaper for which I worked for three decades offered a buyout too good to refuse. As well, Dylan and Robertson had just graduated from university and college, respectively. Still a split-cane Sweetgrass was a wild dream floating amidst distant galaxies.

Unbeknownst to me, however, the stars were in alignment when I visited Grand River Troutfitters founder Ken Collins. I dropped by his home so he could load an Orvis CFO reel I had purchased from him with Cortland 444 double-taper fly line. I wanted the five-weight line to use with my Granger and Montague bamboo rods.

Before loading the reel Ken went into an adjacent room, saying he had something he wanted to show me. I recognized the Sweetgrass insignia (a pair of trout holding in a yin-yang pattern) on the lid of the cream-coloured tube before he opened it. My mouth opened in surprise. 'So you know Sweetgrass?' he asked with a grin. I nodded—somewhat idiotically I'm sure.

He pulled the rod out of the sleeve, revealing a gorgeous seven-foot, nine-inch, three-piece, five-weight. He assembled it and passed it over. I was gobsmacked. Imagine, I was actually holding a sweetly singing Sweetgrass in my very own clumsy paws. Light, yet supple, with some snap, it was like an extension of my right arm. Anglers who assume that bamboo rods are soft or wimpy have never held a Sweetgrass. Words escaped me. I had been playing guitar since I was sixteen and the feeling of holding the rod was comparable to holding the guitar I had owned for thirty-five years until I lost it in a house fire along with every other material possession I held close to my heart, including my library.

Before leaving I confessed that I could not ignore this serendipity. I have been a reader of Carl Jung since university and, if this was not synchronicity, I do not know what the great Swiss psychologist meant by the term. Although Ken had been given the rod to sell on his website, he handed me a business card and told me to talk directly to the rod's owner. It was a generous thing to do.

I called the owner, a devoted outdoorsman, a few days later. He knew a lot about Sweetgrass. He had met Kustich a couple of times at the Grand River bamboo rod builders' get-together, known as Grand Gathering. He had even visited the Sweetgrass shop in Twin Bridges. It was the second custom-built rod he had purchased. He said Brackett had built the blank—a signature, hollow-fluted, hexagonal classic from a modern master.

I refused to haggle over price. It would have been discourteous to him and disrespectful to Brackett and the Booboys. He quoted an amount, I accepted, knowing that it was a fair price for a priceless functional *objet d'art* made by artisans who carry forward the proud tradition of American hand-built bamboo fly rods.

He said he was pleased the rod was going to someone who would appreciate it as 'a superb fishing instrument'. The agreement was struck ten days after my sixty-fourth birthday and a month after I had waded into the tranquil waters of retirement. I put a cheque in the mail; however, he insisted I pick up the rod as soon as I was able, confirming that there are still gentlemen's agreements within the fellowship of fly anglers.

Friendship & Sweetgrass
Synchronicity Reprise

In *Lines on the Water* David Adams Richards equates the Miramichi River with a love and generosity towards others that God required of Old Testament prophets. It is an extraordinary declaration, but it reflects my experience concerning many of the friendships I have made through fly fishing.

Dan Kennaley is one such friend. The closest person I know to a Renaissance fly angler, he has been fly fishing for nearly four decades, travelling regularly to such legendary destinations as Algonquin Park, the Catskills and the Adirondacks. As I prepare this chapter for publication, Dan and his wife, Jan, are enjoying on a year-long RV trip around North America. He is not likely to pass up any water that holds the promise of fish.

Dan fishes mostly for trout and bass, whether wading streams and rivers or paddling a canoe, inflatable pontoon or float tube on lakes. He is a gifted fly tier who mastered some killer patterns, combining the old with the new.

In 2007 Dan won the Greg Clark Award, presented at the Canadian Fly Fishing Forum in recognition of his contribution to the sport, including the column he wrote over two decades for *Ontario Out of Doors*. He felt especially honoured because Clark, a celebrated Canadian journalist and fly angler, is a favoured writer. Dan is also an accomplished photographer (he never goes fishing without his Nikon dangling from his neck). He is a collector by temperament, whether lists of birds, stamps, vintage reels or books.

He is a fly fishing historian who made a significant discovery concerning the earliest record of fly fishing in North America that appeared in *The American Fly Fisher*, a journal published quarterly by the American Museum of Fly Fishing. He is in the process of writing a trio of articles for the journal since retiring in June of 2019.

Dan is widely read in the literature of fly fishing and has assembled an enviable library. And he appreciates artists who are true to the recreational sport, from Winslow Homer to Tom Thomson. Best of all, Dan is a heck of a nice guy. I know of no one more generous when it comes to sharing what he has learned over many years.

His enthusiasm is irrepressible, reminding me of the joy children display before becoming teenaged cynics. Thomas McGuane has fly anglers such as Dan in mind when he observes in *The Longest Silence*, a memoir of a life in fishing told through a series of essays, that angling appeals to an adult's inner child. As friend, mentor and tireless conversationalist, Dan is the angler who has contributed most to my deep love of fly fishing. More than once I have felt like a piscatorial James Boswell to his Samuel Johnson.

* * *

According to Aesop, 'a man is known by the company he keeps.' A man is also known by the books he reads. Given our friendship, it should not be surprising that Dan and I share deep affection for many of the same authors and books. Close to the top of our mutual list is the work of W. O. Mitchell.

One of the highlights of my career as an arts reporter was spending an afternoon with Mitchell for a feature story. I also enjoyed three undergraduate English courses that Mitchell's son, Orm, taught me at Trent University. I bought first editions of *Who Has Seen the Wind*, Mitchell's classic coming-of-age novel set on the bald prairies, for each of my sons. For his part, Dan named his new golden retriever after the Canadian author.

Like fellow Canadian authors Roderick Haig-Brown, Ethel Wilson, David Adams Richards, David Carpenter, Jake MacDonald, Paul Quarrington and Mordecai Richler, among others, Mitchell was a fly angler. A rumour persisted throughout his colourful life that he ignored deadlines. While he steadfastly rejected the accusation, he did concede that he sometimes had more pressing matters—like fly fishing. Although the recreational sport appears in only one of his novels, I have always held that all of his most beloved characters—from Brian in *Who Has Seen the Wind* and Hugh in *How I Spent My Summer Vacation*, through Archie Nicotine and the hired man Jake, to the lively centenarian Daddy Sherry and the philosophizing shoemaker Wullie MacCrimmon—are all fly anglers at heart and in spirit, if not in body.

What do I mean by such a daft statement? After all, Brian and Hugh are boys, embryonic fly anglers at best, Archie has more urgent concerns, Daddy is preoccupied with kites and Wullie prefers a curling rock to a fly rod. Still they share character traits I associate with fly anglers: a contemplative turn of mind at home in the company of elemental questions; a moral compass that points true North; an attentiveness to the manifold wonders of existence; a distaste for anything fake, false or fraudulent—except artificial flies. In other words, these are people with whom I would happily share time on a river.

The passage on fly fishing in *Since Daisy Creek* comprises a set piece of about four pages. The recreational sport makes a cameo appearance in three guises: Casting, Catching and Tying. The protagonist is Colin Dobbs, a delightfully foul-mouthed English professor (sounding very much like W.O.) who is mauled by a grizzly—talk about the all-Canadian horror story. He takes his daughter, Annie, under his piscatorial wing at a young age.

Casting: Like Norman Maclean in *A River Runs Through It*, Mitchell introduces his homespun *Basics of Fly Fishing* with a rudimentary casting lesson. In contrast to Maclean's four-four metronomic count, Mitchell advocates a two-count to accommodate a shorter rod stroke. He instructs Annie to place a beer bottle between her elbow and her side. I was told the same thing as a neophyte fly caster.

Catching: Dobbs's advice on the water is equally perspicacious when he explains what fly anglers refer to as presentation and line management. He tells his daughter to work upstream—the classic dry fly presentation. He reinforces the benefit of mending a line to keep it taught so the hook can be set effectively when a fish strikes. This is what fly anglers mean by the term 'tight lines'.

Tying: Annie is at the tying vise when Dobbs reminds his daughter about the eating habits of trout. It is true, different trout eat different ways at different times, under different circumstances. Fly anglers agree that brown trout are the cagiest, while brook trout are most gullible—or innocent. Cutthroat are easier to fool than rainbow because of their willing suspension of disbelief. Few fly anglers would disagree. I have always taken pleasure in Mitchell applying a literary term to the gastronomic propensities of trout.

When the conversation flows into tying flies Mitchell demonstrates once again he knows of what he writes. Frustrated at the vise, Annie confides to her father in colourful language much like his own. She sounds like Huck Finn in pigtails sitting at a tying vise. (Twain was an important literary influence on Mitchell.)

This exchange touches on the enduring question among fly anglers regarding what flies are more effective: literal imitations of actual insects that are hatching or impressionistic thingamajigs that attract fish for reasons only they understand. Mitchell concludes that shape, colour and movement are the most important factors, in that order. Again, most fly anglers concur.

As so often happens, Dan and I agree that a day off the water *with* a novel by W.O. is better than a day off the water *without* a novel by W.O. Nothing however, not even a novel by one of our favoured writers, beats a day on the water.

* * *

Dan has fished most of his life. He started fly fishing in 1984 when he received as a wedding gift a fibreglass fly rod custom-built from a Fenwick blank by a work colleague. Jan was not impressed. Yet she gave Dan a fly-tying vise as a gift on their first Christmas as newlyweds. Dan purchased his first graphite rod a couple of years later.

In contrast to Dan I came to fly fishing late. I was fifty-five years old and had returned to spin fishing five years earlier. For reasons I can't fathom—and deeply regret—I abandoned fishing in my early twenties. Forsaking it did not stop me from devouring as much fly angling literature as I could long before I was introduced to the recreational sport.

I am close to Dan in temperament and interests. I do not tie flies, I have not travelled as widely, I have never used a pontoon or float tube and my knowledge of the history of the sport is not as comprehensive. However, my appreciation of the literature of fly angling is comparable. When we are not on the water, we are consumed in talk about fly angling literary minutiae that would send most anglers rushing to the nearest river as fast as their waders could take them.

I met Dan at KW Flyfishers which has been providing companionship to anglers since the 1970s. He suggested we get together for an outing and, within the next couple of weeks, we were on the water. Dan introduced me to some of the area's premium fly fishing water, including a couple of secret places which I now cherish as home waters. He never bristled when I asked silly questions, often repeatedly. He gave me flies he knew had a good chance of success. And he never ridiculed something I did, however foolish it might have been.

Early in my fly angling apprenticeship I joined Dan and fellow Flyfishers member Jeff Thomason, himself no slouch when it comes to angling, for a late spring outing on Whiteman's Creek. The water was high, as one would expect for the time of year, and I got a fly hung up on a low branch on the other side of the stream. I had been casting for only a few minutes and I was damned if I was going to lose a store-bought fly so soon in the game.

I gingerly traversed the stream as cold water rose a few centimetres with each step until it exceeded the top of my chest waders. They filled rapidly, causing me to gasp for breath as I succumbed to the cold water that encased my body from the tips of my wiggling toes to my tingling chest hairs. I could have drowned, or so I feared, but survived to face my humiliation.

When Dan found me drying off in the warm chill of spring, I was stone-cold naked. My clothes were spread out on rocks drying in the sun, as was all the paraphernalia from my vest. I had read in *The Complete Idiot's Guide to Fly Fishing* that one of the greatest sins a fly fisherman can commit is allowing the hooks on his flies to rust. Unbeknownst to me, I had lost my car keys, which Jeff miraculously found on the bank some distance downstream.

I am sure that Jeff and Dan shared a hearty chuckle at my expense—who wouldn't—but neither belittled me, despite stupidity and scorn making for cosy bedfellows. Fortunately for me, my baptism as a fly fishing fool did nothing to dissuade Dan from inviting me to join him on other outings, including an annual visit to the family cottage in Muskoka, where we fish for bass from a canoe on a small, secluded lake.

All this is backstory to the day Dan and I headed up to one of our secret places—a slice of paradise in southwestern Ontario. It was a momentous day for me, and I wanted to share it with Dan. I had just acquired my Sweetgrass rod and I was eager to baptize it in holy water.

I was as excited as when I was a ten-year-old heading off on another adventure with my friend Billy Everett, to visit his aunt and uncle on their hardscrabble farm outside of South River, Ontario. This was where I was introduced to brook trout, caught in copious quantities from a small cold spring creek. The specks were caught on black braided line tied to the terminal end of ten-foot bamboo poles, baited with worms from the garden. The specks were beheaded, gutted, dusted in flour with salt and pepper and fried in bacon fat sizzling in a large cast-iron pan on top of a wood stove. Talk about delicious!

Dan and I arrived at our destination about 5:00 p.m. We hit the big pool, which we customarily saved till dusk, so Dan could take a few photos of me catching my first trout on my sweetly singing Sweetgrass. It took three casts and I had a small rainbow. I passed the rod—complete with Orvis CFO reel and Cortland five-weight, double-taper line—to Dan. A couple of casts later, he had a small 'bow.

Dan headed downstream, as is his habit, while I lingered at fishy spots where I expected to find combos of 'bows, browns and, most prized of all, wild brookies. The Sweetgrass drew a graceful arc against a background of rushing headwater and bankside conifers. I caught

one eight-inch brookie among the nine trout I landed over three hours. I handled it gently, as I wanted to get a quick photo of it in close proximity to my bamboo rod, reminiscent of illustrations found in such vintage outdoor magazines as *Field & Stream*.

Just as I was getting the Pentax out of my vest pocket, he spit out the hook and dashed for protective stones on the shallow stream bed. I was disappointed until it dawned on me that catching one of nature's most glorious creations is about living in the moment as the fleeting ghost darted for home. I have come to learn that memories do not require photographic verification to last.

CODA: THE ROD THAT KEEPS ON GIVING

In the previous essay—'Sweetgrass Synchronicity'—I note that acquiring the bamboo rod was synchronistic. When I got home, I checked my emails after pouring a dram of eighteen-year-old Arran malt whisky—with its nose of sweet fruit, vanilla and cinnamon spice dipped in syrup and toasted oak; palate of dark chocolate, ginger, caramelized brown sugar and vanilla dancing on the tongue; and long, luxurious finish. My heart skipped a beat when my inbox revealed an email from Jerry Kustich.

I had sent a link to my blog to the Sweetgrass shop a few days previously, in the hope that Glenn Brackett and the Booboys might be interested in the circumstances that led to one grateful fly fisherman acquiring one of their custom rods. Brackett had graciously replied, asking permission to publish the blog posting on the Sweetgrass website. I told him I would be honoured. On top of that, there was Kustich's unexpected email:

Hi Robert,

The crew forwarded the link to your nicely done blog site and I very much enjoyed your piece about Sweetgrass and your new rod. Also I appreciated your kind words about my books. I am a strong believer in Jung's synchronicity and am pleased you found your rod in that magical way. Bono of the popular musical group U2 would call it Cosmic Rhyme....

Like you I have retired and am exploring life beyond the borders of Montana. I now live in Maryland where I am closer to where I grew up in

Buffalo. Hopefully I will continue to build some rods here for Sweetgrass and continue to write a few more fishing stories about life. I hope our paths cross Robert. Maybe I will make it to the next event in Fergus. Let me know when you catch a fish on the new rod.

All my best,
Jerry Kustich

My Sweetgrass keeps on giving. One of my favourite American artists is Russell Chatham—an angling writer and wild game gourmet as well as passionate fly fisherman. His evocative paintings adorn the covers of the books of his dear friend Jim Harrison. Although I could never afford an original Chatham painting, I have wanted for many years to acquire a good quality print.

I need have looked no further than the Sweetgrass website where I discovered that the company commissioned a poster of a Chatham oil completed in 1989 in honour of master bamboo rod builder Tom Morgan. *Evening Fishing* is an evocative image of a fly angler viewed from behind, fishing at eventide. I purchased the poster and had it framed. It now hangs above my computer desk so I can look up for inspiration when the keyboard defeats true, honest sentences.

Casting on the River of Friendship

Unlike family, we choose our friends—or our friends choose us. Who knows whether it is by random accident, mutual coincidence or preordained design. I have always viewed the emotional transaction and subsequent bond of friendship—especially friendship of long standing—as a form of grace which is not always merited but is bestowed as a gift. It is the blessing life and fly fishing share in common. I do not know whether he chose me or I chose him, but Gary Bowen and I have been friends going on half a century. I have Gary to thank for many things. Foremost he is the improved clinch knot that has tied together a ragtag group of university buddies—Don 'DD' Doyle, Billy Doyle, Randy Mather and Bob 'Herbs' Kidd. I was known as 'RR'. It was Gary who reintroduced me to fishing, which evolved into fly fishing, one of the passions of my maturity.

Gary and I met in 1972 in our first undergraduate year at Trent University in Peterborough, Ontario. We enrolled at the same college: Peter Robinson. Gary majored in biology, while I majored in English. We were both fortunate to build fulfilling careers. He became an authority on fresh water. I worked as a newspaper reporter.

Gary started as an environmental consultant before moving to the Ontario environment ministry. He now works for the Toronto & Region Conservation Authority out of the Duffins Creek office north of Pickering. His expertise is water management. His career has taken him across North America, as well as to Argentina and Scotland. He was appointed by the federal fisheries minister as an advisor to the Canadian commissioner of the Great Lakes Fisheries Commission.

Gary comes from a family of outdoorsmen. His father, Rae—a quiet man with a wry sense of humour—was an enthusiastic hunter and angler, an amateur wildlife painter and carver, and a published author of stories appearing in outdoor magazines such as *Rod and Gun in Canada*, *Fur-Fish-Game*, *Outdoor Canada* and *Ontario Out of Doors*. In the early 1980s I edited one of Rae's stories which won a

Toronto Star short-story contest. Although their dad did not hunt or fish with his three sons when they were young, Gary and his younger brothers, John and Rob, followed in his Gortex footsteps.

One summer while we were at Trent Gary invited DD, Randy and me for a weekend of fishing at an old, dilapidated shack on the shore of a lake on his uncle's property, outside of Havelock in eastern Ontario. We lived on Kraft Dinner, freshly filleted bass and copious quantities of bottled beer chilled in the lake. Although I fished as a kid, I caught more fish over those few days on Lost Lake than I ever had previously—including the biggest bass landed on the trip.

When Gary and his two brothers started working, they purchased property in the vicinity of Lost Lake and built an ever-expanding hunting camp (including maple syrup hut with state-of-the-art equipment). They now own eight hundred acres and have access to another six hundred acres, some of which is owned by extended family. In addition to fishing for bass and muskie on the isolated lake, they hunt deer, partridge, wild turkey and bear (Rob hunts the latter with a bow), as well as the occasional moose when they secure licence tags. Unfortunately ducks that used to populate nearby marshes have pretty much disappeared.

I do not know whether Gary is a remnant of United Empire Loyalist stock—I have never asked. But he is as embedded in the landscape of Eastern Ontario as an Al Purdy poem. He is as solid and honest, as grounded and true as Purdy's Roblin Lake. I have always viewed him as a student from 'that old school of higher standards', to quote Wayne Curtis in *Fishing the High Country*.

In the age of big-box franchise stores, Gary is the equivalent of a small-town, independently owned hardware store that carries a bit of everything, including sporting goods on overstuffed shelves. (Remember the unique smell those stores had?) 'I'm just not into high-end gear,' he said. 'A good rod and gun is what it's all about, even if I pick up some new equipment now and then. I'm cool hunting with my old single-shot 20-gauge.'

You cannot miss Gary on the river. He does not dress to fish. He has no truck with brand names or designer labels. Instead, he prefers a baseball cap (with CAT logo) and T-shirt in summer and flannel shirt in spring or fall (oftentimes short in the arms), along with cheap pair of waders with the boots attached and a faded cotton vest he has worn for more than a quarter century. Rather than nippers, which fly anglers prefer, he has a pair of nail clippers handy. Similarly, he relies on an old pair of needle-nosed pliers instead of hemostats, which fly anglers prefer. He is as far away from an angling fashion plate as a double-haul cast gets. Black powder hunting is a recent interest because 'having only one chance adds to the thrill.' Gary takes after his dad, who died leaving behind a half-empty box of .30-06 cartridges with a note that accounted for every deer and bear bagged with the spent cartridges. To do less would dishonour the sacrament of the hunt.

Since I started writing about my fly fishing misadventures, Gary has ribbed me about writing so much about *not* catching fish. But he confesses that he is not much different, proving that, like an enduring marriage, longtime angling companions start resembling one another.

'I'm getting the same way with duck hunting,' he said. 'I'm good if I get enough for a couple of dinners.' Gary, by the way, is an excellent cook when it comes to game thanks to instruction from his mom. 'As long as I get out hunting or fishing is all that matters—seeing a few birds, making one or two good shots or casting to a rise. If it were just about catching fish or bagging a deer, I'd go out and hit a stupid golf ball around.'

Gary is a throwback to an older breed of outdoorsman, he is a champion of value over price gained through practice in the field and on the stream. He is not a pure fly angler. Most of his fishing is done with a well-oiled spinning reel and durable rod he has owned for more than a quarter century. He tosses minnows from the stern of a fourteen-foot aluminum boat while massaging a cantankerous four-horsepower motor. For his fiftieth birthday Gary suggested 'the Boys' join Herbs in Saskatchewan for a week's fishing on Lac la Ronge. DD flew in from BC while Gary, his brother John, and I flew out from Ontario. It was a week of angling Nirvana in pursuit of lake trout, walleye and northern pike. We stayed in a comfortable rangers' cabin at the far end of the lake with all the amenities—save for indoor bathroom. Every day we enjoyed Herbs's delicious shore lunches. A shore lunch prepared by someone who knows what he is doing is one of life's gourmet pleasures.

Gary has fly fished occasionally over many years, using his father's hand-me-down glass rod and Pflueger Medalist reel. He gave me his father's tying gear, which I treasure even though I don't tie my own flies. I gave Gary a six-weight graphite fly rod and sold him an Orvis Battenkill reel.

Since taking up the recreational sport, I have tried to hook up with Gary at least once every summer. I introduced him to such southwestern Ontario waters as the Grand and Conestogo tailwaters, Whiteman's Creek and Saugeen River headwaters. He has reciprocated by introducing me to some trout and bass waters in eastern Ontario, in addition to Duffins Creek.

I recall spending a day on the Beatty Saugeen. It was the second time I took Gary to the closest place to heaven on earth I can imagine. We caught and released a brace of small athletic 'bows. Gary also landed a brookie.

It was the first trout I had ever caught on an Adams, a traditional trout dry fly designed in 1922 by Michigan tier Leonard Halliday at the request of his friend Charles Adams. I purchased a dozen size 14s at the legendary Dette fly shop in Roscoe, NY.

As fate would have it, we met up with Dan Kennaley and I was able to introduce my two closest fly fishing companions for the first time. It was appropriate for this synchronistic meeting to happen on sacred trout water. Because of their mutual backgrounds, they knew some colleagues in common. The three of us are fans of the late Canadian outdoors columnist Greg Clark—a short man who stands tall in the pantheon of Canadian anglers.

Half a century is a long time to be friends. 'The Boys' have married and raised families. Some have divorced—I more than once. Some enjoy grandchildren. We've buried parents and loved ones. Gary was the last to retire. Collectively we suffer through enough health issues to fill a medicine cabinet. One of us is heroically battling Parkinson's and has been confined to a palliative care facility. Heart disease is a nagging threat. Mortality has proven an adversary with a dark sense of humour.

Through it all, fishing and hunting remain connecting threads. After a glorious day on the water, we began making preliminary plans for a motor tour of some of the great rivers of northwestern Ontario. It would be wonderful were 'the Boys' able to gather again. Heading down the two-lane to Fergus for a late supper and chilled draft Gary remarked: 'We've always had a good time, RR.'

'Right on, big guy,' I replied. Sometimes you don't have to fib about the size of the fish.

Casting on the river of friendship, I am reminded of a poem by Ron Rash, a fine writer, teacher and fly angler from North Carolina. Collected in *Raising the Dead*, 'Speckled Trout' recounts an outing with his cousin, but it is about more than a day of fishing.

Although his cousin died some years previously, Rash's grief paints the poem in solemn hues of mourning. He ends with an accurate description that becomes metaphor. After catching a brilliant trout from the shadows of a dark underwater world, its colours start fading as the poet holds the lovely creature in the palm of his hand.

Eventually we all become trout out of water.

Summer

Cradle of American Fly Fishing
Endlessly Rocking

One highlight of more than three decades of writing about the arts for daily newspapers was reviewing the opening week of the Stratford Festival, in the southwestern Ontario city of Stratford. While nothing could draw me from that cultural privilege, a thin shadow of regret fell over opening week festivities a few years ago when Dan Kennaley started making annual sojourns to the Catskills during the days I was immersed in the myriad splendours of William Shakespeare.

As I was about to begin my first year of retirement in 2015, I found myself in an enviable position. I could accompany Dan and his brother Martin to Roscoe, NY, to cast flies at wary trout during the last couple of days of May and the first few days of June. Since I no longer chased newspaper deadlines, I was able to make arrangements to review festival productions within a couple of weeks of opening performances. This allowed me to have my fish and theatre too.

Although I visited Roscoe for a few days in the fall of 2013, fishing was challenging because of late-season, low-water conditions. So this trip marked my first extended angling adventure in the cradle of American fly fishing. I was like a kid waiting on Christmas. The anticipation was overwhelming.

Most fly fishermen in the same position would be busy tying flies to match late spring hatches, but I don't tie my own flies. What I do instead is immerse myself in fly angling literature. Sparse Grey Hackle said it best in *Fishless Days, Angling Nights* when he observed: 'the best fishing is done not in water but in print.' Consequently, I perused my library prospecting for books and authors associated with the Catskills.

I could not do any better than to reacquaint myself with Grey Hackle's delightful piscatorial anecdotes. Sparse Grey Hackle was the pseudonym of Alfred W. Miller, a New York–born and –bred writer who worked as a reporter for *The Wall Street Journal* and contributed articles to such hook and bullet publications as *Sports Illustrated*,

American Angler, Sportsman and *Outdoor Life*. A conservationist as well as a fly fisherman, he edited a number of early angling classics when not casting a line on his beloved Catskill waters.

Fishless Days, Angling Nights was the only book to bear the writer's pen name. The collection of previously published magazine pieces was published in 1971 by the Anglers' Club of New York. (*An Honest Angler*, a collection of unpublished material edited by his daughter, Patricia Miller Sherwood, was published posthumously in 1998.)

It is a charming book of recollections that paints an affectionate picture of what it was like to fish the Catskills in the first half of the last century. Through humorous stories and tall tales—fish tales?—readers meet the people and the landmarks that defined the region as a pastoral mecca for sportsmen and sportswomen including fly anglers. This is *the* book about fly fishing in the Catskills during its golden age. Grey Hackle knew everyone, from master bamboo rod builder Everett Garrison, through fly angling pioneers George LaBranche, Ed Hewitt and Ray Bergman, to fly tiers Herman Christian and Roy Steenrod, the Darbees and the Dettes.

Grey Hackle begins *Fishless Days* with a tribute to his fly angling wife, Louise, whom he calls Lady Beaverkill. The stories recall an earlier age, gone but not forgotten. But three stories erase the patina of nostalgia and remain relevant to contemporary fly anglers.

'The Quest for Theodore Gordon' demonstrates Grey Hackle's journalistic skills as he interviews Christian and Steenrod, who were friends of Gordon, who is accredited with popularizing the dry fly in America. Grey Hackle not only puts flesh on the bones of a mythic figure, he unearths where Gordon lies buried (accompanying his mother) in New York City's Marble Cemetery. His reportorial quest casts a graceful arc from Gordon, who died in 1915, through Christian and Steenrod, to contemporary fly anglers and readers.

In 'The Perfect Angler' Grey Hackle offers a meditation on the three components of successful fly fishing. Neither a showcase of gear nor a treatise on technique, it conveys the essence of (1) finding a fish, (2) deceiving it into taking an imitation of its food and (3) hooking, playing and landing it. If anyone were to ask me to explain the spirit of fly angling, I would point the enquirer to this fine piece of writing.

'Night Fishing' deserves equal shelf space with the classic fly angling stories that populate the many anthologies devoted to the recreational sport. With unparalleled narrative excellence, the story presents the timeless drama between predator and prey against a backdrop of fear and terror.

Grey Hackle not only paints an evocative picture, he places the reader waist-deep in the river's dark current. The drama he refers to by implication is an essential truth fly anglers are reluctant to acknowledge—that their meditative recreation is, at a basic level, a blood sport. Many angling writers grapple with this ethical dilemma which is philosophical in thrust. A list of contemporary Canadian writers includes David Carpenter, Mark Kingwell, Jake MacDonald, Paul Quarrington and David Adams Richards.

After reading *Fishless Days* I turned to another old literary friend: Dana S. Lamb and his *Where the Pools Are Bright and Deep*, a collection of poetic essays devoted primarily to trout fishing in the Catskills and salmon fishing in Quebec. In the essay 'Season's End' Lamb writes about reading a book with the partial title of *Fishless Days*.

Fly fishing set down roots in Pennsylvania, the Adirondacks and Maine before the Catskills, but the latter is routinely referred to as the cradle of American fly fishing because of the writers who transformed the area, located by automobile two hours west of New York City, into a vibrant literary tradition, according to Tom Rosenbauer in his thumbnail history *Fly Fishing In America*.

The Catskills attracted generations of fine writers, many of whom were based in New York City, arguably the world's publishing epicentre throughout the last century. This literary tradition spans the legendary Gordon, through Grey Hackle, to Arnold Gingrich, the urbane founding editor of *Esquire* magazine.

Born in Michigan, Gingrich was a celebrated fly angler who championed lightweight gear and tackle on a Paul Young 'Midge' bamboo fly rod. A collector of vintage angling gear, he was also a collector of angling literature and became an authority on its history, outlined in his encyclopedic *The Fishing In Print: A Guided Tour Through Five Centuries of Angling Literature*. His *The Joys of Trout* and *The Well-Tempered Angler* are modern classics.

I had *The Well-Tempered Angler* on my library shelf for a number of years. But I didn't read it until eagerly anticipating my trip to the Catskills. Had I known how much I would enjoy the essays, I would have devoured it much sooner. Like the best fly fishing literature, the book is more a meditation on the fishing life, reflecting an approach to living with its concomitant philosophy and moral code, than an instructional manual. However, it does offer practical advice on light tackle fly fishing in addition to a useful bibliography. Gingrich recalls fishing with such angling luminaries as Ernest Hemingway, Ed Hewitt, A. J. McClane and Lee Wulff. He also recounts adventures in Iceland, Ireland and England, as well as Quebec and New Brunswick. But he writes most fondly of halcyon days on Catskill rivers.

As an armchair angler, I especially enjoy Gingrich's observations about the culture of fly fishing and the compulsive nature of collecting, not to mention the meditative sport's literary tradition. Moreover, he is a sophisticated writer; his topics are expressed eloquently and elegantly, with a dry fly wit.

I was pleased to purchase *The Joys of Trout* at the Catskill Fly Fishing Centre in Livingston Manor, a few miles from Roscoe. Its title will mislead readers expecting tips on methods and techniques to be employed on the water. Even more so than its predecessor, *The Joys of Trout* is a miscellany of activities associated with catching fish, which is to say, angling writers with a literary bent, historical lure and lore, angling and conservation organizations.

I challenge anyone to read what Gingrich says about Ernest Schwiebert—a Chicago-born angler who (like Hemingway) vacationed in Michigan—and resist the temptation to hunt down his *Remembrances of Rivers Past*. Happily I succumbed. I even picked up *A River for Christmas and Other Stories* for good measure.

Like Gingrich, Schwiebert is a cultured, well-travelled angling author. Whether recounting early days fishing in Michigan and the midwest, praising legendary Catskill rivers and Pennsylvania limestone streams or travelling the world in pursuit of recreational adventure in the British Isles, Europe, Norway, Iceland, New Zealand or Patagonia, he is both a knowledgeable guide and charming companion.

Anyone who appreciates fly fishing's contribution to literature will be grateful for his account of his trip to Campbell River to visit Roderick Haig-Brown ('The Orchard and the River' in *A River for Christmas*). Schwiebert was one of the first angling writers to tread a path to Haig-Brown's West Coast door. Whether literally or figuratively, others followed, including Steve Raymond, Ted Leeson, Jerry Kustich and Thomas McGuane.

Where Rivers Flow Both Ways

Margaret Laurence wrote one of the great novels of Canadian literature: *The Stone Angel.* She lived in a converted funeral home in Lakefield, Ontario, when I spent four years in the 1970s as an undergraduate at Trent University. While living in the village, she wrote her last novel, *The Diviners,* wherein she poetically writes a river into a symbol of time and mortality by describing it as flowing in opposite directions.

Like the river in Laurence's novel, the trout rivers of Roscoe, New York, flow both ways—at least figuratively—because of the opposing currents of past and present, then and now, history and myth. The metaphor of rivers flowing both ways is enacted in the legendary Junction Pool where Willowemoc Creek flows into the Beaverkill River in the heart of Roscoe, otherwise known as Trout Town, USA. Had Robert Johnson been a fly fisherman instead of a delta bluesman, this would be the crossroads where he bargained his soul with the devil. The notion of rivers flowing in opposite directions is imaginatively sympathetic, at least in my mind, to the tale of the two-headed trout.

According to legend as passed down through generations of Catskills fly anglers who enjoy a dram or two after a day on the water, a migrating trout many years ago paused at the junction of the Beaverkill and Willowemoc to contemplate its route. After inspecting both rivers it could not decide what one to take, both being equally seductive. The trout solved the dilemma quite ingeniously. It settled into the Junction Pool and sprouted a second head so it could spend its days facing up both rivers.

Red Smith, the Pulitzer-winning, New York–based sports writer, knew every fly angler worth knowing associated with the Catskills. As a consequence, he did as much to mythologize the area as a fly angling mecca as any writer, before or since. In his column 'The Beamoc Is a Trout with Two Heads', collected in *Red Smith on Fishing,* he gives the creature an ichthyological name—with tongue firmly planted in cheek. I read the legend as an affirmation of the fellowship of fly angling: two heads are better than one.

Past and present, then and now, converged when I made my first extended trip to Roscoe for eight days of fly fishing straddling late May and early June, 2016. I was on 'the banks of the great tradition' (in the words of Frank Mele in *Small in the Eye of a River*) with Dan Kennaley and his brother Martin, a muskie warrior from Pigeon Lake in Ontario's Kawartha Lakes, who occasionally trades his big stick and large, gaudy lures for a willowy rod and small, hand-tied flies.

Within a couple of days of arrival my thoughts turned to *The Compleat Angler*, which is subtitled *The Contemplative Man's Recreation*. Since its publication in the seventeenth century, anglers have celebrated fishing as a contemplative pastime. This holds especially true for those who view the recreation as a form of meditation or 're-creation'. Despite Sir Izaak's considered opinion, contemplation is a perilous condition for fly anglers—at least for me. Lost in the contours of my sometimes addled mind, I become susceptible to missing strikes. After all, hooking fish requires concentration and focus— not dreamy mental wanderings worthy of William Wordsworth's lonely clouds.

I was fishing a run on the Willow (as locals call the creek) when I was reminded of this piscatorial fact. Long rambling thoughts about writing an account of my trip to the wellspring of American fly fishing had been floating 'on high o'er vales and hills' when a good-sized trout suddenly hit my fly. Blissfully distracted by the poetry of my musings, I flubbed setting the hook. Reflex too late, too sharp. A case of hit and run. I fell back to earth with a mighty thud.

The most memorable every-cloud-has-a-silver-lining-for-some-one-else moment of the trip happened a couple days later when I witnessed Martin landing a fifteen-inch brook trout on a rod with a broken tip and an unnamed fly he tied at home while watching an instructional video on YouTube. I was thrilled Martin caught the trout, I *really* was. Believe me. However, a reader needs to know what led to his thrill of victory to understand the agony of my defeat.

I had failed to catch the rising brookie after more than an hour of diligent effort and frustration on the Upper Beaverkill. I felt like the angler in M. R. Montgomery's *Many Rivers to Cross* who casts repeatedly to the same bored fish boasting an intelligence pitted against me.

Defeated beyond the edge of endurance, I offered the pool to

Martin who caught the lovely gem-like brookie after a few casts. He was over the moon. Me, not so much. Such are the unpredictable wiles of finicky trout. Over beers around the fire back at camp, Dan and I christened the unnamed fly 'the Martykill'.

* * *

Although it predates organized baseball, basketball, football and hockey, fly fishing is the preeminent *postmodern* sport. Nowhere is this more evident than in the Catskills. I use the term non-pedagogically to apply to fly fishing's practice of fusing tradition and innovation, heritage and technology, natural and artificial, memory and expectation.

Against the incessant dissonance of cars and trucks racing along Highway 17 through some of the world's holiest trout water, anglers wade the same tranquil rivers as legends from a hallowed past: Theodore Gordon, Edward Hewitt, George LaBranche, Preston Jennings, Art Bergman, Art Flick, Ernest Schwiebert, Sparse Grey Hackle, Arnold Gingrich, A. J. McClane and Lee Wulff, among others.

The Catskills will remain holy ground for as long as there are rivers and wild trout—and maybe even afterwards when this Good Earth is no more. Sharing water with friendly spirits casts a spell of recognition. Fellowship waist deep in sacred waters heightens and enriches the contemplative experience.

All I need to do is listen to the whispers in the rushing current of time to hear the ghosts of fly anglers past and future in the meeting place of the present. Like a river flowing both ways, I straddle then and now, before and after, by immersing myself in fly fishing's history and tradition through the choices I make. I cast a Sweetgrass bamboo fly rod, carrying forward the dedication to quality exemplified by such legendary New England rod builders as Hiram Leonard, Edward Payne and Everett Garrison.

Likewise, I use a vintage Orvis click-and-pawl CFO reel, a patina bronze beauty made in England (the new models are black and made in the USA) and cherished by anglers for decades. I associate the New England–based company with the heritage of fly fishing in America.

Many of the flies I cast are tied by Dan. Although his comparaduns are based on dressings Al Caucci designed and introduced in his seminal book *Hatches* (co-authored with Bob Nastasi), Dan's designs hearken back to the traditional haystack dry fly of earlier days in the

Catskills. Caucci is connected to the Catskills as owner of the Delaware River Club Flyfishing Resort and Al Caucci Flyfishing School, which have been operating on the West Branch of the Delaware since 1984.

The weather was unseasonably warm during our visit. Hot and muggy is a more accurate description. There was some intermittent rain, but our trip was defined by blazing sun. Sunscreen became a welcome friend. Dan landed the most fish and a higher proportion of big fish; meanwhile Martin and I caught fewer fish and were occasionally skunked. Nothing new in that—at least for me.

It goes without saying that anglers fish to catch fish. But there is more to the experience than what swims below the surface of water. I saw numerous whitetail deer, a couple of porcupines, half a dozen wild turkeys, groundhogs, various birds, including a pair of yellow-bellied sapsuckers, in addition to ducks and Canada geese. I shared water with working beavers and, most spectacular of all, a bald eagle flying at low altitude along the course of the Beaverkill in search of supper.

I am keen to return to the Catskills and its rivers of angling history, legend and myth. I am just as eager to visit Vermont, not to mention Pennsylvania and Maine—places where fly fishing established roots in the late nineteenth century. Then there is Michigan's Upper Peninsula and, of course, Montana, in addition to Quebec, British Columbia and New Brunswick. There is Northern Ontario with Dylan and Robertson. Finally there is the magic trout of the Highlands, with an ancient bard whispering in my ear as I cast to the memory of my ancestors on sruth (stream), abhainnn (river) or bottomless loch.

Recalling the tender words of Scottish-born author Ian Niall in *Trout from the Hills*, these are all places I hope to fish 'until time is with me no more'.

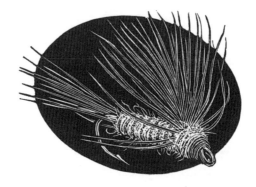

Trout & Art on the West Branch

Henry David Thoreau observes in *Walden* that, 'Many go fishing all their lives without knowing that it is not fish they are after.' I agree with the Yankee mystic on most things, but we part ways when it concerns trips I have made on cruise control with fly gear in the back of the Jeep. With each passing kilometre I become more aware that I am after much more than fish.

What I want is to soak in the landscape, especially its streams and rivers, inhabited by ghosts I yearn to meet. I want to have engaging conversations with people who have swallowed life from a full cup. I want to eat local food without counting calories and drink whisky of good character, dark craft beer and wine that tastes of the soil. I want to smell the rich fragrance of a Habana hand-rolled by women old as the hills (this before my heart attack).

I want to visit bookstores, fly shops, antique emporia, galleries, museums, markets. I want to soak in the history and geography of place. I want to feel the weather and the climate under my fingernails. I want to return home with stories to tell of adventures both on and off rivers. I want memories to keep me company when I am alone in the darkness of night.

The Adirondacks gave me all this, and more, when I made my first trip to one of fly fishing's hallowed grounds. I have described myself as an armchair angler many times. I am also an armchair traveller who tours the globe through the pages of books, fascinated by picture and illustration as much as by text and narrative.

I travelled and fished the Adirondacks long before I dipped my wading boots into the consecrated waters of the state park, which spans much of the northeastern corner of upstate New York. My introduction to the largest park in the contiguous United States was through its conservation ethic, history, literature, architecture, art and rustic crafts—not to mention fly fishing.

From my armchair, Bill McKibben's memoir *Wandering Home*

proved the most congenial introduction to the Adirondacks. His chronicle of an overland hike from his new home in Vermont's Robert Frost Country through the Adirondacks, where he lived for many years, heightened my sense of expectation. I sauntered through Russell Banks's Adirondack novels including *Affliction, The Sweet Hereafter, Cloudsplitter* (about John Brown, who lies buried at his farm outside Lake Placid) and *The Reserve.* I devoured *Fishing the Adirondacks* by fly angling legend Fran Betters.

In the nineteenth century the Adirondacks acted as a magnet for visual artists drawn to the scenic splendour, wilderness romance and fresh air (before the unwelcome arrival of acid rain). By mid-century it became a northern extension of the well-known Hudson River School. In the twentieth century John Marin and George Grosz gave visual expression to the area.

From my perspective there are no better visual guides to the Adirondacks than Winslow Homer, the great nineteenth-century painter, and Rockwell Kent, in my opinion America's most undervalued twentieth-century artist. I agree with David Tatham's premise in *Winslow Homer in the Adirondacks* that Homer's Adirondack oils and watercolours comprise an original investigation into humanity's relationship with the natural world at a time when preconceptions about humans, nature and art were undergoing significant change.

Similarly, I agree with the assessment that informs *Winslow Homer: Artist and Angler* that Homer remains America's most accomplished outdoors painter who transformed picturesque genre pictures into enduring art. With essays by Tatham and renowned angling historian Paul Schullery, former executive director of the American Museum of Fly Fishing, among others, *Artist and Angler* surveys Homer's oeuvre spanning the Adirondacks, Maine, Florida and Quebec. I believe the Adirondacks cut deepest.

Kent painted landscapes bridging such distant places as Newfoundland and Alaska, Maine and Greenland, even Tierra del Fuego; however, his love of the Adirondacks ran as fresh and pure as a spring creek.

Although her connection with the landscape of the American southwest was strongest and most enduring, Georgia O'Keefe had ties to the Adirondacks early in her career. A young O'Keeffe vacationed with her photographer husband, Alfred Stieglitz, on Lake George, where Stieglitz's family owned an estate, before she followed the call of the dramatic forms and intense light of the New Mexico desert.

O'Keefe is reported to have once confided that she would have immigrated to Canada were it not so cold. When I visited the major O'Keefe retrospective at the Art Gallery of Ontario in the spring of 2017 I was struck by qualities—minimalist sculptural forms, limited palette and light as both portraiture and symbol—her work shares with Kent's. I would be surprised if Kent had not influenced the more famous artist.

When I visited the Adirondacks in June of 2017 for five days of fly fishing on its famous West Branch of the Ausable, between Lake Placid and Wilmington, I was reduced to a lovesick pup. The storied river supports a lovely fishery meandering fifty-eight kilometres—much of it at the foot of scenic Whiteface Mountain. It boasts abundant browns and occasional rainbows, in addition to native brookies in its headwaters and smaller, colder tributaries. There is lots of diverse water to accommodate a concentration of anglers, featuring long runs and deep pools, placid stretches and anxious pocket water—all holding fish. There are two catch-and-release zones spanning a total of twelve kilometres. Access is easy because much of its primo water runs adjacent to Route 86 and River Road, which explains why a goodly percentage of anglers I saw revealed tufts of grey hair sprouting from

beneath ball caps and oilskin hats. I saw more anglers using wading staffs than anywhere else I have fished. An inch of prevention is worth a foot of cure in dangerous waters.

The highlight of my most fulfilling eventide of fishing was landing a fifteen-inch brown trout minutes after catching an eight-incher. I caught them in a pool above Monument Falls, with an Ausable Caddis, a pattern designed by Betters, who covered all the piscatorial bases as angler, fly designer and tier, vintage bamboo rod and reel collector, writer and fly shop owner. He is most responsible for putting the West Branch on the fly fishing map—at least in the modern era.

The heartbreak—and there is always an element of heartbreak with fly fishing—came when my camera forsook me. The result: I have no photographic record of landing the pair of brownies. Adding a pinch of salt to the festering wound, I had taken photos earlier in the day; however, I did not check whether they had turned out. Had I done my due diligence, I would have made the necessary menu adjustments before hitting Monument Falls. Talk about a fly fishing fool. Now I face the cruel reality of having no photo to console me during encroaching dotage. On the bright side, I suspect that over time the size of the beautiful trout will grow in my memory archive.

The snafu was compounded by the otherwise dependable Dan Kennaley, a fine photographer as well as angler, not having his Nikon digital camera, which is as much a part of his gear as rod, reel and waders. He mistakenly left his charger at home, so was forced to use his camera sparingly. We were both surprised to learn there are no camera shops in the area. I guess they have become antiquated curiosities in the digital age.

It is always drag on a long dead drift when the mischievous Mr Murphy—you know, the Murphy's Law dude—shows up on a trout stream. When I described my woebegone fish tale to Gary Bowen, my longtime angling pal commiserated sympathetically: 'Why do our cameras screw up on our one big fish and capture every embarrassing thing we do in life?' Why indeed!

Fortunately Dan had a tape to measure the fish after he and his brother, Martin, witnessed the landing. The whole mess proved somewhat ironic because one of the things I appreciate most about fly fishing is its low-tech aesthetic. The simpler things are, the less chance of something going south. That is the theory, anyway.

The abundant hatches of caddis, mayflies and stoneflies on the West Branch follow closely the timing of hatches on the Grand River—perhaps a tad later because of the more northern latitude and higher elevation.

I enjoyed casting famous patterns designed by Betters. In addition to his Ausable Caddis, I used his Haystack—I leave it to fly tying aficionados to debate whether it is the precursor to the comparadun or whether the comparadun is really a haystack—Ausable Wulff and Ausable Bomber. I also purchased a half dozen of his Usuals, which I later used on the Grand where the pattern proves effective.

I was impressed with the two fly shops in Wilmington. They apparently reject combative competition in favour of courteous co-existence. Smart business, that.

When I visited the fly shop at the Hungry Trout in search of the Ugly, a pattern made of raccoon, coyote and muskrat fur, I was informed that, 'the fly shop down the highway' retains exclusive distribution rights. The clerk praised the Woolly Bugger–style fly as 'nothing short of deadly'. Incidentally this is the only place where an angler can pick up a copy of Betters's *Fishing the Adirondacks* for the bargain price of ten bucks.

Our one and only gourmet dinner was enjoyed at the fishing lodge's restaurant festooned with rustic angling and hunting *objets d'art* and memorabilia. Martin and I happily devoured the Guide's Platter, featuring pan-fried trout, medium-rare venison chop and roasted quail, accompanied by a medley of seasonal vegetables, cooked to perfection and delicious.

Similarly the Ausable River Two Fly Shop, which carries Betters's fly patterns masterfully replicated by area tier John Ruff in addition to the Ugly, was equally pleasurable. On my initial visit, Rarilee gave me the rundown on Betters's flies. She also offered to point out sections of the river that had been especially productive in recent days. However, before we discussed the honey spots, I got sidetracked. I mentioned I was interested in Homer and Kent and she told me Asgaard Farm, where the latter lived for half a century, was a mere ten-minute drive away. When I returned the next day, her husband, John, transcribed directions from the farm website.

Dan and Martin share my interest in art and culture and were equally keen to tour Asgaard Farm. We also wanted to take a day trip to the Museum of American Fly Fishing, in Manchester, Vermont, where we also dropped in on the Orvis flagship outlet. We enjoyed a three-hour scenic route on Highway 9N through such historic places as Ticonderoga. We made it back in just over two hours on Interstate 86, which is lovely in its own right.

Visiting Asgaard, which remains a bustling dairy operation spread over two hundred acres, proved memorable. In fact, it was the cultural highlight of the trip. When we arrived I asked a lady working at the farm if this was where Kent lived and she confirmed it was. She said we were welcome to check out his studio, nestled in the woods at the edge of a ridge: 'Feel free to look around. It's open.'

The rustic brown studio with cedar shakes on the roof needed some restoration, but walking around freely was deeply satisfying, like opening a surprise birthday gift. I felt the ghostly presence of the artist, making for a disarmingly pleasant sensation. There were some photos of Kent, a drawing of the layout of the farmhouse on a drafting table, a divan, some chairs presumably rescued from a schoolhouse and racks to hold drying canvases, in addition to some tools in a woodworking shop where picture frames were constructed. I was not sure whether the paint brushes and knives, palettes and other paraphernalia actually belonged to the artist or were period objects placed there to create atmosphere. If they did belong to the artist, it is an acknowledgement of respect that they have not been stolen.

I believe that Kent is unjustly neglected in his own country because of his blend of thorny Yankee self-reliance (he was a New England Transcendentalist in the tradition of Emerson and Thoreau) and communist sympathies (he donated a significant amount of art to Russia in response to neglect at home). My interest in the artist is spurred by his influence on Lawren Harris, a founding member of Canada's Group of Seven.

While the critical chill towards Kent has thawed since the Cold War, a comprehensive reappraisal remains long overdue. A comparison of his paintings between 1917 and 1920 with Harris's paintings from the late 1920s through the 1930s of Lake Superior, the Rocky Mountains and the Far North confirms a striking creative sympathy between the two artists. Although they painted in response to particular landscapes, both artists were driven by a spiritual impulse (as opposed to formal religion). Consequently, their works are as much *soul*scape as landscape. They convey the inner power of nature, featuring highly stylized, sculptural forms and deep, rich colours that reduce nature to its sacred essence.

Although I went to the Adirondacks to fly fish, I caught a lot more than its legendary trout. I am sure Henry would approve.

A River Runs Through Tom

This is as close as I can come to being
salmon, the river's silver soul

& as the white spray rises round me
I know what it is to be

the object of the fisherman's desire,
the subject of the artist's flying brush

— 'Canoeing in the Rapids' by Bernadette Rule
from *Earth Day in Leith Churchyard*

I have admired the art of Tom Thomson since childhood. I remember looking at framed prints of his work, along with those of the Group of Seven, while sitting at desks in classrooms throughout elementary school. These images came to represent the Canadian Shield when I experienced the Precambrian landscape first-hand. They embodied my Idea of North, which was just forming at the time.

My interest in the artist as a fisherman was piqued when I returned to fishing after more than three decades. When I started fly fishing a few years later I became intrigued by the question of whether he was a fly angler. I even began viewing his art differently.

For example, *Northern River* became more than a portrait of an unnamed river. Although it remained emblematic of all rivers throughout the north, I began interpreting it through the eyes and sensibilities of a fly angler. No longer was it just a literal depiction of nature. It simultaneously portrayed an outer state and an inner state of being—what Robert Frost called 'inner weather'.

The painting invited me to 'enter' it metaphorically. I have stepped into this 'picture' many times with fly rod in hand. I recognize the scene from having bushwhacked to promising pools and from portaging with canoe and gear from one watercourse to another.

As with the act of fly fishing, the painting established an intimate connection between me and the natural world. I was not a passive observer looking at nature from a distance—whether panorama from a hilltop or vista of shoreline from a canoe. Rather, I was an active participant immersed in, and enclosed by, nature. I was *in* the forest, *among* the trees. I could hear if any of them fell (in answer to Bruce Cockburn).

The painting acquired a sensuous tactility. It evoked the sensation of wearing wading boots that sink into the soft forest floor of decaying leaves and pine needles. I could smell the moistness of the flora shielded from sunlight by an umbrella of conifers and hardwoods. I could hear the sounds of birds, frogs, maybe even animals scurrying for cover. I felt like swatting at mosquitoes, blackflies, deer flies, horseflies and the tiny bloodsucking insects known colloquially as no-see-ums—the bane of fly anglers.

I realized *Northern River* was not beautiful in a conventional sense. It lacked the majestic splendour of white pine or jack pine so prominent in Canadian landscapes, including Thomson's. Instead, these were spruce or tamarack—northern swampland trees lacking distinctive sculptural form. I saw that the painting recorded a liminal time, as the darkness of night gave way to the light of day. It marked the threshold from forest (terrestrial) to river (aquatic). As a fly angler I was familiar with these transitional periods in the diurnal cycle because it is when insects are most active, which triggers the appetites of hungry fish.

The painting gave me a powerful sense of discovering a landscape in its natural state, unmediated, which was the source of its serene and peaceful mood, always pleasing to fly anglers predisposed to contemplation and reflection. I acknowledged that the river symbolized human existence along the metaphysical continuum of space and time, encompassing the cycle of life, with its intimations of mutability and mortality. And I acknowledged that the sky symbolized infinity. That the light reflected on the water connected the temporal with the eternal, the profane with the sacred. Despite these lofty thoughts, I was grounded in a picture of a deep cold pool holding big trout far from the madding crowd.

Thomson is unquestionably one of Canada's most famous artists, certainly the most famous visual artist. And for many reasons. The mysterious circumstances surrounding his death—whether murder, suicide, foul play, misadventure or accident—play a role in his notoriety. His association with the most famous group of artists in Canadian history contributes to his fame. Moreover, the legend-making machinery kicked into overdrive following his mysterious death, creating a mythic hero who became an iconic national figure, an emblem of the Great White North, at a time when the country was actively shaping its character and identity.

In addition to events beyond the artist's control, the merit of Thomson's creative accomplishment secures him a place in the highest echelons of Canadian art. Yet he transcends the world of visual art. Even people who have no interest in, or knowledge of, visual art recognize his name. Few Canadian artists, irrespective of discipline, are better known—at least among Canadians. It is challenging to name a national creative icon who has exerted more influence across the spectrum of visual, literary (poetry and prose, fiction and non-fiction, scholarly and popular), musical (classical, jazz, folk, pop and rock) and performing arts (theatre and ballet).

Aside from his artistic accomplishments Thomson is celebrated as a fisherman and a canoeist. Although he most certainly fished with live bait and hard lures, I believe he was also a fly angler. By virtue of his unparalleled stature as an artist, he is *ipso facto* one of Canada's most famous fly anglers. Perhaps the country's *most* famous fly angler. Furthermore, he might well have tied his own artificial flies to match the hatch years before it became common practice in North America.

I believe there is a symbiotic sympathy between the artistic temperament and the fly angling temperament. I find it fascinating that so many creative celebrities are dedicated fly anglers: entertainment power-woman Oprah Winfrey; actors (past and present) Jane Fonda, Harrison Ford, Emma Watson, Liam Neeson, Kevin Bacon, Ginger Rogers, Bing Crosby and Henry Winkler (who wrote a memoir about fly fishing); Willie Robertson of *Duck Dynasty* fame (who co-wrote a history of fishing in America); international recording artists Jimmy Buffett, Reba McEntire, Huey Lewis and Eric Clapton as well as Big Band leader Glenn Miller; TV chefs Martha Stewart and Gordon Ramsay; network newsman Tom Brokaw. (These are just the ones I can name off the top of my head.)

There are famous people everywhere, from all walks of life, who are fly anglers. Like Babe Ruth before him, Ted Williams fly fished with the same fierce determination that made him one of the greatest hitters in baseball history. The legendary Boston Red Sox outfielder's second home was New Brunswick's Miramichi River. Annie Proulx, author of *The Shipping News* and 'Brokeback Mountain', is not only a fly angler, she wrote the introduction to an anniversary edition of *A River Runs Through It*.

Many American presidents, Republican and Democrat alike, were fishermen. More than a few were fly anglers, from George Washington, Grover Cleveland and Warren G. Harding, through Herbert Hoover, Harry S. Truman, Teddy and Franklin D. Roosevelt, and Dwight D. Eisenhower, to Jimmy Carter (and First Lady Rosalynn), George W.H. and George W. Bush and, finally, Barack Obama. Not surprisingly, Donald Trump is neither a fisherman nor a fly angler.

Thomson is the spiritual guide of the Canadian wilderness tradition. Like early explorers, he and the painters who became the Group of Seven canoed and fished on painting trips into the Canadian Shield. This places Thomson and the Group waist deep in the current of adventure that flows through Canadian art and culture.

This tradition extends back to European contact with indigenous peoples. It encompasses the exploration of the country and exploitation of its natural resources through westward expansion and frontier colonization. It bridges English and French, Hudson's Bay fur traders and voyageurs. The names of transcontinental adventurers are synonymous with hardship, peril and perseverance: Radisson and Groseilliers, de la Salle, La Vérendrye, Hearne, Mackenzie, Thompson and Fraser. Later came Grey Owl, an English con artist named Archie Belaney who reinvented himself as an indigenous man and conservation pioneer. It continues with such figures as canoeist/filmmaker Bill Mason; wilderness writer James Raffan, author of *Fire in the Bones*, a biography of Mason; and Hap Wilson, a kid who grew up in suburban southern Ontario to become a modern-day Wilderness Man and was a consultant on the Hollywood film *Grey Owl*.

Fishing played a significant role in shaping Thomson—the man and the painter. He fished before he painted. He first visited Algonquin Park—which he later introduced to fellow artists who became the Group of Seven—subsequently determining the course of Canadian art. He fished until the day he disappeared.

No recreation or sport has attracted and inspired more mystery than fly fishing. In part this is because of its heritage, tradition and legacy. It is also the result of the quality of art that has been devoted to it over the last four centuries, especially writing. Since the seventeenth century fly fishing has been practiced by anglers who were for the most part educated, literate and, in many cases, cultured. The fact that he was a fly angler is one small piece in the puzzle of mystique that is Tom Thomson.

Like the narrator in *A River Runs Through It*, Thomson grew up in a fishing household. As Terry Tufts and Kathryn Briggs write in 'Lament for Tom Thomson', one of two songs in the Algonquin Ensemble's otherwise instrumental *Sonic Palette: Tom Thomson's Voice Through Music 100 Years Later*:

> An angler's heart, a painter's eye
> A loving passion for the wild
> His father's son, his mother's child
> Tom Thomson was his name....

As both a fisherman who paints and a painter who fishes, Thomson shared much in common with the nineteenth-century American artist Winslow Homer. Born in 1836, Homer was thirty-four when he first visited the Adirondacks to fly fish and paint in 1870. He continued visiting the area in upstate New York regularly until his death in 1910. Fishing generally, and fly fishing specifically, became an enduring theme and subject—making him arguably the most accomplished angling artist in the history of the recreational sport. (Homer also fly fished and painted angling subjects in Quebec, Florida and the Caribbean.)

As part of the generation that preceded Thomson's, Homer was a Realist. He was predominantly a figurative painter influenced by the Barbizon School. In contrast Thomson was a landscape painter influenced by post-impressionism, art nouveau, arts & crafts and northern European symbolism. Despite differences in influence, both developed distinctive, highly personal styles after starting out as graphic artists. Both were notoriously reticent about their art. Both painted *en plein air* before working up canvases in the studio—Thomson in Toronto and Homer in New York City.

In *Nothing If Not Critical*, the late *Time* magazine art critic Robert Hughes—a passionate fly angler who wrote *A Jerk on One End*—wrote insightfully about Homer and his influence on American sporting art. Hughes points out that remnants of the artist can be readily detected in today's outdoor magazines. He rightly acknowledges that Homer was not only America's first, but its most accomplished sporting artist at a time when the 'wilderness' was praised with religious intensity. Change a few words and Hughes's observations about Homer apply equally to Thomson. I believe Thomson's art would have been much different had he not been a fisherman.

Canadian literary critic Northrop Frye observed in *The Bush Garden* that the artist's design sense was shaped by the trail and the canoe. I would add that his sense of colour was derived, at least in part, from the trout he caught in Algonquin Park. The deep rich palette that defines his paintings is drawn from the iridescent vermiculated colours of native brook and lake trout. I suspect that many of the places portrayed in his paintings resulted not from sketching expeditions, but from fishing outings where the artist cast a fly line or tossed a hard lure or live bait.

Fishing even played a role in Thomson's death. He was reportedly going fishing on the day he disappeared. The importance of fishing to Thomson is indisputable. It is interesting to note that almost all of the archival photos we have of the artist connect him to fishing. But determining whether he fly fished has proven less certain despite incontrovertible evidence.

* * *

Canadian journalist and author Roy MacGregor is the most prominent sceptic regarding the question of whether Thomson was a fly angler. In *Northern Light* he does not conclude *categorically* that Thomson did not cast fur and feather. He is far too cagey for that. Rather, he *implies* the artist did not fly fish by developing a circumstantial argument based on anecdotal knowledge of Algonquin Park. Without offering verification from evidence, he *infers* Thomson was not a fly fisherman.

MacGregor seems torn in regard to Thomson's ability as both an angler and a canoeist. Early on he describes a young Thomson as a fine angler, which concurs with the opinion of many people who knew

the artist. However, he later sides with the provincial park's locals in dismissing the artist as a fisherman and canoeist of average skills. Opinion in the park concerning Thomson's skills as an outdoorsman requires careful scrutiny. On the face of it, men who lived in, and earned a living from, the bush should have been in a position to assess Thomson's woodcraft. Maybe not.

Undoubtedly some would have viewed Thomson as an outsider, an interloper. Although he was country bred and spent a good deal of his early life in the woods, he would have been viewed as a city slicker from Toronto and, therefore, considered little more than a vacation tourist. To tough, untamed, utilitarian men who logged, mined, guided, fought forest fires, trapped and hunted, even poached, for a living, his artistic aspirations would have been ridiculed, if not actively scorned as effete. The fact that he was tall, handsome, and single—making him attractive to women either living in or vacationing in the park—would have made him a threat to men who might easily succumb to jealousy and suspicion.

There is evidence that the myth of Thomson as a master canoeist and fisherman was embellished by friends and champions after his death; however, the opinions of those with possible axes to grind should not be accepted as credible beyond reproach.

I respect MacGregor as a journalist. I have read most of his books with interest and pleasure. His creative fingers have been on the pulse of the Canadian character for many years, as reflected in such books as: *A Life in the Bush, Escape, The Weekender, Canadians* and *Canoe Country*, not to mention *Shorelines* (reissued as *Canoe Lake*), a fictional account of the alleged romance between Thomson and Winnifred Trainor (a distant relative of MacGregor's). His most recent book, *Original Highways: Travelling the Great Rivers of Canada*, includes a chapter on the Grand River.

MacGregor was born in Whitney, just north of Algonquin Park, and he has spent a good deal of his life in the area, which he knows intimately. On the strength of his writing about Thomson (spanning speculative fiction, non-fiction and journalism), he is considered an authority. His opinion carries weight. However, when it comes to the question of whether Thomson was a fly angler, MacGregor gets his line tangled in the reel—what anglers call a backlash or a bird's nest.

In *Northern Light* he observes that there has been a web of romanic notions spun around Thomson—some justified, some not so much. For many reasons people have filtered the artist through a naive and unrealistic prism—what used to be called rose-coloured glasses. Family and friends, including the Group of Seven, were determined to protect his reputation and legacy. Others, including patron Dr James McCallum, had a financial interest. Curators who acquired paintings, sometimes criticized as an unpopular decision, wanted their investment protected.

However, I disagree with MacGregor's inference that those who believe Thomson was a fly angler are engaged in some form of romanticizing. He begins by referencing the photo reproduced on the cover of *Northern Light*, which was taken by Fred Varley's wife, Maud, in 1915. He correctly points out that captions accompanying the photo in numerous books misidentify the terminal tackle as an artificial fly. The error continued uncorrected through successive writers, editors and publishers. He confirms, again correctly, that Thomson is tying on a spoon (likely one he made himself). However, he is casting on dubious waters when he implies the misidentification somehow proves that Thomson was not a fly fisherman. It does nothing of the kind. It simply confirms that the artist sometimes used spoons as terminal tackle, which is not in dispute.

He asserts that anyone who has ever fished in Algonquin Park would recognize the terminal tackle as a spoon, a type of lure commonly used for lake trout and large brook trout. Actually this is clear to most anglers, irrespective of whether they ever fished in the provincial park. It is likely that anyone who has fished for any length of time will be familiar with spoons manufactured by Len Thompson and Williams, not to mention Eppinger's venerable Dardevle.

MacGregor says he has fished 'this part of the country' his whole life, which imparts his opinions with authority. This might be true concerning his knowledge of the area, but it does not extend to fly fishing. His understanding of the recreational sport is superficial when he differentiates the poetic grace of fly angling from the more common practice of trolling with a weighted, triple-hooked lure from a boat or canoe. In fact, early American and Canadian wet flies, designed to look like swimming baitfish, were tied for trolling on lakes, as well as for deep pools in streams and rivers. Thomson would undoubtedly have used wet flies in both angling situations.

MacGregor acknowledges the grace customarily associated with casting a fly rod. But he is describing *one* element—casting a dry fly with a floating line upstream at rising trout on a river. Fact is, fly anglers also cast wet flies, bead-headed nymphs and streamers across and downstream. In times past—when fly fishing was less pure before the catch-and-release ethic gained traction—anglers sometimes combined artificial flies with live bait. For instance, in Ernest Hemingway's 'Big Two-Hearted River' Nick Adams uses grasshoppers on his fly angling rig. On a personal note, a friend's father used to place the fins of the first brook trout he caught on the hooks of his flies. I doubt Thomson was adverse to adopting a comparable practice.

Continuing to wax poetic about fly fishing, MacGregor says it is better suited to the chalkstreams of Britain and the rivers of Atlantic Canada. He is referring to trout and salmon in his pastoral idyll; however, fly anglers target less-revered species, including bass, pike, walleye and muskie, even panfish and carp, in addition to many salt-water species. They also cast flies on sinking tip or full-sinking lines with tungsten 'split-shot' (a term for sinkers, just as fly anglers call bobbers 'indicators'), from canoes, kayaks, drift boats, john boats, Adirondack guide boats and motorized boats. These practices extend beyond his stereotypical description of fly fishing.

MacGregor insists that the small hooks used in fly dressings would get tangled in the park's dense vegetation. Indeed fly anglers do use small hooks—dry and wet fly hooks as tiny as size 28 (one-millimetre shaft), which are impossible to hold without tweezers. But they also use streamer hooks as large as size 2 (eight-millimetre shaft) that can cause a nasty tear to an angler's hand if mishandled. Flies designed for pike and muskie, not to mention salt-water species, can approximate the size of a quarter chicken from Swiss Chalet. They are deadly and awkward as heck to cast.

Thomson might have rigged up two or more flies by attaching a dropper fly to the leader on which the main fly is attached. This compromises the gracefulness of the cast. This practice is prohibited in regulated catch-and-and-release areas where single, barbless hooks are mandatory, but is allowed in Algonquin Park to this day.

Fly anglers get caught up in all manner of vegetation—not to mention human noses and ears—wherever they fish, unless they are in the middle of a lake or wide river. That is why fly anglers employ various casts that eliminate back casts, the roll cast being the most common. Moreover, the bush in Algonquin Park is no denser than the forests of Algoma or North of Superior which are not only popular fly fishing destinations, but areas made famous by the Group of Seven after Thomson died. Ditto for the verdant forests of upstate New York, Pennsylvania and Maine.

MacGregor's clichéd description of fly fishing underscores his remarks regarding the film adaptation of *A River Runs Through It* when he declares that neither Robert Redford nor Brad Pitt would have been interested in transforming the book into a movie had it featured trolling rather than fly fishing.

I concur when he recognizes *A River Runs Through It* as a classic feature film. Not because it celebrates fly fishing, but because it paints a compelling portrait of a multigenerational family saga. It is a coming-of-age story (called a Bildungsroman by literary critics) with timeless, universal themes that touch the human heart: home and family, innocence and experience, devotion and addiction, love and desire, life and death, joy and sorrow, loss and grief. Equal parts spiritual autobiography and wilderness prayer, it is an artistic paradox. While it is the most eloquent expression of fly fishing in world cinema, it has as much to do with the recreational sport as the screen adaptations of *Moby Dick* have to do with whaling. Entertaining as it is, the film is not as multilayered as the novella, which is a blend of philosophical reflection, Western pastoral and modern tragedy. There is a dearth of commentary devoted to Maclean's fictional autobiography. However, those seeking critical appreciations can do no better than two essays: Wendell Berry's 'Style and Grace', and Wallace Stegner's 'Haunted by Waters: Norman Maclean'.

MacGregor is not an academic. When it comes to Thomson, his primary interest is advancing a narrative concentrating on the relationship between the artist and Winnie Trainor rather than evaluating documentary evidence related to other matters. Still, it is disconcerting when he willfully ignores evidence that repudiates his inference that Thomson was not a fly fisherman. This might appear as a tempest in a minnow bucket. For fly anglers like myself, however, it is not an inconsequential matter.

I cannot imagine that MacGregor is unfamiliar with John D. Robins's *The Incomplete Anglers*—either the original 1943 edition or the 1998 Friends of Algonquin Park reprint. Robins, an enthusiastic champion of Canadian art, was a close friend of Lawren Harris.

The memoir chronicles a fishing adventure by canoe Robins—an English professor at the University of Toronto—made with his brother, Tom. Although his brother fished with live bait exclusively, the author was a devoted fly angler. The references to fly fishing are too numerous to delineate. In an early passage Robins lists the flies he wants to purchase—including such classic patterns as Silver Doctor, McGinty, Caddis Drake, Parmachene Belle, Royal Coachman (a famous brook trout pattern) and red hackle (one of the oldest known patterns). Later Robins confides:

I was prepared to worship fly fishing with a pure, exclusive devotion and leave the worms behind. I supposed that true angling aristocrats would be puzzled by the mention of worms in connection with fishing. But [brother] Tom swore that he would have nothing to do with flies.

The reason I mention *The Incomplete Anglers*—one of three fly angling memoirs to win a Governor General's Award, including David Adams Richards's *Lines on the Water* and Roderick Haig-Brown's *Saltwater Summer*—is to confirm that by the 1940s fly fishing was an established tradition in Algonquin Park. The recreational sport, however, occurred in the park long before the Robins brothers. According to documentary evidence, it not only took place in the park when Thomson was there, it was performed by the artist.

Algonquin Provincial Park (established in 1893) and Adirondack State Park (constituted in 1892) share many things in common, including their history of logging, recreation and tourism in an era of rapid urbanization and industrialization when people sought refuge in the untamed 'wilds'. Thomson undoubtedly would have been introduced to fly fishing as a guide in the park when wealthy Americans travelled north to enjoy a Canadian 'wilderness' experience.

American anglers would have been familiar with the fly angling traditions emerging in Pennsylvania, the Catskills, the Adirondacks and Maine, not to mention salmon fishing in New Brunswick and Quebec. The summers Thomson spent in the park from 1912 through 1917 overlapped with the golden age of American fly fishing, when the legendary Theodore Gordon was popularizing the sport. Such master craftsmen as New England's Hiram Leonard and Edward Payne had been making split-cane bamboo rods for a quarter century. New York City–bred Edward vom Hofe had been designing and manufacturing superb reels over the same period. Meanwhile, Mary Orvis Marbury had been collecting original American fly patterns for her seminal book *Favourite Flies & Their Histories.*

In his 1996 pictorial history *Canoe Lake, Algonquin Park: Tom Thomson and Other Mysteries,* S. Bernard Shaw refers to Joseph Adams. The English fly angler and columnist for the prestigious sporting magazine *The Field* visited Algonquin Park in 1910 for the sole purpose of fly fishing. Shaw records that Adams hired chief ranger Mark Robinson to guide him to the Oxtongue River to fish for the park's famous brook trout. The British sportsman enjoyed success with a ten-foot bamboo rod loaded with gut line, while casting two prominent artificial flies (Silver Doctor and March Brown).

Adams would have come to Algonquin steeped in the English fly fishing tradition, including the concept of matching the hatch, as well as the controversy, raging at the time on both sides of the Atlantic, over the supremacy of dry fly versus wet fly, spearheaded by Frederick Halford and G.E.M. Skues, respectively.

The origins of matching the hatch extend back to at least 1643 when Gervase Markam recommended catching flies that were hatching and then imitating them. However, the concept did not start gaining popularity until 1836 when Alfred Ronalds published his seminal *The Fly Fisher's Entomology.* An aquatic biologist and illustrator, he applied scientific nomenclature to insects of interest to fly anglers and, in the process, established a link between entomology and fly fishing. North American fly anglers had to wait a century until Preston Jennings published *A Book of Trout Flies* in 1935.

During the centenary of Thomson's death I visited Algonquin Park's Visitor Centre to take in a modest exhibition, *Algonquin Park in the 1910s—A Tom Thomson Perspective.* I perused the centre's archival photos dating from when Thomson was in the park and—as expected—saw numerous images of anglers with bamboo fly rods resembling the one Thomson is casting at Tea Lake Dam in a well-known photo (more about this photo later).

The riddle of whether Thomson ever fished with a fly rod and tied artificial flies would have been solved had many of his personal belongings not disappeared upon his death. A leading candidate for the light-fingered culprit is Shannon Fraser, owner of Mowat Lodge and one of a number of locals suspected to have accidentally killed or deliberately murdered the painter. Remnants of fly tying material would have settled the matter. But these—provided they existed—disappeared along with Thomson's canoe and paddle, not to mention some painted boards.

Before reviewing the documentary evidence that supports my contention that Thompson was a fly angler—at least sometimes—I want to consider a couple of photos reprinted in *Northern Light*.

The first is a photo taken by Thompson of a well-dressed woman holding a fishing rod and a brace of fish. MacGregor argues persuasively that the woman was long mistaken for Winnie Trainor. He is unable to identify the mystery woman, who remains unknown. Interesting, at least to me, is the fact that MacGregor does not consider what the mystery woman is holding in her left hand. It is undeniably a bamboo fly rod. Yet he does not properly identify the object, but instead passes it off as a generic fishing pole. Most anglers would know the difference between a fishing pole and a fly rod.

I have no evidence to support my speculation; still, I enjoy pondering over the relationship between the mystery woman and Thomson—as it pertains to fishing. It is possible the woman caught the fish, with Thomson acting as guide. However, this is unlikely considering women did not fly fish in significant numbers until after the First World War. The more probable explanation is that the fish were caught by the owner of the fly rod—the man holding the camera: Tom Thomson.

More perplexing is a photo (referred to previously) that provides visual proof that Thomson fished with a fly rod. It is a famous photo of the artist, looking like a lumberjack complete with wool toque, standing on an outcrop of rock and casting into the rushing water below the dam at Tea Lake. The photo was taken in 1916 by Lawren Harris.

Although his knowledge of fly fishing is superficial as revealed in *Northern Light*, MacGregor's knowledge of fishing generally is sufficient for him to recognize that Thomson is holding a fly rod rather than a bait-caster (spinning rods were only invented in Europe, during the Second World War). He also should recognize that the artist is stripping in line in accordance with fly casting practice.

However, most baffling is the caption beside the photo—*Tom Thomson fly-fishing*—which contradicts MacGregor's persistent inference that the artist was not a fly fisherman. Talk about irony.

* * *

Tom Thomson painted at least one fly angler, titled *The Fisherman*. The Toronto painter Harold Town dismissed the painting—in his seminal study *Tom Thomson: The Silence and the Shore*, co-written with David Silcox—because of the figure's apparent awkwardness. Town clearly was not a fisherman, let alone fly fisherman. While Thomson was a demonstrably clumsy figurative painter, the form of this particular figure is a literal depiction of a fly angler playing a fish after it is hooked.

I have not been able to identify the fly fisherman, if in fact the painting is based on an actual angler. Instead, I like to imagine it as a self-portrait: fly angler as artist and/or artist as fly angler. Thomson painted a less distinct fisherman in *Little Cauchon Lake*. While it is not clearly a fly angler, it looks like one to me.

I might be casting on shallow water here, but I suspect Thomson tied his own flies in response to close observation of insects two decades before Jennings published his seminal *Book of Trout Flies* in 1935, not to mention almost half a century before Ernest Schwiebert published *Matching the Hatch* in 1955. Art Flick's influential *Streamside Guide to Naturals and Their Imitations* followed in 1969. I enjoy imagining what Thomson's artistic eye and nimble fingers might have brought to fly tying.

To fuel speculation about Thomson as a fly fisherman, I refer to A.Y. Jackson's maternal grandfather, Alexander Young. The first principal at Kitchener's Suddaby Public School, Young was both a noted entomologist and a fly fisherman. His knowledge of insects might have been passed on to Thomson had the two men ever met. I have no evidence of Thomson and Young ever crossing paths; however, given the interests the artist shared with the fly fishing entomologist, it seems likely Jackson would have talked about his grandfather with his close friend, perhaps while sitting around the campfire after a day's painting or fishing, glowing pipe in one hand and tin cup of Canadian whisky in the other.

More intriguing is a family connection. When Thomson moved

to Toronto in 1905 to embark on a career in commercial art, he spent time with a relative we know as 'Uncle' William Brodie. The relative, who might actually have been a cousin, was a prominent naturalist specializing in entomology. He helped establish the Toronto Entomological Society in 1878 and, from 1903 until his death in 1909, was director of the Biological Department at the Ontario Provincial Museum (later the Royal Ontario Museum). The time Thomson spent outdoors with Brodie fuelled the aspiring painter's passion for nature. The entomology he learned from Brodie would have served him well fly fishing and tying flies in Algonquin Park.

Thomson's early biographers associated the painter with fly fishing. It should be pointed out that the practice was not romanticized at the time. It was just one—albeit less-popular—means of catching fish. In fact, spin casting rods and reels were all the rage when the biographies were published.

Ottelyn Addison—in collaboration with Elizabeth Harwood, a University of Saskatchewan graduate who had studied at the Sorbonne—observes in their 1969 book *Tom Thomson: The Algonquin Years* that Thomson was a fly angler of great skill. In addition to trolling for lake trout from his canoe, he regularly cast for brook trout.

The daughter of Algonquin Park Ranger Mark Robinson (a close friend of Thomson's who spearheaded the search for the artist after he went missing) was a keen naturalist who spent her early summers in Algonquin Park and returned often as an adult. She bases her book on her father's diary. She likely would have understood the difference between fly angling and fishing with hard lures or baits.

She also quotes Park Ranger Tom Wattie, confirming that Thomson could cast in a graceful figure eight, with the fly landing on the water exactly as intended. His description of the artist casting a figure eight might resemble purple prose, but the split-cane rods back in the day were softer—the term 'wimpy' is used by bamboo nerds—than they are today. This makes Wattie's observation even more credible.

In addition to being a park ranger who knew the artist well, Wattie was a fisherman who would have recognized fly angling. There is a photo (credited to Ken Cooper) of him sitting on the porch of what I presume is his ranger's cabin. Over his left shoulder is a bamboo fly rod. Addison (who also wrote *Early Days in Algonquin Park*) writes that Thomson observed, and could identify, the feeding habits of trout. He also knew from experience that trout preferred the coldest water at the height of summer. Finally, a footnote in *The Algonquin Years* includes a letter, dated 16 March 1913, from Leonard Mack, a self-described angling companion of Thomson's who refers to a fishing trip the previous summer during which he took a photo of the artist fly fishing from a rock on Crown Lake. Sadly most of Thomson's photographs, like many of his personal effects, did not survive. In deference to full disclosure, there is a nagging issue in *The Algonquin Years* regarding Addison's portrait of Thomson as a fly angler. The photo that shows Thomson tying on a spoon (referred to above) is reprinted in the book. The caption misidentifies the terminal tackle as a fly.

We do not know whether it was Addison's mistake. She might have been using *fly* as a generic term for all types of lures. This seems unlikely; however, I have read and heard fishermen refer to flies as lures (Scottish-bred writer Ian Niall does this in his classic *Trout from the Hills*) and tackle in a generic sense. She might have unwittingly repeated an error made by a previous writer. Or it might have been an error committed by an editor or publisher. The photo credit belongs to Thoreau MacDonald, son of Group of Seven founding member J.E.H. MacDonald, who might have identified the spoon as a fly knowing that Thomson was a fly fisherman.

Despite the issue of the incorrect caption Wattie is reliable. Likewise we can trust Robinson's credibility.

The piscatorial plot began thickening years earlier with Audrey Saunders's *Algonquin Story*, originally published in 1946 and reprinted in 1963. She was not an amateur literary dilettante, but a pioneer in both oral history and Canadian studies who taught at Montreal's Dawson College and Sir George Williams University (now Concordia). Saunders correctly describes Thomson in the archival photo of the artist at Tea Lake Dam (mentioned above) as *fly-fishing* at the bottom of the lumber dam, which was one of his favourite activities. The artist's posture in the photo is clearly one all fly anglers would recognize as their own. Saunders's book also includes an archival photo, circa 1911, with a caption of 'Fishing trip in Algonquin Park', that shows one of six men (fourth from left) holding two fishing rods, one of which is clearly a fly rod.

Even more significant is her description of Thomson's fly casting skill, which garnered admiration from the guests at Mowat Lodge.

Moreover—and this is critically important—Saunders writes that the artist tied his own flies after observing fish rising to insects. She added that Thomson painted his own imitations on site.

To my mind, this confirms that Thomson—who unquestionably fished with natural bait and hard lures when it suited his needs or when conditions dictated—not only made his own lures, but tied his own flies. The reference to Thomson observing insects that made fish rise and then painting pictures of them on the spot—presumably so he could tie flies later to match the hatch—would place him at the forefront of what became one of the most significant developments in fly angling not only in the twentieth century, but in the recreational sport's long, storied history.

Admittedly this revelation pales beside *Northern River*, *The Jack Pine* or *The West Wind*. Still, as a fly angler, I take deep joy in knowing that an artist I admire shared my passion. It is a connective tissue which, however tenuous, is important to me.

It is impossible to know with any certainty how Thomson being a fly fisherman influenced or shaped his art. But it secures him a prominent place in the history of fly angling in Canada—especially if he tied his own flies to match the hatch. Despite conjecture about his life and his death, his true legacy is no mystery—it rests with his paintings. They will endure long after speculation has been laid to rest. Still, it is clear a river runs through Tom Thomson.

CODA: FISHING FOR TOM

Since becoming friends, Dan Kennaley and I have made a number of trips to Algonquin Park to paddle Canoe Lake in search of Tom Thomson's enduring spirit. We have visited the memorial cairn overlooking the lake and the cemetery where some believe the artist's body lies to this day. (I tend to agree with this opinion.) It remains a curiously spooky place that unsettles the imagination.

One unforgettable day on Canoe Lake we were forced to beach the canoe amidst a fierce thunderstorm, which seemed appropriate in light of the turbulence surrounding Thomson's death. When we finally arrived at a place to disembark from the lake and head inland to the Canoe Lake Cemetery, we encountered a small group of people who said they owned a cottage on the lake.

When we told them of our mission to pay our respects at what some believe is still Thomson's gravesite, they invited us back to their cottage for a drink. They said they were descendants of people who vacationed there during the summers the artist spent at the park. They had stories to tell, so they said. It sounded too good to be true. Did they have information or tales? Were they sincere, or intent on making Dan and me the butt of good-natured joking? We were both interested but we had to decline because we had supper plans with Dan's wife, Jan, a wonderful woman who must not be denied. To this day Dan and I wonder what we might have learned, if anything. We will never know but we never stop speculating about what might have been, could have been, possibly, but not probably…. Thomson remains an unsolved mystery.

We sometimes visit Thomson's gravestone in the cemetery at Leith United Church, outside of Owen Sound, on our way to the Big-head River for a day of steelheading. This is where Thomson's family always insisted they buried the artist after his corpse was transferred by train in a steel casket from Algonquin Park in the summer of 1917. Dan leaves a fly as a memorial. I say a short prayer.

I have been fishing for Thomson for many years. I have reviewed art exhibitions and books, music, films and live performances, based on the artist and his work. I have interviewed writers and artists inspired by Thomson, in addition to art experts. I have written commentaries that relate the artist to recurring themes in Canadian culture and that explore his influence on a range of visual, literary and performing arts. I have written a newspaper feature story based on primary source material about the artist and his mysterious death. I have given lectures at galleries, museums and universities, as well as at fly fishing clubs. Interest in Tom Thomson has no catch limits.

In the summer of 2017, in acknowledgement of the centenary of his death and in honour of his living legacy, I wrote ten articles—one for every day he was missing until his corpse was found—which I posted on my blog. Thomson was Canada's first rock star, an obscure artist throughout his life who became a national celebrity after his death. He painted into mystery. He writes epistles from the grave. He found me as I have been searching for him. He embodies the Idea of North. I will end my days casting my imagination at this elusive artist with the fins of brook trout.

A Hatch Made in Heaven

A minority of fly anglers and canoeists seem bent on impersonating litigants duking it out on the turbulent waters of divorce court. For my part, I embrace fly fishing and canoeing as a 'hatch' made in heaven. As David Adams Richards suggests in *Lines on the Water*, both recreations are declarations of hope.

My chosen form of fly fishing is wading streams and rivers. Nothing surpasses the joy of waving a fly rod while standing mid-river in an embracing current. A close second, however, is casting flies toward the shoreline from a canoe on a secluded lake. I have enjoyed many evenings at the height of summer in the bow of Dan Kennaley's red fibreglass canoe with our paddles and fly rods in synchronized rhythm. There are few outdoor experiences more peaceful.

When I was young I dreamed of owning a canoe. The closest I ever got was when Lois Hayward bought a used one to celebrate her retirement. It was yellow in recognition of the canoe her family kept at their cottage in Lake of Bays. Many of her fondest memories of spending adolescent summers at the cottage involved the canoe.

Despite occasional conflict on the water, there is nothing intrinsic to fly fishing or canoeing that should be adversarial, notwithstanding the stupidity and bad manners of a few anglers and paddlers. Intimately connected by the magic of water, they are compatible, mutually supportive recreations. Any outdoor magazine worthy of the name—from *Field & Stream* to *Gray's Sporting Journal*—features picture after picture, both illustrations and photographs, of fly anglers in canoes. I have long been fascinated by the many attributes that connect these two water-based activities.

The mechanics of casting a fly rod and paddling a canoe share common elements: both are low impact, both are graceful in terms of physical movement, both incorporate rhythm and pace. When done properly, they *appear* effortless—even artful. Like ballet on water or skating away on Joni Mitchell's 'River'.

I first encountered the term *motion pleasure* in Noah Adams's essay collection *Saint Croix Notes*, where he refers to an activity that is 'a whole lot more fun doing ... than watching'. The term—which applies equally to fly fishing and canoeing—is both athletic and aesthetic. Watching a skilled canoeist or a skilled fly angler in action is deeply pleasing, especially when proficiency becomes an expression of elegant muscle memory. Fly fishing and canoeing defy categorization. Both are inclusive in an age of increasing cultural division. Men and women, young and mature, enjoy them equally, irrespective of class, religion, country of origin or socio-economic status.

Both can be done alone or in company. They are solitary activities that welcome companionship. Canadian novelist Ethel Wilson captures this seeming paradox when she writes in *Swamp Angel* that fly anglers share the desire to be both together and apart on lake or stream. R. Palmer Baker, Jr., acknowledges the same dichotomy in *The Sweet of the Year* when he describes fly fishing as both a solitary and a companionable pastime. The same can be said of canoeing.

Fly anglers and canoeists are equally devoted to leaving as faint a footprint as possible on this Good Earth. Fly anglers practise catch-and-release, using single barbless hooks. Most use nets to land large fish and are careful to revive fish before release. Canoeists are careful to remove all evidence of temporary habitation at campsites. Many fly anglers and canoeists, whether individually or as a members of clubs, participate in river clean-up, water rehab and habitat restoration in partnership with conservation authorities and environment ministries. It is not unusual for fly anglers to pick up garbage left alongside waterways during a day of fishing. Canoeists do likewise.

Fly anglers and canoeists seek out wilderness, but they also enjoy pastoral settings close to home. Both appreciate the notion of home water—whether stream, river or lake—to which they are drawn for comfort and peace, renewal and restoration. I concur with Jerry Kustich when he writes of 'the heartbeat of home water' in *Holy Water*:

For all of us, though, these familiar places forever meander through our minds with the timeless capacity of transporting our spirit to another dimension that can be just as comforting as home itself. It doesn't really matter where you are on the journey of life either. Home water is as much a state of mind as it is a state of being, and in one's heart it is always close at hand. Just close your eyes.

When it comes to casting a fly rod or paddling a canoe, simplicity is a beautiful thing. In a world growing increasingly complex, oftentimes bewilderingly complicated, simplicity becomes the mother of necessity. The material properties of fly rods and reels, canoes and paddles, are models of minimalist elegance in which form and function coalesce. Nothing is extraneous. Ornamentation is eschewed. If these were hymns, they would be plainsong. The less-is-more aesthetic of canoes and fly angling gear reminds me of writers I admire, including Sherwood Anderson, Ernest Hemingway, Raymond Carver, James Salter, William Maxwell, Wallace Stegner and Cormac McCarthy *sans* the baroque flourishes. These writers appreciate clarity, precision and lucidity above all else.

Fly fishing and canoeing are rooted in pre-industrial technologies. Although natural materials have been replaced with manufactured materials in many instances, both maintain a low-tech aesthetic which values durability and permanence over obsolescence. The aerodynamic design of canoes approaches perfection. This is design at its most elegant, drawn from the blueprint of nature. Thoreau's comment in the early pages of *A Week on the Concord and Merrimack Rivers* affirms this fact through metaphorical prose. Although he is referring to a boat, I think his description conveys more accurately the essence of a canoe. I replace the word *boat* with *canoe* as he observes:

If rightly made, a [canoe] would be a sort of amphibious animal, a creature of two elements, related by one half its structure to some swift and shapely fish, and by the other to some strong-winged and graceful bird....

Despite changes in regional cultural specifics and materials (wood, birchbark, canvas, aluminum, fibreglass, Kevlar, polyethylene composites), canoe design has changed little over millennia. The same can be said of the design of paddles irrespective of material.

The 'modern' fly rod and reel are industrial inventions dating back to the nineteenth century. Compared to canoes and paddles, they are new kids on the water. Still, they are in large part adaptations of earlier rods and reels. Whether made of greenheart (wood), Calcutta and, later, Tonkin bamboo, fibreglass or graphite, fly rods are essentially long, thin, flexible, tapered sticks that facilitate casting a fly with line and playing fish effectively and efficiently. Initially made of wood, modern fly reels are basically a revolving inner wheel within a stationary outer wheel made from an aluminum alloy. Nothing could be simpler in design and execution. Bliss Perry describes the design elegance of fly fishing gear in his collection of fishing essays *Pools and Ripples* when he observes: 'A three-or four-ounce split-cane rod, with a well-balanced reel, tapered casting-line, a leader of the proper finesse and a well-tied fly or flies, is one of the most perfectly designed and executed triumphs of human artisanship.'

Fly angling and canoeing share a philosophy of wilderness adventure and respect for the natural world. Both activities, which arise from direct contact with nature, are informed by an ecological, holistic approach to the environment, encompassing care, protection and stewardship. When the future of the planet and its inhabitants are under dire threat from pollution and climate change accelerated by industrialization, urbanization and population growth, we need recreational initiatives that remind us of our responsibilities to the health of our global home, now and in the future. A day on the water is a powerful reminder of our duties as citizens and caretakers.

This intimate connection between nature and angler or paddler creates a sense of belonging, of communion with the world around us, both immediate and distant. While much in our modern world separates us from nature, fly fishing and canoeing restore our kinship with nature. In a discordant world, these activities are instruments of harmony. Fly fishing and canoeing help those who feel fractured or broken recover and restore their inherent wholeness. Both activities integrate external nature with inner nature.

When viewed strictly as sport, both activities appeal to 'extreme' or 'gonzo' adrenalin junkies. But at their purest, they are contemplative, reflective and meditative—introverted rather than extroverted, actively passive rather than passively aggressive. They can even be therapeutic. For instance there are fly angling programs for female breast cancer survivors, scarred first responders and military veterans who return from war suffering from post-traumatic stress disorder.

Fly angling and canoeing are experiential activities. They take place in the present, in the pulsating Now. Yet both are memory activities. They are sources of recollection, enriched and enhanced by reflection. Many fly anglers or canoeists cherish sharing their experiences over a pint or dram; recollection informs story.

Fly anglers and canoeists are all about process. There are more effective ways of catching fish than fly angling and more effective methods of water transportation, but catching more and bigger fish is not the primary goal of fly anglers, just as travelling faster and hauling heavier loads is not the focus of canoeists. Both encourage prospecting. Fly anglers seek out the next pool or riffle. Canoeists forge beyond the portage to the next river or lake. The idea of unexplored and uncharted waters is irresistible. This desire keeps us moving forward, it tests our faith in, and hope for, the future.

Fly angling and canoeing have long histories that have inspired rich bodies of literature. The poetics of both activities inspire writers, visual artists and musicians. Many fly anglers and canoeists appreciate the heritage and legacy they carry forward as a living tradition. Therefore both activities shape character and modify behaviour.

Canoeing has deep roots in our national imagination and psyche. I cannot imagine Canada without the canoe. Its deep cultural roots penetrate the country's bedrock and remain a central element of our history and heritage, our character and identity. It is not an exaggeration to refer to this vast country as Land of the Canoe.

The canoe is more than an effective means of transportation—a harmonious blend of form and function, history and geography, design and craft—ideally adapted to the landscape. It played a critical role in nation building by shaping the country through exploration and settlement, trade and commerce, war and recreation, sport and art. It is a link between indigenous peoples and European pioneers.

As opposed to subsistence fishing, fly fishing lacks the deep cultural roots of the canoe. And it does not run as deep in Canada as the fly fishing traditions of New England or the chalk-stream highlands of Pennsylvania. However, the heritage and legacy of salmon fishing in New Brunswick, Quebec and British Columbia are significant.

I was an armchair fly angler and canoeist long before I ever picked up a rod or held a paddle. My library of books devoted to fly angling, canoeing, nature and ecology are literary home waters. The sympathetic relationship between fly angling and canoeing finds eloquent expression through the lives and work of two of my favourite artists.

Though primarily known as an artist, Tom Thomson is also remembered as a fisherman and canoeist. He composed many paintings from the vantage point of a canoe, ostensibly while casting a fishing rod. His distinctive hand-painted canoe is almost as famous as the artist himself. It was the subject of one of his oil paintings, *The Canoe*. The vessel mysteriously disappeared after Thomson went missing in July of 1917.

Winslow Homer painted many pictures of fly fishermen casting and landing fish from canoes (including Quebec). There is a photo taken sometime during the 1890s of the artist, a devoted fly angler, paddling a canoe. Many of his paintings depict guides paddling, running rapids and portaging. Others show anglers casting from guide boats, punts, rowboats and canoes.

Unlike Thomson and Homer, Ken Danby was neither a fly fisherman, nor did he portray anglers in his art. Still, he was a canoeist and completed many works late in his career that underscored a symbiotic connection between watercraft and landscape. He had long been interested in Thomson. In 1997 he painted *Algonquin: In Homage to Tom Thomson* which portrays a lone ghostly canoeist at night on Cache Lake.

Fly anglers and canoeists need not be religious in a formal sense. However, when they talk about nature, their words often carry a sense of reverence and devotion customarily associated with worship. This spiritual awareness is related to the form and rhythm that religious liturgy shares with both activities, as my friend and fellow fly angler Chad Wriglesworth suggested after reading my manuscript.

Chad observed that the word *liturgy* has roots in the idea of a public form of expression. The process of sacred liturgy is connected to rhythm as embodied in the seasonal church calendar. Like liturgical practices, fly fishing and canoeing are committed to the artistry of the ordinary. Whether it be bread and wine, fur and feather or paddle, there is human participation in what already exists as a created gift. Chad added that Norman Maclean, who grew up under the stewardship of a Scots Presbyterian father, gave expression to these rhythmical patterns in *A River Runs Through It*.

Fly fishing and canoeing are rites that lead to the threshold of magic. Likewise, they are 'performed' on the surface of water between the seen and unseen, the known and unknown. This is the threshold where recreation and spirit enter the cathedral of nature.

For me fly fishing and canoeing will always be two chambers of the same heart. Whether standing in a river casting into mystery or on a river paddling into mystery, I feel part of an existential continuum. Intimations of transience and permanence, mutability and mortality await around the next bend. It is at such moments of grace that I feel fully alive and truly connected to this Good Earth.

Fishing Dogs & Patient Poppers

———

Dan Kennaley has a fishing dog. His ten-year-old golden retriever, Maggie, spends hours trying to catch minnows in the shallows in front of the cottage Dan shares with his wife, Jan, son, Ian, and daughter, Erin, on a postcard lake in Muskoka.

Dan often confesses that, while Maggie might not be 'the sharpest knife in the drawer', her understanding of fishing is profound. Her methodology is a model of the Three Ps of Fly Fishing: patience, persistence and perseverance. With the exception of her wagging tail, she stands perfectly still for as long as it takes to spot a trespassing minnow—before lunging. Her powers of concentration are heron-like. She never surrenders to disappointment when she comes up empty. Hope and optimism are her mantra.

Like any devoted dog owner, Dan speaks on behalf of his loyal companion when he remarks: 'After all, it's called fishing not catching.'

Fly anglers can learn a lot from Maggie. Dan and I certainly did during an evening in early July on a nearby lake. The lake—which will remain unnamed for its own peace of mind—is small and isolated, although located close to a provincial highway. At present there are no cottages despoiling its shoreline. We shared its tranquility with a resident loon and a hawk that watched from on high in an adjacent white pine (one of my favourite conifers and a recurring icon in Canadian landscape painting).

When it comes to fly fishing, I prefer the moving water of rivers. But lakes have their own allure as vessels of meditation and repositories of contemplation. I doubt any writer has ever expressed the mystery of lakes more eloquently than Thoreau in *Walden* when he observes: 'A lake is the landscape's most beautiful and expressive feature. It is earth's eye; looking into which the beholder measures the depth of his own nature.'

Dan Gerber—a poet, fly angler and longtime friend of Jim Harrison—takes up where Thoreau left off in 'Tracking the Moment', from *A Primer on Parallel Lives*, when he describes ponds as black pupils through which silent faces peer into distant stars.

About six o'clock Dan and I headed out in his fibreglass canoe on water that was flat, still and serene. Dan has had the canoe—christened *Greg Clark* in honour of the legendary Canadian newspaper journalist and outdoor writer—since his university days. Its bright red exterior has faded with time, having weathered annual brook trout fishing trips to Algonquin Park after the ice goes out and before the bloody blackfly invasion. It was hot and humid in high summer as we paddled to the far shore. We began casting streamers. Dan elected a Mickey Finn, a classic yellow and red streamer his hero Clark named.

* * *

Sportsmen of a certain age, or readers of the *Star Weekly*, a weekend supplement once published by the *Toronto Star*, will recall Clark as a feature writer who wrote comic stories illustrated by cartoonist Jimmie Frise. Many chronicled fishing and hunting misadventures. Few might know that the diminutive writer was instrumental in naming one of fly fishing's most popular streamer flies, the Mikey Finn.

It won't be surprising to fly anglers that so much misinformation surrounds the fly's genesis and evolution. There are many examples throughout the recreational sport's long history of fiction trumping fact. After all, fly anglers are storytellers at heart. Many subscribe to the old saw that a good story should never be compromised by literal truth. Look no farther than the mystery surrounding Dame Juliana Berners for confirmation.

The attractor fly predates Clark's role in the story. One narrative suggests it was originally designed by Quebec fly tier Charles Langevin in the nineteenth century and was initially known as the Langevin. Wrong. The fly's origin remains in doubt; there are numerous competing claims regarding its inventor.

It is widely believed that John Alden Knight, a prominent American outdoor writer, originally called the fly the Assassin. Wrong again. Clark coined this earlier version of the fly's moniker. Knight, however, did popularize an unidentified fly consisting of red and yellow bucktail.

Jock Carroll, author of *The Life & Times of Greg Clark: Canada's Favourite Storyteller*, reports the circumstances under which Clark bestowed the streamer with the name by which it is known today. One summer's day Knight fished Clark's beloved Mad River, just south of Collingwood, Ontario, with a member of the Singhampton fishing club (of which Clark was a founding member). Everyone was skunked, except Knight who caught forty-six trout on an unidentified fly—a memorable outing by any limit standard.

Carroll records that Clark heard about Knight's success the next day in a sporting goods store in downtown Toronto. Upon learning about Knight's 'fabulous fly', Clark insisted on naming the fly by virtue of being dean of the Singhampton Club.

Initially Clark christened it the Assassin. However, a few days later he read newspaper accounts of the death of Rudolph Valentino, allegedly killed (since discounted) by a vengeful bartender in Chicago who slipped Mickey Finns into the Hollywood idol's drinks. Clark renamed the fly in honour of the 'deadly' cocktail. The name of the original fly used by Knight has never been determined, but he gave credit throughout his life to Clark for providing such a provocative name for an enduring streamer.

* * *

For my part on that day at the height of summer, I relied on a black bead-headed Woolly Bugger purchased in a fly shop in Victoria, British Columbia. (By the way, Dan ties a black Woolly Bugger with a red marabou tail that is a killer on the lake.)

Save for a couple of strikes that failed to translate into landed large or smallmouth bass, we were both skunked—temporarily as it turned out. In contrast to Maggie's example of hope and optimism, we were frustrated after a couple of futile hours—if not exactly disappointed. After all, who can be crestfallen fishing on such an evening, on such a lake with a fly rod in one hand and paddle in the other?

Just as the sun was slipping behind the conifers and hardwoods on the western shore, Dan suggested we paddle across the lake to the near side, where we had put in the canoe. We started tossing top-water poppers. Dan and I both chose green frog patterns with yellow and black spots. Mine was store-bought, while Dan's was handmade from rubber flip-flops—tacky as hell (sorry, Dan) but effective. Both patterns sprouted long thin rubbery legs.

I had two determined strikes in rapid succession on the first two casts. Our luck had changed, whether the result of the time—known as the witching hour by some fishermen or as the gloaming by my Celtic ancestors—changing location or changing fly patterns. Or any combination of the above.

Anglers who use bait-casting, spinning or spin-casting reels are familiar with the attraction of hard, top-water lures, whether Hula Poppers, Jitterbugs or Crazy Crawlers to name three of the most popular brands. There is something irrepressibly attractive and delightfully addictive about watching voracious bass leap out of the water to devour poppers. Nothing compares in freshwater fishing, with the possible exception of casting surface lures in shallow water at Great Northern pike with attitude.

The secret to poppers is applying Maggie's Three Ps. Cast to all the fishy places. Think like a bass. Look for structure: pockets among beds of lily pads, edges of fall-offs and weed beds, half-submerged trees, dark holes under overhanging bushes and shadows around rocks and boulders—docks if there are any, but I prefer undeveloped lakes and rivers. (Notice none of these elements require a fish finder, which I abhor because I believe electronics take the 'sport' out of sportfishing. Simply said, techno gadgets have no role in fly fishing.)

On the initial cast I let the popper sit. I took my time; this is part of the Zen of fishing. When the concentric ripples disappeared I gave the rod a short, sharp flick. This was rapid wrist action, causing the tip to jerk suddenly and with authority. The action caused the burble that drives bass crazy—that is the theory, anyway.

William Tapply, the mystery novelist and outdoor writer, claimed it is the sound of prey moving on the water's surface, not its profile or colour, that triggers a strike. He insisted that anglers should impart lifelike noises to bug poppers. Give the rod a sharp tug to make it go *ploop*; a twitch to make it *burble*; an erratic retrieve to make it *chug, glug* and *gurgle*.

I let the popper rest after each rod twitch. I waited until the expanding rings dissipated. Then counted to twenty. Like all accomplished anglers, Tapply veered from the conventional wisdom that advocates rest stops. Instead he recommended little flutters. 'Effective boss poppers are never absolutely motionless,' he contends in *Bass Bug Fishing*. Even at rest they should *shiver, shudder, quiver* and *flutter*. His advice sounds so tantalizingly sexual, I followed it with the enthusiasm of a young buck in rut.

I took Tapp's wisdom to heart. My popper fell *upon* the water with a muffled *splat* or soft *plop*. If it had landed soundlessly, bass would not hear it; if it slapped like a tossed rock, they would hit the road, Jack.

Dan and I landed five bass apiece. We also entertained plenty of hits we failed to set, which is par for the course for anglers of all dispositions and inclinations. I missed a respectable bass that was spooked as soon as it spotted the canoe—a common angling liability.

All of my landed bass were largemouths (aka bucketmouths), ranging from nine to fifteen inches. The thirteen-incher was exciting. The fifteen-incher was thrilling. He took off like a diminutive linebacker on performance-enhancing pharmaceuticals. He put an impressive bend in my Colorado-made, seven-weight Scott by pulling the canoe around as I tucked the rod butt into my gut for leverage. I am not kidding! On two occasions Dan and I choreographed doubleheaders—a term denoting two strikes at the same time. TV anglers crow collegiately when they land a pair of fish simultaneously. Had a camera been pointed at Dan and me, we would have had to exclaim the obligatory: 'Talk about fun. This is what it's all about, buddy.' Thankfully, we were paddling on a solitary lake out of earshot of angling celebrity.

CODA: NATURE IN RETREAT

The tenth anniversary outing to our thin slice of bass paradise confirmed two maxims: (1) life's only constant is change and (2) every good thing must come to an end.

Maggie had passed the previous autumn at the age of thirteen and Dan was still grieving. (Dan had not yet welcomed a new golden retriever into the family. Mitchell arrived later in the fall. The family had a lengthy discussion about what their new pet would be named. They eventually deferred to Dan's wish to call him Mitchell in homage to W. O. Mitchell.)

On our way to the lake, Dan informed me that the property had been sold to a buyer with deep pockets. Rumour had it that the new owner intended to build a quartet of cottages along the shoreline. It might not be Joni Mitchell's asphalt destruction of paradise, but it was still unsettling and more than a little sad.

After we arrived across from a locally owned hunting camp that had been sold recently to outside interests, we paddled to the far side of the lake, as is our custom. We each caught a couple of small fish before a bank of menacing thunderheads announced its intention. We made it back to the car before an onslaught of rain obscured our view of the lake, no more than a few metres away. It was the first time precipitation had ever chased us off the water.

We waited out the downpour by washing down granola bars with bottles of Sleeman's Cream Ale. When we returned to the water we were greeted by a pair of serenading loons against the backdrop of a luminescent rainbow smiling across the lake's eastern shore. The wind, which had been persistent before the shower, had dissipated, turning the lake into a sheet of isinglass.

I took the charmed fusion of sight and sound as an omen and decided to use one of the few flies I have ever tied—a black Woolly Bugger with a red marabou tail. I had retired the fly after catching a bunch of bass on an earlier trip, but decided to reactivate it—for some unknown reason. I thought of it as a superannuated hockey player recruited for the last game in a Stanley Cup playoff series. I caught three bass including a thirteen-incher. (I have since retired the beat-up fly tied with my very own hands permanently.)

At dusk Dan suggested we paddle back across the lake and try some poppers. Good thing we did, especially for Dan, who landed a personal best on the lake—an eighteen-inch brute. Both of us caught a dozen bass, making for a satisfying outing. I thought of Thoreau's description of a 'delicious evening'.

While making our way to the car in the embrace of darkness I felt a shiver of melancholy. I knew that everything has its season, and I was deeply thankful that Dan and I had this small, generous lake to share in a fellowship of two for a decade. Still, the thought of this being our last trip before bulldozers arrived to guzzle our wee dram of paradise left my mouth as dry as a brittle leaf falling on hard ground.

Bassin' on the Grand

Mention the Grand River over a frosty pint in a local pub and most fly anglers assume you are talking about the stocked brown trout fishery in the tailwater between Shand Dam at Belwood Lake and West Montrose, twenty-eight kilometres southwest. But the 280-kilometre river—which meanders through southwestern Ontario from Luther Marsh in the Dufferin Highlands (one of the largest inland wetlands in southern Ontario) to Port Maitland on the north shore of Lake Erie—supports a diverse fishery.

The Canadian Heritage River is the longest river entirely within southwestern Ontario, boasting more than eighty-two species of fish, comprising more than fifty per cent of the species found in Canada. Not all are gamefish, according to *Fishing Ontario's Grand River Country*, edited by Steve May and published by the Grand River Conservation Authority. But in addition to brown trout, there are pike, walleye, rainbow trout, steelhead, perch, crappie, mooneye, smallmouth bass, carp and channel catfish (on an outing to the portion of river running through Brantford, a bait fisherman showed me a photo of a fifty-pound catfish he caught at Wilkes Dam. What the brute lacked in beauty he compensated for in size).

When water temperatures exceed seventy degrees—the point at which it is inadvisable to target brownies—the enthusiastic fly angler need not put away rod and reel until water temperatures cool down in September. The Grand between Cambridge and Paris is a smallmouth bass (aka bronzeback) factory.

Few fly anglers disagree with James Henshall's well-known assertion in his classic *Book of Black Bass*, published in 1881, that 'inch for inch, pound for pound' bass are 'the gamest fish that swims'. The Grand does hold what good ol' boys in the Deep South gleefully call 'hawgs'.

The majority of Grand smallmouth do not grow much beyond thirteen inches—at least the ones I have caught or the ones I have seen caught with the exception of Dan Kennaley's eighteen-incher—a personal best on that stretch. No matter. Like bantamweight boxers punching their way out of poverty, it is the size of the fight rather than the size of the fish that lands the knockout.

The smaller ones—those in the eight-to-ten-inch range—jump acrobatically as though catapulted from an aquatic trampoline. I recall catching a ten-incher that cleared the water by at least 1.2 metres (four feet). These qualities make for an evening of high summer fun with a four -or five-weight fly rod and a box of juicy nymphs, small minnow patterns and streamers (including Woolly Buggers and Clouser minnows) for subsurface prospecting, and Dahlberg divers and small poppers for exciting top-water action.

Fishing for trout in large streams or small rivers remains my most satisfying form of fly angling. But I love catching bass, either from a canoe on sun-dappled lakes or wading in the flowing current of coursing rivers. Depending on conditions—when you get to my age cold water becomes less inviting—wet-wading in shorts and an old pair of sneakers brings back the boyhood thrill of summer angling.

I recall one mid-August evening I was on the Grand with Dan Kennaley and Jeff Thomason, a professor at the University of Guelph when he isn't fly fishing (not only in Ontario but in such lovely places as his native England, Scotland, the Catskills and the Yucatan Peninsula). Dan and Jeff have been fly fishing companions for a quarter

century. They are competitive in a friendly way. In fact Jeff proved the exception to the rule on this stretch of river by landing a 'hawg' exceeding twenty inches. Dan documented the trophy with a photo later published in *Ontario Out of Doors*.

I once hooked a big one on the same stretch as Jeff, but the wily bronzeback escaped as I bent down to lip him. Excitement eclipsed by disappointment—the angler's curse. Another time, I landed eighteen pint-sized (under ten inches) bass in a span of forty-five minutes. Exhilarating despite the modest sizes.

It was a lovely evening, hot but not as humid as it had been in recent days. Because of much-needed rain, the river was a little higher and stained more than ideal. Wading was relatively easy, however, considering this portion of river has some unexpectedly deep pools and aquatic garden of large submerged rocks that demand alertness and care.

Dan and Jeff each caught bass numbering in the low teens, with a couple each exceeding twelve inches. I landed seven, the largest measuring (according to my outstretched hand from tip of baby finger to tip of thumb) nine inches. The outing was memorable for me because it was the first time I had a camera to snap a couple of photos.

Crayfish patterns proved the ticket. Dan's custom two-legged Woolly Crayfish was effective. (He also likes to use a Mickey Finn.) Jeff preferred a juicy crayfish pattern with lead eyes. I relied on a beige crayfish pattern and a black, bead-headed Woolly Bugger, with a couple of slivers of red tinsel and four pairs of thin rubber legs extending from both sides of its body—a steelhead pattern I bought in a fly shop in Victoria, BC. The fly had been successful a couple of weeks previously on a Muskoka lake I fished with Dan. As usual I took a minimalist approach by casting across and letting the fly swing down and around. I mixed up my retrieve. Jeff, who likes experimenting outside the box, had success casting his streamer upstream.

This is rich farm country. I enjoyed the pastoral tranquility; however, we were not the only ones savouring the Grand. During the three hours we were on the water a couple of foursomes of canoeists took advantage of the high water and paddled downstream, complete with hearty greetings. I have canoed this scenic stretch and it is clear to me it would be both productive and rewarding to paddle or kayak downriver, floating and fishing at promising pools and runs along the way.

Canoeists were not our only companions. A great blue heron took flight upon our arrival, and before we left, a small rambunctious chevron of Canada geese flew along the river's flight path, with a lone straggler pulling up the rear. Funny how annoying geese are when pooping all over city parks, but they remain icons of Canadian wilderness in their natural habitat.

'It was a great evening of fishing,' Jeff rhapsodized as we walked back to the cars as the sinking sun bled into the treetops. 'We all caught something.' Later, at a pub, he rephrased his tribute to Grand River bronzebacks: 'What a lovely evening.' I agreed. Sipping on a frosty Boddingtons, Dan nodded. Sometimes silence really is eloquence.

Size Really Does Matter

It started with a short email sent by cell phone. 'Give me a call.' The email came from Dave Whalley, former professional guide and past president of KW Flyfishers. The subject line was promising: FISHING TOMORROW. When I called, Dave asked if I had plans. 'Nope,' I replied. My partner at the time, Lois Hayward, was in England on a choir tour of hallowed cathedrals. She had left me in the care of our two girls—nine-year-old Labradoodle sisters, Abby and Mandy. Dave invited me to join him for a muskie and bass outing from his drift boat on the Saugeen River, a pleasant, ninety-minute drive from my Waterloo home.

I confirmed that I would be happy to tag along, adding I had neither fished from a drift boat nor targeted muskellunge, a prehistoric Goliath whose home is confined to the Great Lakes region. Its name originated in the late eighteenth century from the French masquinongé or maskinongé, which itself was derived from the Ojibwa maashkinoozhe (meaning elongated face).

'What time?' I asked.

'How about six,' he replied. 'Is that too early?'

'It isn't,' I said, fibbing through clenched teeth.

My consternation might need explaining to anglers who pride themselves on rising at the blush of dawn. Meeting at 6:00 a.m. means getting up at 4:30 (I never leave the house without a morning shower). I know, lots of good people besides farmers leave the comfort of their beds before sunrise. But not me. Still I could not refuse Dave's offer.

* * *

In *Where the Bright Waters Meet*, Harry Plunket Greene identifies three types of fish: 'friendly, indifferent and sinister'. In my capacity as intrepid fly angler I have met my share of the first, far too many of the second and too few of the third. I had never fished for muskie with an artificial fly; however, I knew what muskies were all about, firsthand—sort of. I had a memorable close encounter with one some years previously when a newspaper colleague invited me to the dilapidated family cottage his father and uncles cobbled together four decades earlier from railroad boxcars on a rocky point overlooking the French River.

One torrid August day we portaged to a small lake that feeds into the historic river. We canoed into a bay that looked like a fish haven, brimming with lily pads, windfall, deadheads and much else that appeals to ravenous bass. We cast hard lures, including all manner of spoons, crankbaits, buzzbaits and spinnerbaits, with optimistic urgency. Nothing. We could not believe that the bay was a barren piscatorial wasteland. There just had to be fish, we both asserted repeatedly. Then—slowly, silently, sinisterly—a massive muskie rolled alongside and brushed against the side of canoe, almost tipping us into the cold, tobacco-stained water.

Hell! I gasped—awestruck, dazzed and shaken. 'What a bloody monster.'

The beast was scary. I swear we heard the menacing soundtrack from *Jaws*. The solitary marauder explained the dearth of fish, which had either high-tailed out of Dodge City or had been 'devoured' out of the bay through a cannibalistic cycle of breakfast, lunch and supper.

In hindsight I admit I was not thinking straight. I hastily retrieved my eight-pound test monofilament and replaced the crankbait with a no. 5 red bucktail Mepps spinner, the largest lure in my tackle box.

I was shaking like a wilting leaf as I tossed the spinner over the side of the canoe. It was immediately inhaled. I was connected to the antediluvian, chthonic leviathan for as long as it took to lower his massive head and lumber away, showing as much concern as a super-sized trucker tonguing a toothpick after downing an all-day breakfast platter in a roadside greasy spoon. It is not cowardliness to confess that we paddled a little more carefully until we were able to shake the after-effects of our close encounter with Precambrian prehistory.

With our courage bolstered we returned to what we now nicknamed Muskie Bay over the next three days to no avail. We were back, energized by a cocktail of dermination and resolve, a few weeks later after buying some recommended muskie lures in a tackle shop. We never got a bite, never saw a rise and never saw a fish of any kind, including the rapacious apex predator. But we knew whenever we returned—we could sense somewhere deep within our being—that the finned beast was there, brooding, lurking, waiting and watching in the dark northern myth-haunted water.

* * *

Dave and I met at a designated location and headed out on an empty two-lane amid darkness and fog. We arrived at our destination about 8:00 a.m., just as the warming sun was burning mist off the river. We put in the drift boat and started casting 'fuzz and feather' (so named by American outdoor writer Charley Waterman).

My preferred game species is trout. Hatchery-raised browns and rainbows are fine. But catching native brook trout, which I called speckled trout or 'specks' when I first fished for them in Northern Ontario as a youngster, is as close to piscatorial paradise as I can imagine. I also enjoy fishing for largemouth and smallmouth bass while wading rivers or casting to shore on lakes from a canoe.

I cast trout flies proficient distances on three-, four-, or five-weight bamboo and graphite rods. Here, accuracy and finesse are more important than distance. I cast small streamers, usually Woolly Buggers on six- or seven-weight graphite rods well enough to catch my share of bass. But casting hefty ten-weight rods with enormous muskie flies took me out of my comfort zone—big time.

Dave rigged up one of Steve May's Quarter Chicken articulated muskie streamers. The provocatively named fly is made from various synthetic materials, with a rattle, rotating joint, big nasty hook and other sundry doodads. Casting it is like heaving a rubber boot tied to the end of butcher twine. Still I persevered, determined not to be deflated or defeated during my inaugural drift boat adventure. There is no room for wimps when fly fishing for muskie.

I struggled to cast and reached far short of desired distances. I worked harder than I needed to through sheer incompetence. Dave, a superb caster whose effortless tosses propelled large, awkward flies optimum distances, was generous in sharing what he had learned over a lifetime of fishing. He did not ruffle easily. He remained phlegmatic and casual, with a ready smile.

He demonstrated how I could improve my casting. It is all in the 'rhythm and timing', he explained. I listened dutifully and watched intently—with no appreciable improvement. I failed to duplicate

Dave's form, let alone rhythm and timing, as my arm grew weary, melting into jelly by the cast. (In my own shabby defence, I should report Dave is at least a decade younger, bigger and stronger than me. This does not explain my failings, but it massages my tender ego.)

I soon came to the conclusion that targeting muskie with a fly rod is a young man's game. Unlike the low-impact quality of most freshwater fly fishing, casting gaudy, unwieldy muskie flies requires muscle strength and stamina. A few months' prep in a gym with a Navy Seal or Marine was the ticket, I reasoned.

Miraculously my bungling did not prevent me from hooking a Great Northern pike. I landed a forty-four-inch leviathan a few years back on a spinning outfit while slowly trolling on a small lake in Temagami, but this was by far the biggest fish I had ever caught on the fly. It will likely remain so.

While trout are revered, bass admired, steelhead praised and salmon worshipped, northern pike are feared. These apex fresh-water predators match size and ferocity with beauty—an olive base highlighted with short, yellowish slashes. Their sleek body and long snout make them look like thick water snakes with razor blade teeth.

No less an authority than Izaak Walton describes pike as 'the tyrant of fresh water'. In *The Compleat Angler* he observes that they are 'solitary, melancholy' fresh-water wolves 'by reason of [a] bold, greedy, devouring disposition'. Their stealth nature has inspired the work of many poets, including Americans Theodore Roethke and James Wright. English poet Ted Hughes—a passionate fly angler who spent many hours sharing water with the Queen Mother—wrote most memorably about the aquatic carnivore. He captures the creature's frightening ferociousness in 'Pike', a poem that examines inherent violence in all animal species including mankind.

I would like to report that the vermiculated beauty fought like a crazed behemoth on steroids—Captain Ahab's mythic whale incarnate in a lazy, hazy river at the height of summer. But it was more of a heavy, sluggish dead-weight than a ferocious fight. Imagine landing a discarded car tire. There was more battle in a gorgeous six-inch brookie or feisty nine-inch smallmouth than in this gorgeous brute.

That is, until he saw the boat. Then freaked out. And all hell broke loss. The river ignited into a concentrated boil. Talk about wild!

I landed the mighty leviathan shortly after 9:00 a.m. I was elated.

Apologies to the men reading this essay. Size Really Does Matter. To put the time of day in perspective, it is usually when I am still in my bathrobe and slippers, sipping my first cup of freshly ground java with a book in hand. Dave subdued the forty-incher (an estimate in the absence of a measuring tape) using a powerful pair of lock grippers that held fast to its intimidatingly toothy yap.

Of course—all too typical for me—I did not have a camera, so Dave snapped a few photos on his cellphone while the exhausted beast languished, sulking, alongside the boat. I could tell he was pissed. I knew he was catching his breath, biding his time to get even. Erupt into revenge mode.

But, man, what a magnificent specimen, every inch worthy of the title Great Northern. He reminded me of a heavyweight prize fighter on the mat, down for the count in the dying seconds of the fifteenth round, in days gone by when boxing commemorated sacrifice in the name of honour.

Dave adeptly lifted it out of the water and passed it over for a couple of quick trophy shots. I struggled awkwardly, trying to hold the primordial monster for a couple more photos to add to my piscatorial memory book. Then Dave revived it, allowing it to return to the dark, muddy subaquatic world out of which it came, seemingly eons ago.

Trophy photos are part of angling tradition. One of my most prized possessions is a photo of my two sons sitting in a fourteen-foot

aluminum boat after an evening of fishing with their dad. Dylan, who was eleven at the time, is casually holding a bass by its mouth, striking the standard angling pose. In contrast, I resemble Robertson, who was seven and struggling mightily to grip a big ol' bass by its floppy tail. Their smiles are reflected on the face of the fly angler sitting in the bow of Dave Whalley's drift boat more than fifteen years later.

Summer on a Secret River

Pity the fly angler who does not have a secret river—or a secret stretch of river—in which to fish. It need not be exclusive; it need only be restricted to a fellowship of angling companions bound by an oath of fidelity. Here I offer an account of one summer on a secret stretch of river which I revere beyond all other rivers and lakes.

I had a bottle of 12-year-old Glenrothes tucked away in the back of the Jeep a few days before the summer solstice as I drove an hour north of Waterloo to Clifford, Ontario to pick up Wesley Bates. This was a special single malt. I developed a taste for whisky four decades ago after discovering Glenrothes in its distinctive apothecary-shaped bottle, raised embossed lettering and handwritten label. I was delighted to learn that in September 2018, the Speyside distillery introduced a 12-year-old from its Soleo Collection, so named because the whisky ages entirely in seasoned sherry oak. I was eager to introduce my angling companion and creative partner to its aroma of banana and vanilla and its taste of banana, citrus and hint of cinnamon, capped with a long sweet finish of melon and light spice.

Wesley and I had fished together once before, but he was preoccupied, snapping photos in preparation of the engravings for our book. This was our first outing devoted solely to what Bliss Perry in *Pools and Ripples* calls 'the art and mystery of fishing with a fly'.

Wesley was introduced to fly fishing by his father, a career Mountie who had retired to British Columbia. Wesley's father enjoyed trolling with a fly rod and streamer from a canoe, an activity his son also found appealing. At the time Wesley was living in Hamilton and was transitioning from salaried working stiff to freelance commercial engraver. He was undergoing physio and his therapist confirmed that the recreational sport served as an effective therapeutic treatment. His parents gave him a seven-weight fibreglass fly rod the following Christmas, which he was still using more than a quarter century later.

I had been accompanying Dan Kennaley to this private stretch on the Beatty Saugeen for more than a decade. He and angling companions Jeff Thomason and Craig Wardlaw had been frequenting the headwater for three decades. I introduced it to Gary Bowen and I was keen to initiate Wesley to its myriad wonders.

I knew its location like the back of my hand. Or so I thought. Wesley's directions did not prevent me from driving too far north of the two-lane hardtop that would take us to a gravel road and then to a pockmarked, twin-rutted, dirt path through a thick copse to the river. Consequently, it took us an hour to wind our way through a warren of backroads to arrive at a spot no more than twenty minutes from Wesley's storefront gallery and studio. Like a standup comic angling for laughs, I insisted that we were not so much lost as exploring one of my favourite areas of southwestern Ontario. He graciously went along with the ruse. Before arriving at the river we paid our respects to the property owners. Wesley gave them one of the engravings he had completed for our book. They were surprised and delighted. After parking in a small, secluded field of tall native grasses, we geared up and I led Wesley through an entrancing arbor of cedars that seems lifted from the pages of a medieval romance.

Forests, of course, have long been viewed as embodiments of enchantment. In theme and setting, form and figure of speech, forests are simultaneously literal and symbolic as they recur in literature, music and visual art, religion, psychology and mythology. I know of no woods more pleasurable or more delightful than these. They attracted and fascinated me the first time I passed through them—and I remain under their spell.

Headwaters are equally magical. In *Spring Creek* Nick Lyons observes that headwaters are *numinous*—the perfect word with which to describe them. I do most of my trout fishing on the tailwater of the Grand River. However, I find headwaters more alluring. Headwaters and wild trout—especially brook trout—are synonymous. If a wandering pilgrim were to ask directions to a Lost Garden, I would direct him upstream toward the headwater to the source.

I am intrigued by the differences between tailwaters which are essentially communal, and headwaters which are essentially private (I am not talking property rights here). I associate tailwaters with the head: rationality, logic and reason. In contrast, I associate headwaters with the heart: intuition, feeling and emotion.

Tailwaters are manufactured. Their flows are regulated by dams constructed to serve such functional purposes as flood control, irrigation and the needs of agriculture, industry and urbanization. As a fly angler I am thankful for the bottom-draw Shand dam at Belwood Lake, east of Fergus, which provides stable flows of cold water throughout the summer to sustain a world-class brown trout fishery.

In contrast, headwaters are organic, which makes them poetic. They are fountainheads of mystery. Pristine and wild, fecund and vital, they follow their own course, dictated by rock and soil, climate and weather. They are not only geographical sources, but sources of wonder. More than contours on topographical maps or boundaries on survey maps, they are limnological features of the imagination. They entice fly anglers around the next bend.

We heard the river before we saw it, drawn onward by its music, our expectations rising with each step. Emerging from the cloistered shade of the magical arbor, we stood before a watercourse that steals an angler's breath. I cannot decide whether it is a large stream or a small river, so I prefer the Scottish term *burn*. 'This is unbelievable,' Wesley whispered. 'And so close to home. Amazing.'

In *The Old Ways* the brilliant British writer Robert MacFarlane talks about transitions in the landscape from the known to the unknown. He calls these perceptual thresholds *border crossings*. They are not so much geographical as metaphysical. Crossing over makes a person feel and think differently. The ancient Celts sanctified such places in a landscape they viewed as holy. In *A Summer on the Test* John Waller Hills describes this portal experience from one realm to another as stepping 'into a different plan of life'. Here was such a place, exuding 'an air of expectancy and new life'. We looked on three branches of flowing water that converge below a small island and tumble over a low rocky ledge. The cascading water has carved out a deep pool where big trout reside. A ragged line of cedars stands guard over this clean, well-lighted place (with a nod to Ernest Hemingway).

Of all the places I fish, this oasis of solitude and serenity has the surest hold on my heart. Although located no more than a couple of kilometres from paved roads as the osprey flies, civilization has retreated into insignificance. The sense of a path giving out to a secret stretch of river is not dependent upon distance. Tranquility is a matter of *further*, not *farther*.

I put down my knapsack containing the bottle of *usage beatha*. When I fish with Dan we customarily go our separate ways before reuniting at the big pool at sunset. But I suggested to Wesley—who has not done as much fly fishing as I have despite beginning years earlier—that we might prospect together. The river was a tad high, a little boisterous, which I interpreted as a promising sign. Dan and I had last visited eighteen months previously, in late September after a brutally torrid summer. The river was ailing so severely that we feared climate change had permanently damaged our liquid sliver of paradise. I was thrilled to see that nature's healing powers were so clearly and abundantly evident—at least for now.

'Let's get at her,' I chirped.

We both noticed a few Isonychia mayflies fluttering about. I tied on one of Dan's comparaduns to match the hatch and began casting my split-cane Sweetgrass five-weight. I changed to an Adams dry fly after catching a couple of fish on the comparadun. Nothing gives me more pleasure than catching native trout on flies of pedigree and tradition. For his part, Wesley tied on an Isonychia dry fly he had purchased a couple of days previously and began casting.

By dusk Wesley had caught a trio of trout, one rainbow and a pair of brook trout. Meanwhile, I landed eighteen rainbows, a couple exceeding eleven inches (which is good for the headwater), and a lone brookie. Dan and I had caught precious few brookies in recent years, so their return to the watercourse was welcome because it confirmed a healthy habitat. A pool below a rocky ledge a short distance upriver, not much larger than a small backyard wading pool, proved especially generous. It also compelled me to rethink my reading of shadow-casting as depicted by Norman Maclean in *A River Runs Through It*. I have always interpreted Paul's signature cast as an elegant metaphor for the creative process—all artists shadow-cast when they pick up a pen, paintbrush or musical instrument.

I did not follow Paul's example of casting a long graceful line over the water, thus fooling gullible trout into believing that a hatch is on. Instead, I made short sharp steeple casts (utilizing vertical backcasts high over my right shoulder) to direct a fly at the water, suddenly retrieving it centimetres above the surface. Unsuspecting trout actually rose to the phantom hatch. I was amazed by the prospect of life imitating fiction.

When an angler encounters a pool for the first time it is like meeting a new friend bearing unexpected gifts. Over time it evolves into a cherished old friend. A pool has its own personality. As an angler becomes acquainted with its temperament and moods, it becomes more generous, sometimes even more forgiving. Lyons—an English professor as well as a fly angling writer and publisher—evokes John Keats in *Spring Creek* when he notes that a pool serves as an 'objective correlative' for an angler. I agree. My old friend gave me a half dozen trout before introducing it to Wesley. He was greeted with his first fish of the evening. He responded with a celebratory arm-pump. '*Yes!*'

This was where I caught the nine-inch brookie, a specimen of rare beauty that fills me with joy and gratitude every time I am fortunate to land one. Also known as speckled trout or specks, brook trout are actually a species of freshwater char in the genus Salvelinus of the salmon family Salmonidae.

Ichthyology aside, they are my *very* favourite fish. I recall with delight the first one I ever caught on a fly, which happened to be on the Rocky Saugeen, the Beatty's sister. I tell anglers and non-anglers alike that God created brook trout as His supreme achievement before working his way down the Great Chain of Being, ending with humanity at the bottom.

Wesley was inconsolable when he confided that one of the brookies he caught had swallowed the fly. Despite his best efforts he could not save the fish—as sometimes happens despite artificial flies with single barbless hooks being far less injurious than treble hooks or live bait on barbed hooks which fish devour. However careful a responsible fly angler is in reviving and releasing fish unharmed, the activity retains elements of a blood sport. Unintentional death remains a regrettable, but nonetheless inevitable, consequence of fishing. There is no honest way of sugar-coating this fact.

I remember catching a robust smallmouth bass that had inhaled the fly so deeply that it got entangled in its gill plates from the inside. Seeing it floating inert and sideways on the lake after releasing it was distressing in the extreme. Knowing that it would provide food for a natural predator offered neither consolation nor comfort.

I understand why some people condemn fishing. I acknowledge that, while subsistence fishing for survival is acceptable, fishing for sport remains inescapably controversial. I lack the philosophical turn of mind to defend sportfishing on ethical grounds. I contend, however, that corporate agriculture and factory harvesting of the oceans harm the environment far beyond responsible recreational angling. Fact is, the food chain is a killing machine, wherever the food source (animal or vegetable) is positioned.

Moreover, I do more harm to the environment driving my Jeep or heating my apartment than I do casting my fly rod. Fly fishing reminds me that I am an integral part of the rhythms and cycles of nature. Consequently, I am a more devoted steward of a sacred trust over which I do *not* exert dominion.

As the sun slipped silently behind western treetops, Wesley and I sat on the bankside with our wading boots dangling in the river, like kids sitting on a dock beneath an expanse of distant stars piercing the enveloping darkness. Against a backdrop of river music and flickering fireflies dancing like notes on sheet music we witnessed voracious trout wolfing down vulnerable insects. This drama of life and death was played out on the liminal surface of water as black as obsidian.

I brought out the Glenrothes and poured a dram in pewter demitasse cups embossed with Celtic scrollwork. We toasted the trout and the river, our friendship and our creative partnership.

CODA ONE

LOSING YOUR WAY IS NOT BEING LOST

If only the evening had ended there, in a state of gratitude. The Glenrothes was so smooth, however, that Wesley and I shared another dram—and then another. The darkness was palpable by the time we decided to head back through the arbor of cedars to the Jeep. Normally it would have taken no more than a couple of minutes. But we lost our way—somehow. Thanks to my LED pen light we impersonated extras in the *Blair Witch Project*. An hour later we made it to the Jeep, laughing uproariously as we took off our gear before heading home under a crescent moon resembling a lingering smile.

* * *

It had cooled off by Midsummer's Day when Dan and I were on our way to picking up Wesley en route to our secret stretch of trout headwater. I was eager to share an evening with Wesley and Dan. Moreover, Wesley wanted to talk to Dan about artificial flies, some of which he intended to transform into engravings for our book.

Rain had begun when I got into the Jeep at home. It continued after meeting up with Dan in Arthur and picking up Wesley in Clifford. It turned to drizzle after we geared up and waded into the headwater at 6:00 p.m. By sunset the rain had stopped but not before putting the damper on all but sparse, intermittent hatches.

Despite changing fly patterns and sizing down, I had numerous looks and rejections from snooty trout. Still, Dan caught ten rainbows including an eleven-incher. Wes caught a single brookie. And I caught three rainbows, including an acrobatic eleven-incher, and a lovely ten-inch brownie.

We lowed the curtain on a pleasurable evening by sharing a couple of drams of twelve-year-old Singleton of Dufftown. Tirelessly innovative, Wesley served the malt whisky in white porcelain eggcups purchased at an antiques shop. Featuring a stylized leaping salmon on its label, the Singleton was delicious, with a nose of brown sugar, espresso and roasted walnut, complemented by a palate of orange zest, oak and toffee. Its dry finish with a fruity crispness sent a trio of happy anglers on their merry way.

* * *

It was the last day of the inland trout season in southwestern Ontario when I joined Wesley for a couple of precious afternoon hours on the Beatty. We shared a mutually celebratory mood.

Wesley had a new five-weight, graphite fly rod which he was eager to christen. He had purchased it a couple of months previously; however, finishing the engravings for our book had kept him off the water. For my part, I had spent the previous week sweating over the final draft of my manuscript after receiving proofs from the editor.

For the first time in more than a decade there were other fishermen in the small field where I park the Jeep. They introduced themselves as Al and Carl. Turns out they had spent the morning 'drowning worms', Al joked, adding that they have been coming to this stretch of river on the last day of trout season for many years. They were tossing back chilled frosties while perched on the tailgate of Al's pickup. It was obvious when Wesley and I fished the big pool a while later that Al and

Carl were not catch-and-release anglers. They clearly had more than beer in the plastic cooler Al was leaning against when we were chatting. They were obviously counting on a platter of pan-fried trout for lunch or supper.

Entering the cloistered shade of the arbor of cedars held its customary magic. And coming on the open stretch of *burn* was as transporting as ever. We had arrived at our peaceful point in a troubled world. After tying on a beadheaded Pheasant Tail Nymph, I took Wesley downriver to introduce him to another pool that had been generous over the years. I caught a dozen rainbows ranging from squiggly fingerlings no longer than my pinky finger to a respectable eight inches. Wesley did not catch any fish, but he familiarized himself with his new Fenwick rod.

Fly rods have their own topography which an angler comes to understand through the feel of motion, like a hiker breaking in a new pair of Gortex boots. 'Remember, you don't teach the rod, the rod teaches you,' I teased. 'Like an end-grain of wood, it tells you what it wants you to engrave, you don't tell it.'

After a couple of pleasant hours we made our way upriver to the big pool. It was cleaned out of trout, of course. Neither nibble nor bite. Unfazed, we sat down at bankside. Wesley poured a dram from a pocket flask into a couple of collapsible telescopic cups. (They brought back memories. When I was a boy my grandfather gave me such a cup, which had been given to him by his father. Like so much in life, it had slipped through the cracks of time.)

Wesley's offering was a delicious three-year-old wheat whiskey

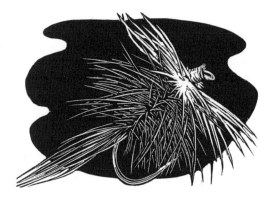

called Dry Fly, named in recognition of the legendary salmon steelhead and trout waters of the American Northwest. Double-distilled and aged in American oak barrels, the hand-crafted whiskey is made from grain grown on a century-old homestead farm forty-eight kilometres from the distillery in Spokane, Washington. (The mustard-coloured fly painted on the bottle seems to dance in the amber liquid.) Its nose reveals dry candied fruit with notes of honey and toffee. Despite its slightly higher alcohol-to-volume ratio than regular malt whisky, it is warm and easy on the palate, with a gentle finish that lingers on the back of the tongue, with a pleasing touch of vanilla and toasted oak.

As we were getting up to leave, Wesley said softly, 'Thank you, river.' Then we entered the magic arbor on our way home.

CODA TWO
ONE MAN'S JUNK IS ANOTHER MAN'S TREASURE

After dropping Wesley off in Clifford I noticed that the Rooster Perch, the antique store across the street, was still open. Wesley had told me that the owner, Nick Oleksandriw, not only bought and sold items of interest, he was a passionate collector. He recognized me, even though we had never met, and he knew of our book, so it was obvious that Wesley had talked to him about our project.

The store (which is a converted funeral parlour) is not so much a commercial business as an abundant treasure chest of remembered things from the past. More than a shop owner, Nick is a magician who deals in memories and nostalgia as if these were rabbits pulled from a hat. We talked of vintage fishing tackle (Heddon River Runts and such), malt whisky (Nick is a Macallan's man) and sports memorabilia (especially pertaining to his beloved hometown Montreal Canadiens and my cherished Detroit Red Wings). The names Richard, Harvey and Plante, Howe, Lindsay and Sawchuck skated on our tongues.

Because he only deals in cash, Nick gave me a Canadian-made Eckmier fly reel, which I intend to pass along to Dan, a collector of vintage reels among sundry fly fishing memorabilia. I will complete the barter transaction with some vintage tackle I acquired when I still tossed Rapalas at bass and Mepps spinners at brown trout.

* * *

Casting a backward glance over the summer on the secret trout headwater, the most affecting trip occurred on the Canada Day weekend. I tell anyone who will listen that fly angling is about more than catching fish. Sometimes it is pilgrimage—what the early Christianized Celts called *peregrini*. A fly rod is more than an agent of beauty, it provides comfort and solace. I was on such a journey with rod in hand when I returned to the Beatty with my eldest son.

Dylan and his fiancée were hoeing a tough patch, which would eventually land him in a bed of stinging-nettle heartbreak. They had agreed to take a time-out to give themselves space to assess the situation. He did not know it at the time, but temporary separation would harden into permanency. My son was distraught. He had bravely endured eighteen months of turmoil, including an urgent health crisis with lingering consequences. He quit his job and returned to school to pursue an enthusiasm that would ultimately lead to a new career.

Dylan brought his tackle with him when he returned to Kitchener to stay a few days with his mom. He phoned me shortly after arriving and asked whether I could get away for a few hours of fishing. We made plans for the next day. Nature proved sympathetic when I picked him up. It was raining when we left and it was raining when we returned but, miraculously, the couple of hours we spent on the water were rain-free.

When we parked the Jeep, Dylan realized that he had left his reel behind in London. When the world turns vengeful such unintentional oversights are the accoutrements of anguish. I suggested we return to Waterloo, but he was intrigued by this secret stretch of river I had talked about so often and which he had never visited. I am sure he intuited its restorative potential.

I recalled a similar situation that occurred a decade earlier. It was my first birthday after separating from Dylan's mom after eighteen years of marriage. I was entrapped in suffocating grief. Feeling alone and isolated, I gathered my fly gear and headed up to a part of the Beatty Saugeen I had never fished before—nor have ever fished since. Casting lines on a headwater in the area where my wife had spent her childhood neither comforted nor consoled. However, it did give me something I desperately needed. Although I was unable to identify what exactly that 'something' was, it kept me on course and moving forward when I feared I was lost and had no place to go.

Dylan was enthralled by the arbor of cedars. He said it reminded him of the landscape J. R. R. Tolkien creates in *The Hobbit*. Dylan was a more precocious reader than I was in early adolescence. He was making his way through Tolkien, including *The Lord of the Rings* and *The Silmarillion*, while I was reading Scott Young's *Scrubs on Skates* and Jack Hambleton's *Temagami Guide* (the latter of which I lifted from my grade seven classroom library, the only book I ever pilfered).

My son was on to something. Leaving the dark enclosure of cedar and coming upon the bright expanse of water is like opening a door onto a different realm of imagination. Such a landscape is not only an external reality; it is an inner reality. It invests consciousness with conscience and bestows grace on anyone who is *aware* of crossing a threshold.

'It's like stumbling on a new world, a magical world, a mysterious world,' Dylan said. I agreed, adding that the experience always reminded of Tom Thomson's *Northern River*, which makes viewers feel like they are coming on a pristine river for the first time after bushwhacking through a forest of cedar and tamarack.

Dylan is a spin-fisherman so I asked if he would like to try casting a fly rod. We spent some time at the big pool. I showed him the basics and he made a series of casts, turning instruction into practice. He said he would like to see one of the elusive trout I cherish so much. I suggested moving upriver to the pool that had been so generous on previous outings.

I made a few casts before hooking a brace of cooperative trout. Dylan was fascinated by the ghostly torpedo shadows that transformed into gem-like materiality after emerging from the shimmering pool below the ledge of rushing water. His troubles were momentarily forgotten as he concentrated on the squirming, twisting flashes of luminescence before they regained their freedom. He was thrilled to glimpse the fierce affirmation of life they embodied in cold flesh.

Before heading home we sat on the bankside overlooking the big pool. I poured us a dram of Highland Park, the smoked honey of Orkney, where the ghosts of Celt and Viking continue to roam across an austere minimalist landscape on the northern edge of Europe. 'Hey, Dad, isn't strange how the Reid Boys are drawn to water when things turn to shit,' said Dylan. 'There's something soft and soothing and cleansing about a river, especially a river at sunset.'

Without knowing the full extend of his words, Dylan intuited that fly fishing is equal parts recollection, connection and commemoration. It is the means through which I struggle to make sense of myself and the world. It gives me the vocabulary to tell my story and the stories of those I love.

As the secret river surrendered to the darkness of eventide, we lamented how sorrow pierces like a rusty hook in a tender lip. Then father and son, sharing a dram of the water of life, toasted the awful beauty of letting go.

Autumn

Getting It Right

Despite severe storm warnings, I decided to head out on the Grand River for a couple of hours after supper. With the constant rain we have had all summer across southwestern Ontario, surrendering to inclement weather forecasts dramatically reduced my time on the water. Not tonight; no way. Caution to the wind and all that.

It was early September, a month when I especially enjoy fly fishing for brown trout. I went to a spot that has been generous to Dan Kennaley and me. I had the river to myself but I was not alone. I enjoyed the company of a few scattered ducks, a chevron of Canada geese, a kingfisher and a pair of blue herons. A cedar waxwing, reminding me of an oiled baseball glove from my youth, wheeled and pirouetted above the river—I love these handsome birds. A sleek marten patrolled the shoreline. My Partagas Serie D No. 4—cigars are best enjoyed on the water—reached the band as darkness seeped through the trees at eventide. I stripped in line for the last time before heading back to the car under distant stars. Then I saw it; not once but twice. Twice.

Holy shit!

A large fish catapulted out of a pool adjacent to a riffle beneath a large willow tree twelve metres upriver. The picture he painted reminded me of a pair of Winslow Homer's Adirondack watercolours: *Jumping Trout* and *Leaping Trout*.

The fish was obviously hungry, undoubtedly relishing one of the cream caddis flies that were fluttering about. If he was a brownie— and why wouldn't he be—it would be one of the largest I have ever seen with the naked eye on the Grand's tailwater. I began shaking with excitement, but hesitated to cast. The darkness deepened at the close of day. The reel seat of my Sweetgrass five-weight bamboo rod needed attention; I did not want to risk catastrophe.

Reluctantly I retreated, determined to return the next day. We have all read or heard tales about big, territorial fish protecting aquatic turf. I was confident this guy was not going anywhere.

It was an interminably long twenty hours or so, with rising expectation. The next afternoon I once again drove through Mennonite Country. The weather was cooperating. Excited and anxious, I felt like a primeval predator on the hunt. Instinct on high alert. I had Bruce Springsteen on the car CD player—*The Ghost of Tom Joad*. I had a trio of acoustic Boss albums on constant rotation since I went to the funeral of a friend who lost his battle with an especially virulent cancer. Bill Walker was a young fifty-two years of age, sports editor of the *Owen Sound Sun Times*, beer league goalie and indefatigable community volunteer. He was the husband of a colleague, sports reporter Christine Rivet, whom I sat across from during my last decade at the *Waterloo Region Record*. He was father of two teenage girls. And he was a Springsteen fan, as am I. Some years previously we had worked together to bring a union to the *Sun Times* to protect his fellow reporters, editors and photographers.

When I arrived at the river, Springsteen was soulfully meandering through 'Oh Shenandoah', the heartsick American folk ballad dating from the early nineteenth century and believed to have originated with French voyageurs who paddled southward from the North Country. For me this song of longing and hope is about travelling beyond the hard life, about passing over to a new land, a new world, a new existence, brimming with the promise of salvation.

I got into my gear and slowly made my way to the home of the mystery fish I had come to slay. It took willful effort to take my time, to wade cautiously and carefully. I crossed the border, left the mundane world behind and entered the magical world of piscatorial expectation and potential wonder.

When I arrived I tied on a cream Usual dry fly originally designed by Adirondack fly tier Fran Betters. Although there was no rise, I spotted an occasional cream caddis fly madly fluttering about. After twenty minutes or so I tied on a Possie Bugger, a nymph Steve May recommended in his powerpoint presentation—'Versatile Fly Patterns for Ontario Waters'—at a recent meeting of KW Fly Fishers.

I stealthily made my way upriver and began casting down a current seam, allowing the fly to swing into the adjacent eddy—the spot.

After a few casts—WHAM.

I set the hook. I was ecstatic. To think, I had hooked the fish I came to catch. I was the alpha predator. Me.

I played the fish and carefully led him out of the riffle into the placid water of the eddy. I had him; he was mine. My knees were shaking. I gulped a deep breath. I began thinking about my waterproof Pentax camera in my vest pocket. Thoughts jumped to the blog I was going to post, recording My Big Fish Adventure.

Sonofabitch!

'What the hell is that?' I asked myself.

It was beyond doubt the fish I had seen the previous night. I could tell by its girth, its silhouette, its length. But, wait a minute.... Could it be? I'm far from an ichthyologist, but it looked like a walleye.

A walleye!

I confess: I was pleased to accomplish what I had set out to do; but the result was not what I expected, what I anticipated, what I wanted, what I dreamed on (to paraphrase Will Shakespeare).

Damn!

Eventually I settled down. Then I started brooding. It occurred to me that in our daily routine we too often fall into the trap of chasing perfection. We aspire to be the perfect son or daughter, the perfect spouse, the perfect father or mother, the perfect friend, the perfect employee.... Of course we fail, as we must. It is our condition. I have failed miserably, many times, over and over. Regrets? Too many to count. In contrast fly fishing is not about perfection. It is about getting it right—mostly, at least occasionally, fleeting as a hummingbird's wingbeat. The right cast, with the right fly, at the right spot, at the right time....

This is one of the things fly fishing shares with writing. When Ernest Hemingway, a man who knew more than a little about both writing and fishing, was asked what he thought he was doing by rewriting the ending of *A Farewell to Arms* thirty-nine times, he replied: 'Getting the words right.'

This is what I try to do every time I sit at the computer keyboard or wade a river, waving a fly rod—or apologize to someone I love and have hurt. It is what my friend did so well. He was not a fly angler, although he once confided that he would like to try it. Sadly we never got out on the water. Like my son Robertson, he was a goalie in a game he loved. Had we ever made it out, I know he would have risen to the challenge of getting it right. After all, that is how Bill Walker lived.

A Good Day to Live

I started the day as I usually do, with a coffee and a book. Today I was reading *Hemingway on Fishing*, a compilation of writing, both fiction and non-fiction, dedicated to one of his great passions. My interest in the much maligned and misunderstood American writer was rekindled with the publication of Mary V. Dearborn's *Ernest Hemingway: A Biography*.

I admire much, but not all, of Hemingway. Writing 'Big Two-Hearted River', one of the best stories ever devoted to fishing, would have been enough. But he did not stop there—his observations about writing short stories reflect an ecological philosophy, with which fly anglers can identify. I cherish what he said in *A Moveable Feast* about writing the short story: 'What did I know best that I had not written about and lost? What did I know about truly and care for most? There was no choice at all.'

So much to unpack here. He touches on the mystery of writing about something he had not written, but knew intimately, with his whole being. And had lost. So writing was a creative act of recovery, a kind of memory rehabilitation. What he had lost had to be something he cared about deeply. So writing was about heart more than mind. Writing is not about words on the page but about soul made manifest. How he expressed these thoughts without sounding sentimental or disingenuous is a mark of his grace under pressure.

Hemingway was more than a one-cast wonder when it came to water, fish and angling. A reader does not have to spend much time with him to realize how much Hemingway knew about these subjects. Angling was an enduring passion; fish and water were mistresses he never betrayed.

'I could never be lonely along the river,' Hemingway writes in 'Fishermen of the Seine'. I am moved every time I read this confession from a writer who was profoundly lonely throughout this life. Despite success, fame, wealth, four marriages and friendships with the rich, famous and notorious, I believe loneliness fuelled the writer's destructive obsession with celebrity.

I believe the bombastic braggadocio was a disguise for a deeply insecure introvert who suffered from physical and mental pain for most of his adult life. Read 'Big Two-Hearted River'—it is clear as a freestone mountain stream that fishing provided comfort and solace he found nowhere else.

Hemingway was young and pure when he fly fished and subsequently wrote about trout and bass. His personality began deteriorating—causing him to become a pathetic cartoon of the man and the artist he truly wanted to be—when he abandoned fly fishing after his tackle trunk was lost or stolen en route to Idaho by train in 1940. This personal tragedy marked Hemingway's loss of innocence and the beginning of his cartwheel into disgrace. He confused tabloid celebrity with the man he was once destined to be.

I wish Hemingway had devoted more writing to fly fishing for trout. I wish there was more of 'The Best Rainbow Trout Fishing', which he wrote for the *Toronto Star*, or 'The Clarke's Fork Valley, Wyoming', written for *Vogue*.

Canada's legendary newspaperman Greg Clark once took Hemingway fly fishing for trout when the two worked at the *Star*. Clark later confessed that he did not have much use for the American's writing. Hemingway did not have much use for Toronto and the newspaper that bears the city's name. The most accomplished Toronto writer Hemingway befriended was Morley Callaghan, even though the two met in Paris. Hemingway became estranged from Callaghan after losing to the more diminutive writer in a famous boxing match with Scott Fitzgerald as timekeeper. In contrast, the American held Clark in esteem throughout his life.

I have little interest in salt-water fishing, so Hemingway's deep-sea angling exploits leave me cold. I find the photographs of 'Papa' boasting unapologetically beside magnificent marlin and shark tethered to racks on docks grotesque—even considering that the ethics of fishing-to-kill have changed dramatically. Still, I can be moved when he writes about the sea. This short passage from 'On the Blue Water—A Gulf Stream Letter' is eloquence born of understanding. Likening the ocean to the last wild country is genius:

In the first place the Gulf Stream and other great ocean currents are the last wild country there is left. Once you are out of sight of land and of the other boats you are ... alone ... and the sea is the same as it has been since before men ever went on it in boats....

Hemingway is not only poetic, he is prescient. The deep ocean is the planet's last frontier. Its health is the key to survival—the earth's and all its living creatures, including humankind. This makes fish the barometer, the canary in the mine (or maybe mind), the finned prognosticator of our future.

After spending a few hours with Hemingway in the comfort of my armchair I was primed to hit the Grand River. It was time to put literary theory into angling practice. Dan Kennaley and I had been out the previous evening. We each caught a pair of brownies (nine to eleven inches). It was a good outing, followed by supper at a favourite pub. We both washed down schnitzel the size of dinner plates, made from locally-raised pork, with pints of chilled craft beer. I don't know why, but draft beer is best when enjoyed after a few hours on the water.

Summer across southwestern Ontario had apparently waited until September to announce itself as I drove to the river. Nature had started underpainting trees in deep rust, preparing the palette of dramatic reds, oranges and yellows that were soon to follow—the brushstrokes of autumn. I wound my way through Mennonite country as farmers applied manure to fields. A thick, pungent aroma permeated the inside of my Jeep despite closed windows.

It was late afternoon on a Friday. I saw three or four cars and pickup trucks at access points along the river. I expected to have company. After arriving and gearing up I sauntered to a favoured spot, the same location Dan and I had fished the evening before. Surprisingly I was alone except for another solitary fly angler far upriver.

I started casting. I got hits on my first couple of lyrical lobs but had no fish to show for it. There is an old fly fishing adage that the first casts are the most important. It was two strikes and I was out. The fish were clearly not baseball pitchers familiar with the three-strike count.

I continued casting for twenty minutes or so and caught nary a trout. But I did land a bug-eyed, foot-long walleye—the second I caught within two weeks on the Grand's tailwater. I was beginning to worry about the deleterious impact they might exert on the brown trout population. I feared that hatchery-raised fingerlings would decrease after serving as breakfast, lunch and supper for these voracious, sharp-toothed predators.

Later when I raised my concern with Gary Bowen, a fresh-water specialist, he reminded me that walleye are native to the Grand, whereas stocked brownies are an introduced species. Still, I could not help worrying about the health of the trout fishery in the tailwater.

On another recent outing to the same stretch of river I caught two small yellow perch for the first time. (I swear the next walleye or perch I catch is going into a buttered frying pan, despite the catch-and-release aesthetic I honour.)

I emailed Steve May, a fellow member of KW Fly Fishers who knows the tailwater well. Walleye were not present in Belwood Lake until the new millennia, he explained. 'It's suspected someone introduced some egg-and sperm-laden fish to the river above the lake and they knew what to do from there.' Walleye are now leaking from the lake into the tailwater. 'This can be expected as once fish travel below the dam, they can't get back to the lake. I wouldn't worry too much about them. They're a river predator like bass, pike and trout.' And, as a bonus to some anglers, are legal to eat.

'I expect they're migrating down from the dam as there's better habitat for forage fish down in the mid-stretch,' Steve added. 'The substrate is better for spawning chub and shiners which walleye eat. The upper river above Fergus does not have as many baitfish and they're mostly sculpins, at least this is what I found when studying it for the Ministry of Natural Resources.'

Echoing Gary, Steve confirmed that genetic testing has verified that the walleye are Grand River stock. 'They're native to the watershed, whereas the brown trout aren't.' Steve has caught yellow perch in the river for years. But they were usually closer to the dam. 'There's a healthy population up there. I say enjoy the diversity; others may have a different opinion.'

One of the attractions of this section of river is that an angler can cast to riffles, runs and pools within fifty metres of one another, presenting a different casting challenge, both upstream and downstream, with dry and wet flies, nymphs and even streamers.

I prefer dry flies, but readily employ wet flies and nymphs. Casting upstream to rising trout is the ideal. But fishing is seldom about ideals. So I often cast dries downstream. I know, purists will wag judgmental fingers. In defence, I have never been much of a purist in anything, save for drinking malt whisky neat.

Despite the technical demands of casting upstream at rising fish, I did *exactly* that and landed my one and only brownie of the evening. It was a ten-incher, the picture of health. I was pleased that I caught it on an Ausable Caddis, designed by Fran Betters. I purchased a dozen from a contemporary tier in the Adirondacks earlier in the year. I am delighted that a fly designed for one of fly fishing's iconic rivers works so well on the Grand.

I do not tie my own flies, despite receiving from Gary his father's tying vise and box of materials. Consequently, I enjoy using patterns tied by others, whether Steve's Full-Motion Hex or Ian Colin James's Brass Ass. Dan ties deadly Grey Fox, Green Drake and Isonychia comparaduns, keeping me in generous supply.

Similarly, one of the things that pleases me about my Winston five-weight is knowing that Harry Middleton fished with Winston rods. He might be a bit rich for some anglers who enjoy reading about the sport because, like Hemingway, Harrison and McGuane, he was a serious literary author who wrote about fly fishing, rather than a fly fisherman who wrote.

I prize as much as any books in my library *Rivers of Memory*, *On the Spine of Time*, *The Earth is Enough*, *The Bright Country* and the posthumous *In That Sweet Country*. These should not be confused with angling fiction. Rather they are literary memoirs of distinction. Middleton writes as beautifully about fly angling as any author I know.

Reading about fly fishing enhances my experiences on the water. Writing about those experiences deepens my enjoyment of angling because it encourages me to be more attentive, thoughtful and contemplative. Reading and writing are the rhythmical equivalent of the back and forward motion of a cast. Both are essential to placing a fly on the water with a semblance of grace.

I resumed casting, content in every way. I heard voices and saw a father and his daughter descending the tall limestone embankment to check out the river. I continued casting, a little self-consciously. Rivers are not the private domain of anglers.

I made a short cast downstream into a current seam and allowed my fly to swing into softer water. I got a substantial hit; it was a heavy fish. I set the hook and stripped in a little line. But I pulled the hook out of its mouth.

Damn!

I immediately recognized the error I committed while playing a big fish. And I told myself in language that would peel paint that it *must* be corrected. Or else. I was momentarily shattered. *Disappointed* is too weak a word to convey how I felt. But I knew the feeling of dejection would pass. In contrast to the regret, sorrow and grief we all suffer, fishing reminds me that the possible, the potential, if not the probable, awaits with the next cast.

That was pretty much it for the evening. A murder of crows circled slowly, expressing their displeasure at some unknown irritant. A few minutes later a chevron of Canada geese flew low over the waterway, their wings whistling. They came to rest for the night downstream.

When I arrived home, I poured a dram of twenty-two-year-old Bruichladdich—a scrumptious unpeated single malt with a nose of banana and marzipan, followed by a honied medley of vanilla and butterscotch on the tongue and a long, luxurious finish.

I once attended a Scotch-tasting conducted by Jim McEwan, former master distiller at both Bowmore and Bruichladdich, distilleries located on the isle of Islay. He praised malt whisky as 'the blood of Scotland'. I have never heard a more eloquent description.

I sat down at the keyboard, waiting on the right words.

My mind circled back to starting the day in the company of Ernest Hemingway. Then my thoughts drifted to another great writer with even deeper roots in Michigan's Upper Peninsula, where, like Hemingway, he learned to fly fish as an apprenticeship in living. Jim Harrison was born in Grayling and raised in Northern Michigan, where he resided much of his life. He never really left, even when he relocated to Montana and southern Arizona. He is an all-time favourite writer of mine who remained a passionate fly angler until the end of his life.

Harrison lived big. And wrote big. A celebrated gourmand, he wrote poetry, novels, short fiction and essays between bird hunting and fly fishing. He bit off large sinewy chunks of life. He wrote elegantly about the recreational sport we share. He once observed that it was comforting to fly fish for trout because cares and worries evaporated.

He suggested that a river flows at the speed of life, so compels anglers to reflect on such big matters as mortality and mutability.

So, with apologies to Jim Harrison—who titled an early novella *A Good Day to Die*—I drew the curtain, turned down the duvet and got ready for bed after quietly declaring it *a good day to live*.

CODA: THE LURE OF NORTHERN MICHIGAN

Northern Michigan, especially the Upper Peninsula (commonly called the UP), has always pulled at the loose threads of my imagination. I have never visited the area, so it remains a promise I am determined to keep before the common infirmities of advancing age conspire to make the trip inadvisable. I became interested in writers with ties to the state when I began reading seriously as an undergraduate in English literature. I became *more* interested in them when I returned to fishing, and subsequently took up fly fishing.

Not surprisingly my point of entry was Hemingway's early short fiction collection *In Our Time*, which is built on a number of Michigan-based stories including 'Big Two-Hearted River'. Hemingway spent his summer vacations throughout his youth with his family in Northern Michigan. A mediocre early novel, *The Torrents of Spring*, is set there.

My eyes were open bug-eyed to the state's literary charms when I discovered Jim Harrison. He attended Michigan State, where he befriended longtime fly angling compadre Thomas McGuane.

McGuane was born in Wyandotte and raised in Michigan before relocating in Montana via Key West. He has written about angling in both fiction and non-fiction throughout his long career. *Ninety-two in the Shade*—his National Book Award–nominated third novel—is a picaresque romp about an aspiring salt-water fishing guide who gets in over his head with the wrong people. It was the work that set McGuane on the road to becoming one of the most important American authors of his generation, equally adept with the novel, short fiction, screenplay and essay.

Like all of the best authors of fly angling literature, he does not really write *about* the recreational sport. Rather fly angling inhabits his literary world like a trout inhabits a river. Fly fishing is a living presence more than a topic or subject.

Ninety-two in the Shade reminds me of *Tarpon*, a fly fishing cult film shot in psychedelic 1970s Key West, which McGuane characterizes in *The Longest Silence* as 'a great and corrupt gardenia of an island in a wilderness of shoals and mangroves.' McGuane stars in the film along with literary sidekicks Richard Brautigan and Harrison. (Brautigan, author of the counterculture classic *Trout Fishing in America*, serves up the best line when he remarks that when an angler releases a fish, 'you have him in your mind forever alive.') The film, featuring terrific footage of fishing for tarpon, is directed by Guy de la Valdene, another member of the merry angling/literary pranksters. It features an original score by fly angler/musician Jimmy 'Margaritaville' Buffett (McGuane was once married to Buffett's sister).

A couple of McGuane's essay collections feature some of the best writing ever devoted to fly fishing. Many of the pieces in *Outside Chance*, and all of *The Longest Silence*, acknowledged as a fly angling classic, are about the sport (including pieces reprinted from the earlier volume).

Richard Ford attended Michigan State and remained in the state long enough to publish his first two novels. Born and raised in Mississippi, Ford is a lifelong angler and hunter, as well as an authority on bird dogs. One of his dearest literary friends, Raymond Carver, was an avid fly angler who wrote wonderful poetry about fishing, fish and rivers. Still, Ford's pen has seldom crossed paths with a fly rod (at least as far as I know), which is a shame since he is one of America's finest literary stylists.

Theodore Roethke was born in Saginaw and attended the University of Michigan before relocating permanently to Washington State. He did not write specifically about fly angling, but his visionary poetry of introspection and exultation draws heavily on nature (including rivers and fish) as both source and subject. Roethke was a gifted and influential teacher who provided the kindling that ignited the creative flames of many fine poets. Some, including James Wright and Richard Hugo, were fly anglers who wrote memorable poetry about the contemplative sport.

Like many fly anglers who are insatiable readers, I am very fond of John Voelker who wrote under the pen name of Robert Traver. Born in Ishpeming and a graduate of the University of Michigan law school, he capped his career as a State Supreme Court justice. He wrote the courtroom drama *Anatomy of a Murder*, adapted into a seven-time Oscar nominated movie directed by Otto Preminger, with score by Duke Ellington, and featuring a powerhouse cast of Jimmy Stewart, Lee Remick, Ben Gazzara, Arthur O'Connell, Eve Arden and George C. Scott.

Traver is much admired as a fly fishing tale-spinner. *Trout Madness* and *Trout Magic* are classics. His humble-pie narrative voice and backcountry wit cannot disguise a piercing intelligence and cultivated sophistication. His North Woods autobiographical essays are endowed with the easy grace of a well-placed cast to rising trout.

Traver was the first writer to solve the mystery of the identity of the river Nick Adams fishes in 'Big Two-Hearted River.' Turns out Hemingway applied a name he liked, with undeniable metaphorical appeal, to a river he fished and knew well, and in the process, wrote a masterpiece. A lot of gifted authors have dedicated beautiful words to fly fishing. But it would be hard to find the essence of the recreational sport compressed in so few elegant words as in Traver's 'Testament of a Fisherman', a prayer more than a few fly anglers know by heart.

In the 'Testament' angling readers hear the voices of Thoreau and Twain. Every sentence fragment expands like riseforms to comprise a chapter in the Holy Book of Fly Fishing. If readers want to know what this thing called fly angling is all about, all they need do is take in these words, study their meaning and reflect on their significance. And wonder why they are not fly fishers, too.

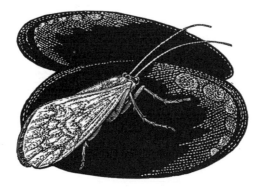

O Brother, How I Love
Those Fishless Nights!

If I play hockey and don't score any goals, I lose. If I play baseball and don't hit any runs, I lose. Conversely, if I fly fish and don't catch any fish, I still win. 'What?' shrieks the competitive sceptic. 'What the hell are you going on about?'

Don't get me wrong, I like catching fish as much as the next angler. Number and size matter. Wild or native are better than hatchery or stocked. But catching fish is not the be-all and end-all. The essence of fly fishing lies elsewhere. I am not the first fly angler to praise the merits of 'fishlessness.' After all, Sparse Grey Hackle called his compendium of stories, tall tales and humour about fishing and the outdoors *Fishless Days, Angling Nights*.

I should explain my fishless contentment by tracing the contours of an evening on the Grand River. I was fishing for brown trout in the tailwater between Elora and Fergus. Autumn had tentatively started dabbing her way across the margins of southwestern Ontario, dripping her palette of russets, oranges, yellows, ochres and umbras like an abstract expressionist. Trout season was winding down for another year. A sweet fragrance of pensiveness was in the air. I was fishing solo because my regular angling buddy was enjoying a couple of weeks' vacation at the family cottage. On that particular evening the river was my cabin in the woods. There was another fly fisherman at a good spot a couple of pools upstream. It was serene; there was space enough for both of us, each alone in mutual solitude but not lonely.

The evening began with my driving to the river after supper—forty minutes through rolling farm country. The driver's-side window was rolled down. I could smell the rich funky earthiness of crops readying for harvest. Tony McManus, a world renowned acoustic fingerstyle guitarist who moved to Elora from his native Scotland a decade previously, was on the CD player.

This is Mennonite country. I passed a couple of black, horse-drawn buggies rambling along the side of the two-lane. The life of simplicity followed by the Old Order reminded me of the simplicity of casting an artificial fly tied by hand on a vise. Similarly, I know of nothing simpler than a reel consisting of a metal cylinder rotating inside a stationary metal cylinder, attached to a long, willowy, tapered rod. On this evening I was using my Sweetgrass five-weight, hand-made in Montana from Tonkin bamboo harvested in China and constructed by craftsmen who value time-honoured quality above mass-produced quantity.

When I arrived at the river, the sun was continuing to slip away in the west. Daylight receded as twilight slowly asserted itself. This was the gloaming, a time in the diurnal cycle caused by the earth's rotation and celebrated by my Celtic ancestors as well as poets, visual artists and composers—romantics who live close to nature in heart and imagination, even if not in actuality. W.D. Wetherell describes this time in his memoir *Vermont River* as 'the peaceful edge of beauty' between day and night.

There was little insect activity either on the water, which was a tad stained, or in the air; consequently there were precious few rises—the intoxicating elixir for fly anglers. Still, because I had my beloved bamboo rod I insisted on casting dry flies.

I lit a Partagas Serie D No. 4, a fine Robustos cigar hand-rolled and wrapped in Cuba and aptly described by cigar aficionado Charles Del Todesco in *The Havana Cigar* as 'worth savouring in peace and quiet'. I inhaled between casts, establishing a pleasant rhythm of shallow breathing and graceful motion. Occasionally, I stopped casting for a few moments to enjoy the pulsating current flowing around my waders as I stood thigh-deep in cool water, listening and watching, in rhythm with the world around me.

The temperature cooled as the sun set and shoreline shadows inched silently across the river, which I shared with a small flock of frisky ducklings, a darting reconnoitring kingfisher and a magnificent osprey holding a small fish like a torpedo as it gained ascendance along the river's flyway.

I had no hits, even though a couple of fish contemplated and subsequently rejected my Usual fly pattern and otherwise reliable Elk Hair Caddis. Both are efficient dry flies on the Grand—but not tonight.

The darkness lengthened. It was time to head home, with the window down as the sweet melancholy of eventide seeped into the car.

McManus accompanied me once again with the sweet melancholy of ancient Celtic airs. Playing an acoustic guitar and casting a bamboo fly rod share much in common. Both are instruments of imagination, extensions of the body that touch the soul.

The darkening horizon was illumined by slivers of burnt orange, rust and dusty rose. I looked forward to a nightcap of Bowmore Devil's Cask, a small-batch single malt from Islay aged in Oloroso and Pedro Ximenez sherry casks to impart a deep mahogany colour. I anticipated the taste of Christmas pudding soaked in toffee sauce that would evoke sitting in front of the hearth in a stone cottage awash in the cold, salty spray of the North Atlantic.

I was reminded of Andrew Greig's observation in his poetic memoir *At the Loch of the Green Corrie*—which chronicles a fly fishing trip he made with a couple of friends at the behest of revered poet Norman MacCaig to Assynt in the northwest Scottish Highlands—that enjoying a dram is 'like drinking the landscape'.

As many an angling scribe has noted, fly fishing is about more than catching fish. To paraphrase an old adage: A trout in the pool is worth two in the hand. The recreational sport is really about squeezing delight out of what we have in our grasp. And giving thanks for the bountiful fruits provided by this Good Earth. *O Brother, how I love those fishless nights!*

The Fish That Flew Away

He was perched on a limb, high in a bankside tree when I got to the river—immobile, intense, fierce, impressive. A confident, solitary, wild sentinel, the osprey was patiently waiting on supper. He showed little interest in me. Before I made my first cast, I retrieved my waterproof Pentax camera out of my vest and snapped a couple of photos using the telephoto option. I wanted to get as close to the predator as I could. He remained still, implacable. Describing him as majestic is not hyperbole; it is fact.

Watching him brought to mind some superb poems by Robert Penn Warren, a Kentucky-bred poet, novelist, critic, teacher and historian who I admire unreservedly. Sadly he is not as well known today as he deserves to be. He was a giant in American letters when I attended university. He was an intellectual who straddled North and South, city and country, academia and the natural world. His poetry is deeply influenced by the rhythms and texture of nature which he studied with a keen, sympathetic eye.

Hawks meant a great deal to him, and he thought deeply about them as living creatures and as poetic symbols. They soar through the best of his poetry. I know of no poetry more worthy of its subject. His hawk poems—including 'Evening Hawk', 'Red-Tail Hawk', 'Pyre of Youth' and 'Eagle Descending'—are not only profound and transcendent, they are sublime. Warren, a great American Metaphysical poet of nature, came to identify with hawks as visionary emissaries with Time in their talons.

Ospreys are unique among North American raptors for their diet of live fish and their ability to dive swiftly into water to snatch up their finned meals. On an episode of the last season of the television series *Longmire*, a wise medicine woman explains to Sheriff Walt that ospreys are more efficient fishers than eagles. Diving ospreys are models of intense concentration, plunging headlong, their yellow eyes focused along ferocious, expectant, outstretched talons.

They are seen regularly soaring over treetops, meticulously patrolling the Grand River. The local conservation authority has built platforms on tall poles along the watercourse that house large, untidy stick nests. These big, rangy hawks do well in the company of humans. Happily, they have rebounded following the ban on DDT.

While tying a fly to my leader I reflected on one of the most pleasing aspects of fly fishing—experiencing nature up close and personal. Fly angling, especially while wading, offers a more intimate contact with birds and critters than other types of fishing. I cherish my close encounters with otters, beavers, martens, muskrats, wild turkey, deer, moose, turtles, frogs, snakes, herons, sandhill cranes, kingfishers, swallows, swifts, grosbeaks, red-winged blackbirds, cedar waxwings, hawks, osprey and ravens. (I worry about how many of these critters and birds will be around when the children of my two sons are my age. I no longer see the meadowlarks, orioles and bobolinks, butterflies and honeybees that I saw when I was a child.)

* * *

I remembered one eerily surreal evening on the Beatty Saugeen, north of Mount Forest, Ontario. Dan Kennaley and I drove through torrential rains to get to one of our favourite spots. Fortunately the rain stopped when we arrived. We apprehensively put on our gear.

We entered a charmed circle of serenity when we hit the water, despite ominous clouds against a dramatic backdrop of menacing skies—a blend of the red and orange of wildfire and the yellow and purple of bruised skin. At about seven o'clock I was casting into a run off a small island when I was joined a few feet downstream by a nurse of raccoons consisting of mom and trio of playful kits intent on supper. I did not bother them; they did not bother me. Our communion was not interrupted by a single drop of rain.

Dan and I were unnerved when we left for home and journeyed through a ravaged countryside of ruined farm buildings, downed trees and flattened fields no more than a couple of kilometres from the river. Turns out we had been fly fishing in the calm eye of a tornado.

* * *

On this evening on the Grand River near Inverhaugh, downriver from Elmira, I cast a cream-coloured Usual in pocket water in a long riffle.

It was early evening on the threshold of the equinox, overcast, with a refreshing breeze. Temperatures had cooled over the previous few days and nights, allowing water temps to drop to the mid-sixties, making it safe to fish for brown trout in the tailwater. Dan and I had spent an enjoyable summer fishing for smallmouth bass between Cambridge and Paris. One memorable evening I caught thirty-two bronzebacks, between six and fourteen inches, over a couple of hours. On another outing Dan caught twenty-eight spanning the same length over a comparable period. The constant rain—caused by the same global climate change that had left drought-stricken British Columbia vulnerable to wildfire—prevented us from targeting trout through the prime weeks of late May and June.

I turned my attention from the osprey, but remained aware he occasionally left his perch and took flight, leisurely surveying the river with his nervous, high-pitched *chirp*, ready in a split second to take a lethal dive at an unsuspecting fish.

Soon Dan arrived and I pointed out our feathered companion. Dan, a birder as well as a fly fisherman, always has his Nikon digital camera hanging on his neck whenever he hits the river. We fished for an hour or so, both aware that we were sharing the water with one of nature's supreme anglers.

After catching a dozen pesky chub, I finally landed a small brownie, about seven inches in length. Dan had a couple of hits. Things were looking up for both of us. I waded upstream a few feet and cast at some quiet holding water between a couple of converging currents. I got a strike. My Winston five-weight snapped out of slumber with a sudden, throbbing arc. I was on to a good fish. I shouted to Dan: 'Fish on!'

I raised my rod and began stripping in line. The fish broke the surface, flashed and splashed, exposing himself momentarily. The battle was on. Then, suddenly, I heard the heavy wingbeat of the osprey. Out of the corner of my eye I glimpsed him diving with speed and precision at *my* fish.

What the hell!

The opportunistic river-hawk snatched up my lovely brownie in his powerful talons and hightailed it upriver. With its head facing forward in a streamlined position, the trout resembled an iridescent torpedo launched from a submarine. If ospreys could smirk, I know this smug bastard was smirking—*at me*—pleased with his angling prowess which would soon translate into a delicious sushi supper.

But my fly was *still* attached to the captive trout's lip.

Shit!

My reel pained as my line took off in a blazing trajectory aimed at the highest treetops along the riverbank. The line peeled down to the backing in the blink of an angler's anxious eye. I feared I was going to lose my precious fly, maybe even my line as my reel continued to *schreeeeech*. I gave my rod a mighty yank and, fortunately, released the fly from the fish's mouth—taking delight in my improved clinch knot holding. My line snapped back as *my* beleaguered fish rose higher and higher, firmly gripped in the osprey's mighty talons.

The sequence of events, taking fleeting seconds to unwind, was not so much shocking as unbelievable. I was dazed, stunned, amazed more than disappointed—that feeling would come later. Dan stood downriver—a witness to the ordeal—incredulous. 'Did I actually see what I think I saw?' he asked. If only he had had time to snap a photo.

The whole surreal episode put me in mind of poet and avid fly angler Richard Hugo's poem 'In Your Blue Dream.' After being skunked on an outing somewhere in the American West the narrator is given advice from a group of veteran anglers to view fishing through the eyes of an osprey. Interestingly, this contradicts Paul's advice to Norman in *A River Runs Through It* to think like a fish. Based on personal experience, I suggest both are equally judicious.

I have heard it said that fishing is like love—it is the ones that get away that cut the deepest, that leave wounds festering so they never completely heal. But it is not all heartbreak. I remembered bass fishing with Dylan and Robertson, when they were still young, at the invitation of my old friend Gary Bowen. Late one morning Dylan caught a bass and was reeling it in when a proprietary loon decided it was lunchtime and snapped the fish from my son's silver Rapala minnow.

Many years later we still talk about that act of piscatorial larceny. Dylan has long forgotten about the bass he landed so long ago on Lost Lake, but the memory of the stolen fish remains sharp and precise, like all remembered losses. I know I won't soon forget *the fish that flew away* on the tailwater of the Grand River on the cusp of autumn.

The Music of Rivers

In *Lines on the Water* David Adams Richards sounds like Norman Maclean in *A River Runs Through It* when he writes about stories blending into one another on a river. Rivers are stories, as stories are rivers. Both flow like music.

I have always been intrigued by how fly anglers interpret the sound of moving water as music, oftentimes as classical music. Fly anglers learn that to be successful they have to develop the ability to see the natural world, especially rivers. This is more than passive look-ing *at*, but active seeing *into* what escapes the eye under 'normal' conditions and circumstances. This is seeing with the imagination as well as the eye.

Similarly, many fly anglers develop a heightened sense of active hearing that is more refined than passive listening. They hear music when others perceive a discordant jumble of disconnected sounds, the noise of moving water rushing over rocks and around boulders and fallen trees in a river. Like seeing, hearing is a sympathetic act of imagi-nation, born of respect and understanding, requiring an ear tuned to the reality of wonder.

John Randolph, longtime editor and publisher of *Fly Fisherman* magazine, makes the same point in *Becoming a Fly Fisher* when he confides that he spent five decades trying to learn the libretto of fly angling. Eventually, he realized the secret was listening to what tran-spired between the notes

In 'Hospital', the opening poem in his final collection, *Dead Man's Float*, Jim Harrison reports that he heard cellos among the voices of songbirds when he was trout fishing. An appreciation of the music of rivers is shared by literary authors who write about fly fishing, as well as by fly anglers who write about the recreational sport.

Ted Hughes, the twentieth century's great mythic poet of nature, evoked the music of rivers in his beautiful poem 'In the Dark Violin of the Valley', collected in *River*. Hughes expresses the unifying and harmonizing power of spirit as a kind of night music that embraces both the living and the dead because spirit is transcendental, sewing body and soul, soul and sky, sky and earth, river and sea.

W. D. Wetherell is an author of novels, short stories and essays. He reflects on the music of rivers in 'Symphony', a chapter of *Vermont River* (the first in a trio of memoirs including *Upland Stream* and *One River More*). Comparing the sounds of a river to a symphony, he hears Bach cantatas. Like Harrison, he hears the notes of a cello, the instrument which is closest to the human voice, in the motion of water bubbling over a riverbed.

James R. Babb is the former editor of *Gray's Sporting Journal* and author of a quartet of fly fishing books including *Crosscurrents, Fly-Fishin' Fool* and *Fish Won't Let Me Sleep*. In his sophomore volume, *River Music*, he recalls the cadences of a springtime symphony. He not only hears the music of Handel and Purcell, even Wagner, but the songs of French-Canadian voyageurs.

A river is the melodic umbilical cord—or shall I say chord?—that connects fly anglers to the natural world beyond its banks. Fly anglers are not only immersed in the music of rivers; they are surrounded by the stereophonic sounds of nature. I do not wade a river seeking silence, but rather multifarious melodies. Noise strikes my ear; music strikes my imagination. Above and beyond the syncopation of moving water is the cadence of a breeze caressing fluttering leaves in the tall branches of trees, accompanied by the refrain of birdsong and the incessant hum of insects.

I seldom spend a day or evening on the river without playing over in my mind the music of Ralph Vaughan Williams, whether his *A Pastoral Symphony* or one of his many chamber pieces or song suites that draw on nature, including *Serenade to Music, The Lark Ascending, Fantasia on Greensleeves, English Folk Song Suite, In the Fen Country, Norfolk Rhapsody No. 1, Fantasia on the Theme of Thomas Tallis, The Wasps* or *In Windsor Forest*, among others. While many commentators have described Williams as a quintessential English composer, to my Canadian ear, he is one of the last century's great classical composers of nature. I realize sceptical readers might be perplexed when I confide that I hear the music of Vaughan Williams on the rivers I fish. This requires explanation, I know. Fly angling encourages metaphorical thinking. For fly anglers, metaphor is not simply a figure of speech; it is 'a habit of thought', as described by Steven J. Meyers in *Seeing Nature*. Meyers was a professional fly fishing guide and photographer before he became a writer of metaphysical angling books and a creative writing teacher.

Viewing the natural world metaphorically enables fly anglers to discern patterns of order in what at first appears chaotic, to discern patterns of harmony in what at first sounds discordant. Metaphorical thinking enables fly anglers to perceive relationships that otherwise remain obscure. Metaphor penetrates the literal and opens eyes and ears to the reality oftentimes obscured by appearances. In *Becoming a Fly Fisher* Randolph suggests that anglers graduate through a series of levels, with the lucky ones finally reaching 'that mature melding of knowledge and perceptions that create metaphor'.

When a fly angler's senses are tuned to metaphor, he or she feels incorporated in and integrated with, rather than separate from, the natural world. A sense of alienation is replaced by a sense of communion. This is the peace and hope that forms the riverbed of fly angling. This is casting into mystery. All this might seem abstract, but it is why I hear Vaughan Williams—a composer I deeply admire and respect—in rivers of music.

I was moved to contemplate the sympathetic link between music and rivers one afternoon on the cusp of autumn in early September. After attending a noon-hour concert, I spent a leisurely afternoon fly fishing on a pastoral stretch of the Grand River, west of Elora.

The concert, titled *Earth Peace*, presented a program of instrumental and choral music incorporating the stories of women. It was performed by a chamber ensemble made up of members of the Renaissance Singers, a community choir founded in Waterloo Region in 1972, augmented by a string quartet, a soprano soloist and a trio of female readers including the composer.

The music was composed by Carol Ann Weaver, professor emerita at Conrad Grebel University College at the University of Waterloo. Weaver has spent time in Africa and has been influenced by that continent's rich music. *Earth Peace* was compiled and composed in South Africa and Namibia. The work is a dialogue between humanity and the natural world, bridging such urgent global issues as peace, social justice and environmental stewardship.

With such titles as 'Gloria', 'Laudamus', 'Dona Nobis Pacem',

'Kyrie', 'Lament' and 'Peace to Our Planet', the choral pieces are drawn for the most part from the Latin Mass, with lyrics written by the composer. The instrumental pieces, with such titles as 'Hartebeest', 'Wild Dog Dervish', 'East Timor', 'Springbok Lamb Ode' and 'Ring Out Peace', are short, poignant reflections in response to the choral text. The narratives cover a range of experiences and emotions from conflict and pain, to resolution and joy.

Later, as I waded thigh deep in the Grand with the music of its tireless currents sweeping in and around, over and under my senses, I began reflecting on *Earth Peace* with its blend of sacred and secular music that presents humanity and nature as two sides of the same spiritual wafer. I use the word *wafer* deliberately, as a reference to the thin disk of unleavened bread used in the Eucharist. I was not thinking of myself as pagan, but as I stood in the river casting my fly rod as gracefully as I was able, I felt as intimately connected to the essence of things as I ever do. It felt as if I were taking communion.

As someone who has been reading literature for many more years than he has been fly fishing, I cannot stand in a river and cast without thinking of rivers figuratively as well as literally, symbolically as well as experientially. For me, rivers are where the seen and unseen, the known and unknown, meet on the surface of Mystery. It is where I hear the voice of Creation singing in the ear of my imagination.

For me the music of rivers is the harmony of peace. I believe peace is impossible so long as the planetary ear of nature continues to be assaulted by the cacophony of neglect and disregard. Humanity will not make peace among its diverse people until it makes peace with this Good Earth. It is what I prayed for on that beautiful September afternoon as I cast in time with the sonic backdrop of river music.

CODA: HIGH-BROW RIVER MUSIC

I am not an authority on classical music, but I have been listening to it, and enjoying it, my entire adult life. I routinely read fly angling literature against the aural backdrop of classical music. It is a beautiful thing when the great rivers of literature and music merge.

Izaak Walton is undoubtedly the best-known angling scribe to incorporate music in his work. *The Compleat Angler* abounds in high-spirited folksong, including the charming 'The Angler's Song'.

Many prominent classical composers have devoted works to rivers. A few have written music in praise of fish. Sadly angling has rarely been addressed. In *Where the Bright Waters Meet*, Harry Plunket Greene—who was a classically trained festival and oratorio singer who happened to write a fly angling classic—lamented the dearth of music and song in the classical repertoire; however, he acknowledges 'Angler's Song', by Charles Stanford, himself an avid fly fisherman.

What follows is neither comprehensive nor definitive, but a compilation of the works I have in my music library. It is a pleasant pool at which to begin casting on the river of music.

I am delighted Franz Schubert had a thing for fish and rivers. His 1819 composition 'Forellen Quintett' ('Trout Quintet') was his first chamber work to achieve widespread popularity. 'Die schöne Müllerin' ('The Lovely Maid of the Mill') is one of Schubert's greatest song cycles based on poems by Wilhelm Müller. Conversely, 'Die Forelle' ('The Trout') is a pedestrian *lied* about sulky trout darting to and fro. Other river songs I much prefer include 'The River', 'By the River' and 'On the River'. One of Franz Liszt's signature virtuoso piano showpieces is 'Au bord d'une source' ('Beside a Spring'). Bedřich Smetana's symphonic poem 'Vltava' ('The Moldau') traces the river from its source in the mountains of the Bohemian Forest, through the Czech countryside, to the city of Prague.

A couple of European giants wrote popular compositions inspired by British natural landmarks. George Frideric Handel's 'Wassermusik' ('Water Music Suites') is a court composition written for Thames water parties in the dawn of the eighteenth century. Felix Mendelssohn's moody 'Hebrides Overture' ('Fingal's Cave') remains a favourite. Those who share my passion for English music from the first half of the last century likely know George Butterworth's melodic idyll 'The Banks of Green Willow', inspired by a folk song. His death at the age of thirty-one in the trenches of the First World War imbues his compositions with a bittersweet poignancy. E.J. Moeran's 'Lonely Waters' is based on a fragment of a Norfolk folk song. Inspired by France's famous Seine, Frederick Delius's 'Summer Night on a River' is a meditation on peace and serenity.

Frank Bridges's 'There's a Willow Grows Aslant the Brook' is a late work. Then there is 'Deep River' by Samuel Coleridge-Taylor (the composer, not the poet).

Contemporary British composers have played the tradition forward. Eric Whitacre's 'The River Cam' is a pastoral piece for cello and strings inspired by Elgar and Vaughan Williams. A founding member of the English rock band Genesis, keyboardist and composer Tony Banks's 'Still Waters' is from his suite *Six Pieces for Orchestra.*

On the other side of the Atlantic, composers have responded to the vast and diverse riverscape of America ever since its origins along the Eastern seaboard. Some favourite compositions include Ferde Grofe's 'Hudson River Suite'. I much prefer the 1955 composition over his better known orchestral works 'Mississippi Suite' and 'Grand Canyon Suite'.

Aaron Copland's 'At the River' is the fourth song in his *Old American Songbook* set to the popular hymn written by Baptist preacher-turned-hymn writer Robert Lowry in 1865. Arguably his most popular work, Virgil Thomson's 'River Suite' has proven more enduring than the 1937 documentary film for which it was written. Amy Beach was the first successful American female composer of large-scale art music. Her 'By Still Waters' is a lovely chamber piece for piano set to the twenty-third Psalm. Only three minutes in length, it loses nothing for being brief.

John Luther Adams's 'Become River' is a chamber work for orchestra and a companion to 'Become Ocean'. Finally, John Cage's wonderfully idiosyncratic 'Water Walk' is another recent work inspired by rivers (at least I think Cage's multimedia performance piece is inspired by rivers; listeners can judge whether it is possible to catch fish in a bathtub).

Elusive Steelhead Under a Frosty Moon

Maybe it is my Celtic soul, but autumn is my time of year. This is why sad songs always make me glad and elegies are the poems that speak to me most deeply. I prefer the gunmetal skies of November over the sun-soaked skies of August. I love walking beneath the skeletal architecture of deciduous trees after their many-coloured leaves have fallen and covered the earth for another long winter's sleep. I welcome the feelings evoked by Robert Frost in 'My November Guest':

> My sorrow, when she's here with me,
> > Thinks these dark days of autumn rain
> Are beautiful as days can be;
> She loves the bare, the withered tree;
> > She walks the sodden pasture lane.
>
> . . . .
>
> The desolate, deserted trees,
> > The faded earth, the heavy sky,
> The beauties she so truly sees,
> She thinks I have no eye for these,
> > And vexes me for reason why.

Frost, who lived most of his life in New England, knew a thing or two about 'bare November days'. He knew instinctively that autumn is not one, but rather two distinct seasons within a single season—autumn and fall.

The days of late September and October are *festivals* of riotous colour, comforting sun and cooling temperatures. This is when trout are most beautiful, clothed in deep spawning colours. In contrast, the days of November and early December are *presences* of monochromatic sombreness, fading sun and advancing cold. Fall is the season of steelhead burnished chrome, mirroring the cobalt of pensive skies.

Since childhood I have always experienced a shiver of excitement as the hours of daylight shortened, creating a unique beauty that appeals to a sweet latent melancholy. When I began reading Celtic spirituality I was not surprised that my ancient ancestors celebrated the beginning of a new year on the first of November.

Situated halfway between the autumn equinox and the winter solstice at the apex of the fall, Samhain marks the end of the harvest and the beginning of the dark half of the year. It is a time of celebration and preparation when cattle are brought back from summer pasture, edible plants are stored and livestock are slaughtered. Ceremonial bonfires are lit, around which protective, cleansing rituals are enacted.

Samhain is a liminal date on the Celtic calendar when the border between the natural world and the supernatural world (Otherworld) is gossamer-thin and is easily traversed. Anglers know this experience well because so many elements of fly fishing are threshold activities that penetrate barriers and boundaries.

Offerings of food and drink are provided for the *Aos Sí* (nature spirits or fairies) who cross over. Souls of the departed are believed to return to their earthly homes where they receive hospitality—the Celts were big on hospitality, including in monasteries and abbeys after the arrival of Christianity. Feasts are held, during which souls of dead kin are welcomed. An extra place is set at the family table while such community rituals as mumming (which survives in such Celtic outposts as Newfoundland) take place.

Fly anglers do not have to be Celtic to mark the opening of steelhead season with a sense of ritual and celebration. Although I do not count myself among devoted steelhead brethren, I have come to associate November with steelhead chrome, despite the fact that the season continues through early spring. It has often been said that more fly anglers spend more time casting at fewer muskellunge than at any other freshwater gamefish. While this might be true, I can say the same about steelhead.

Admittedly I have gotten out on rivers in search of elusive migratory rainbow trout no more than a couple of times each fall. In the decade or so I have been fly fishing this translates into a mere two dozen outings. Still I have never had so much as a nibble, let alone a strike to rouse my seven-weight Scott to life.

I have witnessed float fishermen catch steelhead in the same pool

I have been duly casting black Woolly Buggers (with a little flash) or glowbug egg patterns—in vain. I have witnessed from close quarters Dan Kennaley catching a steelhead. Seldom was envy more palpable.

I have never felt the thrill of a muscular silver bullet torpedoing into the current, let alone landed one with its tail drooping over the rim of a net. Just when I was ready to blame my lack of success on ineptitude, I stumbled across 'The Addictive Allure of the Steelhead Tug', an essay in Chris Santella's *The Tug Is the Drug*. I was relieved to learn that he understood my plight, insisting that steelheading is an act of faith. Reading his consoling words comforted my irritating affliction, which when reduced to simple terms was: casting *endlessly* without catching *anything*. All of which has made steelheading the most contemplative of angling challenges. Failing to land this magnificent fish has given me lots of time to think and meditate, reflect and brood, imagine and dream.

This has coincided with my love of November's fifty shades of grey, complete with pewter skies and slate duvet of clouds. The Orcadian Scots identify such skies as *glamsy*. Referred to by the Cree of North America as 'the month of the frosty moon', it is when trees surrender their splendour as persistent drizzle, bone-chill gusts and intermittent flurries fall amid temperatures 'just above the ice point', in the words of William Faulkner in one of his hunting stories collected in *Big Woods*.

An outing on the Bighead River on the outskirts of Meaford, Ontario—where the great naturalist and conservation writer John Muir lived for a couple of years during the American Civil War—proved emblematic of my chronic steelhead frustration.

Dan and I hit the river together in early afternoon. We immersed ourselves in the 'faint, cold, steady rain, the grey and constant light' (Faulkner again). Following a familiar pattern, we went our separate ways; I headed downriver while he made his way upriver. We agreed to meet at my Jeep at 'the dimming of the day'—to use English songwriter Richard Thompson's phrase which also, to my mind, applies equally to November as the dimming of the year.

I usually reserve my consumption of alcoholic beverages till I am off the water. A beer never tastes better, whether cooled among rocks in the river or enjoyed in a local pub with a hearty meal. However, I never go steelheading without a small flask of malt whisky or

American bourbon in my vest pocket. Reflecting the mood of the day, I customarily prefer an Islay single malt, perhaps Lagavulin, Bowmore or Bruichladdich. On this day I was fortunate to have an Arran eighteen-year-old, boasting a nose of sweet orchard fruits with syrup and toasted oak, a palate of chocolate, ginger and caramelized brown sugar and a long, lingering finish.

While I enjoy a cigar while casting a line in all manner of weather, a Cuban Habana is never more welcome than when November skies turn gloomy, to paraphrase Gordon Lightfoot. I was happy to have an old favourite—a Partagas Serie D No 4, a fine hand-made Robustos with a profile of rich aromas to thaw the chill in my bones. Its notes of spice, cocoa and cedar evoked the flavours of fall.

My mind began wandering as I leisurely made my way through a promising run—aren't all runs promising? Until the promise is broken, that is. I divided the stretch of water into geometric squares and covered it as systematically and methodically as I could. I pulled on my cigar in synchronicity with my casting, maintaining a satisfying rhythm that would have made Norman Maclean proud. (This was before my heart attack reshaped my hedonistic habits.)

Later I sat on a large rock at water's edge and scanned the withered branches of trees along the bank in a landscape of line and lengthening shadow. In my suspended state of quietude I searched for birds I welcome as winged soulmates. I took a warm swig of Arran from my flask and waited a few minutes in these skeletal woods before taking another run *at* the run. Time relaxed and I felt content and at peace.

It pleased me to consider how much of my time fly fishing is woven into the tapestry of recollection. A fly rod is an instrument of memory. Paradoxically the more I focus on the living present, the pulsating Now, the more my mind ranges freely over people, places and events from the past. For me fly fishing unfolds at the intersection of past and present, promise and fulfillment, actuality and daydream.

One of the attractions of the recreational sport is that it encourages travel to some of the most beautiful places on this Good Earth. While I have visited the Catskills on two occasions and the Adirondacks and the Blue Ridge Mountains of North Carolina once, most of my fly angling is done no more than four hours from where I live.

Of course this does not take into account the thousands of miles I have logged as an angling tourist casting lines of imagination on literary waters. If only readers received frequent-flyer points. The pull of memory nudged my thoughts toward the people and the places embodied in talismans I wear, cast or carry with me in my vest that enrich and enhance my experience on the water. I cherish these and cannot imagine fishing without them.

Not unlike many athletes, fly anglers are notoriously superstitious. They see omens, both good and bad, in all manner of things. In *Lines on the Water* David Adams Richards goes where anglers fear to wade by confessing that it was unlucky to fish without a plug of tobacco nestled in his cheek. I think of the pilgrims who leave small charms on Tom Thomson's headstone in Leith Cemetery and at the shrine to his memory on the shore of Canoe Lake in Algonquin Park. Dan leaves a fly whenever we visit one of these sacred memorials. I bow my head in prayer.

I carry with me Christmas gifts including a stainless-steel flask; an Italian tan leather case in which I keep my cigars; waders and wading jacket that protect me from the elements; and waterproof camera which I will use if I ever land a steelhead. There is the fading shirt that fits more snugly than it did when it was given to me as a birthday present more than thirty years ago. These are significant because they were given to me by those who reciprocated my love—at least for a while. Finally there is my Ross reel, purchased with a gift certificate I received from my union in recognition of more than a quarter century of service.

As I considered these talismans I grew more appreciative of the bare-bones of November. The passage of time between the closing of trout season (end of September) and opening day (end of April) can seem interminably long. Bass season, which opens at the beginning of July, overlaps with steelhead season for a few weeks before closing at the end of November. However, it is the latter that brings the angling year in southwestern Ontario full circle. Without steelheading the long winter would strike the heart as more desolate for fly anglers who eschew ice-fishing. There is fly tying and reading, of course, but these worthy pastimes are not substitutes for moving water.

Fall steelheading is a period of transition, a time of diminishing light as the Northern Hemisphere tilts farther away from the sun and much of the natural world prepares for slumber. The translucent light of fall differs from the transparent light of autumn, closer in tone and texture to the opaque light of winter. Fall rivers follow a different rhythm from autumn rivers. Their characters change, become more temperamental, more stubborn, in some cases even threatening. Caution becomes a fly angler's sixth sense.

I change clothes and gear, tactics and techniques as insect activity wanes. My time on the water contracts in response to climate and diurnal circumstance. My thoughts follow suit, drifting further into introspection. I begin the ritual of retreat from rivers to the sanctuary of the hearth. The element of fire replaces the element of water.

I returned to the Jeep at eventide, a few minutes before Dan. I removed layers of flannel and fleece, wool and GoreTex as three chevrons of raucous Canada geese flew overhead. These were not the belligerent, ill-mannered nuisances that desecrate city parks and university lawns, but true creatures of the wild, heading south after summering in the North, following a migration pattern extending back ten million years to the Miocene period.

A long moment after the skein vanished, a lone straggler who had lost his way passed with a plaintive honk in the gathering darkness, when the 'essence of winter sleep is on the night,' in the words of Robert Frost, that lovely dark and deep poet of the back end of the year.

Sláinte! Ian

————

To Rob: Keep the tip of your rod nice and high. *

— *Your Big Bald Buddy, Ian Colin James*

Like a custom bamboo fly rod, Ian Colin James was one of a kind. His death on 29 June, 2015, left Canada's fly angling community bereft of one of its most oversized personalities.

Taking his cue from W. B. Yeats, Marshall McLuhan once pointed out that a passionate life doesn't produce subtle characters. Ian had no truck with subtlety in any shape or form. That wild Irish mystic Yeats was fond of quoting Goethe's observation that we learn not by thought, but by action. Ian was a man of action who gave expression to his life through a tying vise and fly rod. Ian was a big man with a big appetite for life, as brash and brawny as his most famous fly pattern, Ian's Brass Ass. The pattern was a perennial bestseller for Orvis. The Brass Ass was one of a number of innovative flies Ian designed, including his Smack 'em Spey and Crunchy Caddis patterns. Made of copper wire and translucent epoxy and originally designed to attract steelhead along breakwalls on the Great Lakes, the Brass Ass was a magnet for brown trout that turned up finicky noses at more traditional patterns. Bass could not refuse the nymph either. When Czech nymphing became the flavour of the month, it served as a deadly point fly or mid dropper.

Ian was born in the Scottish Lowlands, where he was bitten by the mayfly bug as a youngster. After immigrating to Canada he graduated from the University of Guelph with a degree in agriculture and lived in London, Ontario, for many years. He died a day before my sixty-fourth birthday in the month I began my early retirement, which made me feel a little closer to the angler.

————

* Inscription in my copy of *Fumbling with a Fly Rod*.

I was privileged to spend a day with him on the Grand River about a decade ago. He taught me a great deal—not always orthodox, but always BRILLIANT, to use one of his favourite words. He was one of the first professional guides, if not the first, on the Grand tailwater. Since a day of guiding did not include lunch, I came with two helpings of homemade clam chowder and generous chunks of old cheese from Dublin, Ireland, on thick slices of sourdough bread baked fresh from a local bakery.

'Are you trying to kill me?' he boomed before accepting a sandwich and some chowder in a tin cup. He wore a broad smile when he explained that he had suffered a heart attack a few months earlier. Sadly it was a subsequent heart attack that brought the big man down. Since suffering a mild heart attack myself, I can better appreciate Ian's first encounter with mortality.

Unconventional, contrary and opinionated, Ian had no truck with the gentlemanly—some might say effeminate—side of fly angling with roots on English chalk streams. And he considered himself an adversary of any misguided fly angler who viewed the sport as a privilege reserved for snobs and elitists. In contrast, he was a bred-in-the-bone-Scots egalitarian—and bloody proud of it. His language was sometimes akin to that of a sailor or longshoreman, spiced with obscenities enough to make a placid trout stream boil.

Ian had his own way of doing things on the water. Here are some of his angling quirks which are sure to raise eyebrows among angling cognoscenti and delight those who take a more common approach to the contemplative sport.

• He ridiculed tapered leaders, favouring six-pound monofilament fishing line bought at Canadian Tire.

• He scorned fishing vests as a sissified affectation, preferring an old canvas rucksack.

• He disdained strike indicators, which he gleefully denigrated as 'bobbers'.

• He dismissed false-casting and double-hauling as the work of the fly angling devil. 'Can't catch fish if your fly is out of the water,' he reasoned with blunt eloquence.

• He condemned bead-headed nymphs in favour of traditional, soft-hackle, wet flies which he learned to tie in Scotland.

• Instead of using commercially made 'gunk' to sink his wet flies, he mixed a concoction of river mud and liquid detergent. 'Why pay exorbitant prices at fly shops when you can make your own goop for pennies?' the resourceful iconoclast asked. My Scots grandparents would have approved of Ian's frugality.

• Finally no species of fish was too lowly to escape his fly, even such bottom feeders as carp and gar. He championed the lowly carp, a respectable game fish in Europe for centuries, making it acceptable to target with a fly rod in North America.

The Rebel with a Fly Rod was a dedicated environmentalist and generous teacher. He taught the first credited course in fly fishing in Canada, at Fanshawe College. His public talks brimmed with jokes, not always politically correct, and were punctuated with raucous laughter. He wrote the hilarious memoir *Fumbling with a Flyrod: Stories from the River*, now a collector's item cherished by armchair fly anglers. He was working on a sequel, but never got it finished in time.

Only fifty-five when he died, Ian parlayed his larger-than-life personality into celebrity, talking fly fishing with Peter Gzowski when he was the voice of Canada on CBC Radio's *Morningside*. He appeared on CBC TV's *Rick Mercer Report*, attempting heroically to teach its klutzy host the intricacies of casting a fly rod. He also appeared on *The New Fly Fisher* TV show. He fished as he lived—wading a path all his own, in his own time, at his own pace. His like will not fish these waters again.

Ian gave me good advice about casting. As always, he had a few tricks up his sleeve, which was always rolled up to his elbow. He could effortlessly cast to his backing (I saw him do it), aided by copious amounts of Armor All spray to his line. 'Some fishermen claim it'll rot the line, but that's a load a crap,' he burred.

Even though I do not tie my own flies, I took a workshop he conducted at McDougall Cottage in Cambridge. The patterns to which he introduced me were simple to tie and ugly to look at, but he assured me they would catch fish. BRILLIANT.

A few months before his passing he gave a talk at KW Fly Fishers on fishing for alternate species. With his tongue planted in his cheek he began with slides of dogs, fowl and other critters as alternate species before turning his wry eye to an assortment of fish that would turn the likes of Frederick Halford, G.E.M. Skues or Theodore Gordon convulsing in their graves. But I think Sir Izaak would approve, with a wink and a nudge.

I am left with a persistent question: Were the fly anglers wading the rivers of Paradise ready for the likes of Ian Colin James? I seriously doubt it. Like many who cast lines on waters across North America, I miss him.

A toast of malt whisky, the water of life, to you, Ian. *Slàinte!*

The Celtic Way

For much of its long history fly fishing has been invested with religious significance. Two of its most eloquent spokesmen have expressed opinions as renowned as anything ever written about the recreational sport. In *The Longest Silence* Thomas McGuane notes that angling and religion have been connected for thousands of years. And as Norman Maclean observes in the opening paragraph of *A River Runs Through It*, religion and fly fishing formed a bond in his family.

Many of fly angling's most eloquent practitioners have discussed the contemplative sport in the context of nature religion and living tradition. No less renowned an authority than Roderick Haig-Brown observed in *Fisherman's Spring* that fly fishing is an exploration of an inner world beyond the apprehension of non-anglers.

In 'Cohorts', an essay collected in *One River More*, W.D. Wetherell acknowledges trout as spiritual. In *Lines on the Water* David Adams Richards does not shy away from his Christian convictions. He states unapologetically that he views rivers as made by God, that the music of rivers is God speaking through the rhythms of nature. In another passage, he invokes the visionary poetry of William Blake when he suggests that every moment on the water flows into eternity. This is the English visionary's 'Auguries of Innocence' filtered through the imagination of a literary fly angler.

No literary fly angler is more attuned to our Good Earth than Harry Middleton. In *Rivers of Memory* he celebrates catching his first trout on Starlight Creek as a moment of excitement, of joy and wonder, of magic and mystery, which triggered both exhilaration and exaltation. I read this as an expression of rapture, of ecstasy, at the moment of conversion.

I get that non-anglers might have difficulty appreciating the sheer happiness that washes over me when I hook a trout, even one no longer than my index finger. My heart skips a beat, my breathing increases. Although an adult, I feel once again the polymorphous joy of childhood. I feel embraced in the arms of wonder, of being connected to nature, to a world beyond my existential self which was created not by accident, but by design. With the exception of witnessing the birth of my two sons, this is the closest I have ever come to experiencing intimations of the Divine.

I have tried many times to find spiritual enlightenment and solace in formal religion. And failed. I cannot get beyond the fact that religious sects and denominations continue to excuse and condone desecration of the planet by interests that distort and corrupt scripture to justify rapacious exploitation and wanton destruction.

That is why I am so grateful to have found refuge in Celtic spirituality which I have been studying for more than three decades. The pagan Celts and early Christian Celts answered many of the questions with which I wrestle, not through dogma and doctrine but through a worldview or cosmology that reflects my reverence for Nature, which I believe is sacred. One of the primary reasons I took up fly fishing was because I sensed it would allow me to actively participate in the worship of Creation.

* * *

Of all the great poets in the Western canon none wrote more movingly or more beautifully of rivers, fish and fishing than W.B. Yeats. The word *beautiful* has fallen on barren waters in contemporary literary discourse, but it is the right word when applied to such poems as 'The Song of the Wandering Aengus', 'The Fisherman', 'The Stolen Child', 'The Fish', 'Why Should Not Old Men be Mad', 'The Wild Old Wicked Man' and 'The Tower', among others.

Yeats had a Celtic sense of the spiritual potency of rivers, fish and fishing, to which he gave expression in poems by turns magical, mystical and haunting. Readers who take to heart the title of this book will surely be enchanted, entranced and transported by the opening stanza of 'The Song of the Wandering Aengus', an early poem rich in innocence and romance. Seldom has fly fishing been wrapped in such fanciful garb:

> I went out to the hazel wood,
> Because a fire was in my head,
> And cut and peeled a hazel wand,

And hooked a berry to a thread;
And when white moths were on the wing,
And moth-like stars were flickring out,
I dropped the berry in a stream
And caught a little silver trout.

From what I know of the poet, Yeats fished occasionally in his youth and seldom, if ever, in his adulthood. But he was born, raised and lived much of his later life on Ireland's west coast, home to some of the country's prime sea trout, native brown and salmon waters. He also cast his imagination into the wild and miraculous waters of Irish folklore, legend and myth and was intimately aware of the role fish, especially salmon, play in traditional verse, story and song.

Although he cloaked rivers, fish and angling in metaphor, symbol and allegory, he was familiar with the mechanics and practice of fly fishing which gives his poetry an authenticity which is not lost on readers who are fly anglers, or fly anglers who are readers. In his poetic iconography the fly angler is a figure of honour, decency and nobility in a world that does not always value these natural character traits. In 'The Fisherman' the fly angler represents the best that is Ireland (and by extension, the best in all of us):

Although I can see him still,
The freckled man who goes
To a grey place on a hill
In grey Connemara clothes
At dawn to cast his flies....

The fly angler took refuge in the poet's imagination until his final poems. Eager to escape the manacles of old age, he begins 'The Tower' by recalling his boyhood (and William Wordsworth):

… when with rod and fly,
Or humbler worm, I climbed Ben Bulben's back
And had the livelong summer day to spend.

Similarly in 'Why Should Not Old Men Be Mad' the poet looks back on a greener time before disillusionment, disappointment and grief coloured his life in shades of melancholy and despair, when he 'had a sound flyfisher's wrist'. Yeats knew that the secret to a graceful cast is not breaking the wrist.

* * *

My friend Sherry Wolf does not overtly adhere to any system of Celtic beliefs, ancient or otherwise. Nor is she a fly angler. But her world-view, which includes devotion to the natural world, is Celtic in temperament. She embodies and enacts the Celtic spirit in the way she conducts her life, every single day. Make no mistake, she is a Celtic warrior, whether or not she knows it.

Sherry thinks about the forest close to her home—which she affectionately refers to as 'my forest'—the same way I think about rivers. She views her forest as a sentient thing, albeit under threat. I view rivers as sentient things, also under threat. Sherry has integrated her forest into the very fibres of her mind and body, heart and soul, as I have integrated rivers into mine. Her forest has helped shape her as a person and helped define her values and attitudes, as rivers have helped shape and define me. Her forest and my rivers are mentors we both heed. Her forest is a teacher through which she learns the lessons of the natural world, as I learn lessons from rivers.

What most distresses Sherry is the tree-slashing that clears the way for residential and commercial development. I recall fishing my favourite trout headwater a couple of years ago only to discover that a torrid summer had decimated the trout population. The sorrow I felt was overwhelming. Sherry mourns the death of trees as I mourn the death of fish—for are not trees rivers that reach toward the heavens?

When I join Sherry on walks in her forest I feel the same way as I do when I wade rivers. I share her deep respect, her empathy, her search for understanding, her sense of awe and wonder. And we grieve together when we witness the death of what we cherish.

Sherry draws spiritual sustenance from the services she attends every Sunday, even though they are not conducted in the church into which she was born and raised. Still her beliefs regarding the natural world are sympathetic to, and compatible with, the beliefs I have gained through Celtic spirituality. She walks the Celtic way.

Like a duckling that transforms into a swan, Sherry is a self-made woman. Born and raised in poverty in my hometown of London,

Ontario, she endured unbearable emotional hardship that would have broken most children. She started working before the age of sixteen and has succeeded in a range of careers.

When you meet Sherry professionally, she exudes sophistication. She is intelligent, creative and confident. She seems intimidating because of her low threshold for fools. She surrenders no ground to laziness or incompetence. Her uncompromising honesty pits her against those who sport in lies and deception. She appears tough; but her tender heart makes her vulnerable in ways few people suspect.

Sherry radiates an elegance born of self-awareness. But like a river with a deep current, she is more than she appears. To know her, you have to accompany her in the forest when she is wearing her 'walk-the-dog clothes', including mud-caked hiking boots, weathered jeans, dollar-store mittens and hooded coat, complete with pockets bulging with balls, treats and biodegradable poop bags.

Sherry is a canine magnet. Her instinctual understanding of dogs is so uncanny I often call her the dog whisperer. She has had dogs—purebred and mutt, large and small and everything in between—all her life. Her current companions are a pair of male Shih-poos, Hagrid and Miko. She most often walks her 'boys' in her forest, which she lays claim to not to exert dominion, but to protect. This is not ownership, but stewardship.

A walk in the woods with Sherry and her boys is a lesson in attentiveness. She is observant about the ways of her forest. She notices things others miss. She is an irrepressible conversationist. Her stream-of-consciousness thoughts flit from topic to topic like chickadees in flight. Sometimes her mind-leaps are hard to follow. She is always one thought ahead. The experience reminds me of the joy Thoreau expresses in his essay 'Walking' when he describes the activity as being bathed 'in such a golden flood, without a ripple or a murmur to it'.

Sherry is fearless. Late one spring evening she was escorting her boys home when she heard a pack of coyotes yipping in the midst of a killing party. She knew they were close, but was still shocked when a pair of them slipped out of the darkness. Unfazed, she shone a flashlight in the direction of her uninvited guests and shouted, 'Oh no you don't. You aren't having *my* boys for dessert.' The creatures stopped in their tracks, calmly assessed the situation and sauntered off, returning to their interrupted meal. She confessed later that she did not start shaking until she and her boys had returned home.

Another time, when two dogs attacked gentle Miko, she threw herself into the fray, sustaining painful injuries, while the owner of the two aggressors stood by and watched, stupefied and useless. She insisted on going to the vet before she sought medical attention.

One winter day Sherry was walking her boys when she came across a Doberman she recognized that was in distress. It was losing its battle with the icy currents of the Grand River. Ignoring her own safety, she waded into the frigid water and rescued the dog. Fearing that it was suffering from hypothermia, she wrapped the dog in her coat and headed for home. En route she came across the creature's owners who were scouting the neighbourhood by car. Sherry gave them their traumatized pet, still wrapped in her coat, with a stern warning to take it to the vet immediately. The dog survived and the owners returned Sherry's coat a few hours later.

Sherry is a stickler for rules, not for regulation's sake, but as a code of ethical conduct. She is quick to report despoilers who defile her forest by dumping garbage, tires, leftover concrete and used paint cans rather than recycling them at the municipal landfill. She responds to willful degradation not only with rage but with a sense of violation.

In *The Bone Pile* Maximilian Werner wrestles with the moral dilemma of people who are devoted to doing what they can to protect the planet, while living in ways that are harmful. He concludes that, though it is preferable to support the environment, the cause cannot be so all-consuming that it isolates a person from the most important obligation of all: to live out each and every day responsible to the planet. Sherry lives these wise urgent words, as do many fly anglers of my acquaintance.

Sherry has given me a number of handmade Christmas gifts with a fishing theme. One year she gave me a Celtic ceramic plaque of three salmon entwined in a circle. Its mossy slate colour suggested submerged river rocks. With it she gave me a card confirming a donation to the Grand River Conservation Foundation to develop a metre of trail commemorating all of the 'wonderful walks' we have shared with Hagrid and Miko.

* * *

Like Sherry, fly anglers have much in common with the Celts—whether they know it or not. I delight in the fact that casting lines into mystery puts me in touch with the worldview espoused by ancestors who inhabited the 'pure shattering beauty' (in the words of W.D. Wetherell from his essay 'Two Places Well') of the Scottish Highlands.

Even heathens and pagans, not to mention atheists and agnostics, among fly anglers must concede that it is as easy to be caught in a spiritual net as it is to catch fish. The sacred worldview of the ancient Celts offers insight into why fly fishing has accrued meaning and purpose beyond other methods of fishing. This is why I refer to it as a *calling*.

Water, fish and fishing have symbolic meaning in many religions and mythologies. Long before fish were appropriated by Christianity, the pagan Celts revered salmon (*Salmo salar*). They play a vital role in the Celtic imagination as vessels of otherworldly wisdom, notes the *Dictionary of Celtic Mythology*.

I have never landed a wild salmon—a dream as yet unfulfilled. And while I have felt none the wiser for landing a trout, bass, pike or pickerel, I never feel more intimately connected to the fierce, elemental life force (Eros) than when I hold a fish in the palm of my wet hand as I remove a single, barbless hook and release it as carefully as I can. The primeval shock of recognition has nothing to do with the size of fish. For me, this makes fly fishing an act of reverence.

Although salmon swim from salt to fresh water to spawn, in the very water in which they were born, Irish and Welsh traditions depict them as inhabiting sacred wells, pools and waterfalls as well as rivers. No wonder fly anglers habitually hold pools, riffles and runs in reverence. These are holy places, which are often given local, familiar names—in other words, christened—by anglers who share a common creed.

The life cycle of the salmon is symbolic of the soul's journey to the source of life, the source of being. When a fly angler wades into a river and casts to salmon he or she partakes in the journey toward union with the Divine. This *unio mystica* is the path of the mythic quest.

Most anglers experience powerful feelings when they wade a river and cast a fly rod, especially at dawn or at dusk. Beyond the physical sensation of wading in flowing currents and the rhythm of casting, rivers are figurative as well as literal. They represent the flow of chronological time, past, present and future; the continuum of life from birth to death to rebirth; the currents of memory and desire; the bridge between the unconscious and consciousness; a link between nature and humanity, both profane and sacred.

Anglers might not be consciously aware of these symbolic associations, but that does not diminish their potency as they cast *to* fish rather than *at* fish. This epistemological difference recognizes that a fly rod enables an angler to examine the true river—its essence, its personality, its soul. This makes a fly rod a divining rod.

Humans and salmon interact in various ways in the Celtic imagination. There are legends in which humans are transformed into salmon (a popular adaptation is T. H. White's 'The Sword in the Stone' chapter in *The Once and Future King*, when Merlin transforms young Arthur into a fish as part of his initiation).

It is difficult to explain the mythic power of salmon. But it is apparent the instinctual act of swimming between salt and fresh water implies a capacity for passing between worlds. No wonder fly anglers gravitate toward the threshold—or liminal—times of dawn and dusk (known in the Celtic world as the gloaming), when the boundary between our world and the 'otherworld' is gossamer thin—fly anglers might think of 8X tippets, the smallest diameter available.

Jim Harrison, a longtime fly angler as well as accomplished writer, embraces encroaching darkness as a primeval companion. In the introduction to his collected non-fiction *Just Before Dark* he expresses his affinity with magical mystical twilight. Similarly, the early Celts revered 'thin places' as sites in the landscape where the border between the sacred and the profane is thinnest. These are where spiritual experiences occur—not unlike trout steams.

Viewing fly fishing in spiritual terms, Celtic or otherwise, might be too much of a leap out of familiar water for some fly anglers. But there is a powerful connection between the way the Celts related to the natural world and the way ecologically aware fly anglers relate as well. The ancient Celts made no distinction between the secular and the sacred, believing they lived in a hallowed world. Consequently, all of Creation, including nature, was invested with spiritual significance.

Celtic spirituality is rooted in the Stone Age, long before the Romans brought Christianity to the British Isles between the second and seventh centuries—often called the Age of Saints. While inhabiting the outermost margins of the civilized world in what is wrongly dismissed as the Dark Ages, Christianized Celts viewed nature as both a physical manifestation and a poetic expression of the sacred. They read from the Book of Nature as they read from the Bible, especially the Gospels of the New Testament. For these Christian converts the presence of God was an immediate reality.

Celtic spirituality should not be confused with pantheism. In contrast to such English Romantic poets as William Wordsworth and Samuel Taylor Coleridge, or to such New England Transcendentalists as Ralph Waldo Emerson or Henry David Thoreau, this is not nature worship, but Creation worship. Its connection to nature is cosmological in thrust. Pagan Celtics venerated the landscape which was confirmed by sacred groves, trees and stones. The poetry of early Celtic Christian writers was drawn from nature because nature was revered as part of God's Creation.

Celtic spirituality is both ecological and holistic, which accounts for its popularity among people, including fly anglers, seeking a relevant eco-cosmology as the planet slowly melts through what threatens to be irreversible climate change. The relationship the Celts maintained between nature and grace has powerful appeal. To quote William Blake, who was not a Celt but wrote poetry like one: 'Man without Nature is barren.'

Ancient monolithic stone rings and later high crosses, not to mention monasteries and churches, were built on consecrated ground. The Celtic crosses that continue to endow the landscape with a haunting beauty often feature Scriptural imagery (gospel narratives) on one side and Creation imagery on the other.

The pagan Celts celebrated a close relationship to the creatures of land, water and sky. This is not a Disney fantasy world, but acknowledgement of the ferociousness inherent in both the natural world and the human heart. Many Celtic saints followed the example of their pagan brethren by nurturing close relations with wild animals, fish and birds.

Their images are prominent in Celtic art. When written language began to be developed the Celtic alphabet, known as Ogham, incorporated three sets of vowels comprising twenty letters with each letter bearing the name of a tree or a plant. Imagine trees serving as the planet's lexicography, not to mention the calligraphy of plants.

By following the spirit of my Celtic ancestors, I do not worship rivers and fish, birds and animals, rocks, trees and plants when I am waist deep in water. I am neither Wordsworth nor Thoreau waving a magic wand. By casting on the altar of nature, I acknowledge the creative force that is with me, before me, behind me, in me, beneath me and above me—to paraphrase the beautiful Irish prayer 'St. Patrick's Breastplate'. Consequently, I feel more spiritually alive casting into mystery on a river—of which I am a part, now and forever—than I do kneeling in a stained-glass church.

The Celts lived not only close to nature, but *in* nature. They were *of* nature and their spirituality was a creative response to that intimate contact. Although not a Celt himself, Thoreau acknowledged the Celtic notion of *wildness* as a vitally potent element in the human heart, mind and soul. 'The wildness and adventure that are in fishing still recommend it to me,' he says in *Walden*. Let us all say a resounding YES to wildness.

I believe that Celtic spiritually remains relevant at a time of crisis when the planet is under siege. History is getting the upper hand on biology. A second does not pass without the planet losing more of its furred and feathered wildlife, more of its trees, flowers and grasses, more of its rivers and lakes, more of its fish. As we lose these natural forms of life, we are at the same time forsaking beauty, freedom and meaning. Celtic spirituality gives humanity a vocabulary to warn and caution, champion and defend that which we are losing, or have already lost. Language is a tool by which we protect. Words are emblems of love. Fly anglers have a moral and ethical obligation to act as responsible stewards in return for the gifts we receive from Nature. Our *calling* demands action, now.

We need to hold this Good Earth in a caring, reverential embrace. We need to follow Sherry Wolf's example of love and courage, empathy and moral passion. We need to practise what the visionary poet William Blake recognized at the dawning of the Industrial Revolution when he declared in *The Marriage of Heaven and Hell*: 'For every thing that lives is Holy.'

Winter

Books for a Winter's Night

For many creatures in the natural world winter is the season of sleep. For me, winter is the season of reading. It is when I am most fully awake. A good book is a lamp that lights a winter's night. Reading keeps the darkness at bay.

I take to heart what the guiding father of fly fishing in America once observed. Theodore Gordon was on the threshold of the last year of his life when he wrote in the *Fishing Gazette* that, 'There are few things that give one more pleasure on a winter's night than a good work on fly fishing.'

While many fly anglers spend hours at the tying vise, I pass the nights of wintertide in my Mission-style armchair with book in hand and dram of malt whisky within reach. A fireplace is nice but not necessary; however, I enjoy company. Like fly fishing, reading need not be a solitary act. First it was a collie named Parker, then a black lab called Leia and, finally, a pair of labradoodle sisters Abby and Mandy. Now my reading companion is Callie, a calico cat who likes to cuddle on my desk while I sit at the keyboard in search of that one true sentence.

I should clarify what I mean by fly fishing literature. I do not use the phrase euphemistically; I use it literally. These are books that need not aspire to serious literature. They *are* serious literature of demonstrable quality. Many of the writers in the genre are literary authors or teachers of English literature who are fly anglers and who happen to write about the contemplative recreation. Irrespective of how they identify themselves on income tax forms, their stories and poetry share equal space on my shelves with works of serious literature.

There is nothing like a good mystery to keep the imagination warm and cozy as the dying year turns cold. Murder mysteries comprise one of the most rewarding tributaries feeding into the twin rivers of fly angling literature and mystery genre.

Again let me clarify what I mean by fly fishing mysteries. I do not mean books about fly fishing framed in the mystery genre—usually awkwardly and ineptly and boringly. I have read some of these, not always from cover to cover, and discarded them like aggravating chub in a trout stream. Sometimes donating them would be a disservice to a worthy charity. What I mean by the phrase are mysteries, well-written with engaging plots, characters and setting, that give pleasure and are deserving of multiple readings, like any work of serious literature. In other words, mysteries that happen to include elements of fly fishing.

The connection between mysteries and fly fishing is intriguing. All good fly anglers are sleuths. Conversely all good sleuths are fly anglers. Not only do fly anglers 'read' the water to understand the habitat and habits of fish, they need angling technique to be successful. Writers develop comparable 'reading' skills and literary technique in order to be successful.

The sympathetic link between fly fishing and detective work helps explain why the recreational sport flows into crime fiction and why, equally, crime fiction is refreshed by fly fishing mysteries. Such classic mystery writers as Agatha Christie, Ngaio Marsh and Caroline Graham featured piscatorial mayhem in their work long before contemporary crime writers got in on the act.

I was introduced to the 'boutique' genre when I picked up a Max Addams mystery at a second-hand bookstore in Peterborough, Ontario. I was vacationing with Lydia, Dylan and Robertson in a rustic cottage on an island in a small lake, brimming with large and small-mouth bass, east of the village of Bancroft.

I forget which was the first of the three paperbacks by David Leitz I eventually purchased. However, I enjoyed all of them including *Casting in Dead Water*, *Dying to Fly Fish* and *Fly Fishing Can Be Fatal*. Even when I dropped one down the hole in an outhouse—um, the details do not matter—I was able to find a replacement.

Max—our fly fishing guide, turned sleuth—operates Whitefork Lodge in the highlands of northern Vermont. The setting is enough to hook me because New England remains one of my favourite places. Appropriately Max never has to go looking for murder; murder always finds him at his scenic fishing lodge.

Like an angler in unfamiliar water, I began prospecting for fly fishing mysteries in bookstores, both new and used. I searched out intriguing titles on angling websites and through online book retailers. I eventually assembled a collection of mystery novels to enhance my fly fishing library, encompassing novels, short story collections, poetry, essays and memoirs, in addition to instructional non-fiction.

William G. Tapply was a double-haul caster when it came to writing. He was not only a fine crime novelist (his Brady Coyne mystery series takes place in Boston and around New England), but also an excellent outdoors writer of both memoirs and instructional books. Although fly angling seeps into the Coyne series, the recreational sport is at the heart of three late mysteries featuring Stoney Calhoun, a fishing guide with a mysterious past who lives in Maine (*Bitch Creek, Gray Ghost, Dark Tiger*).

John Larison is a river steward, guide and teacher in Oregon who has written a couple of mystery novels set in the Northwest including *Northwest of Normal* and *Holding Lies*. Another Oregon writer, Warren Easley, has written a pair of mysteries (*Matters of Doubt* and *Dead Float*) featuring Cal Claxton, a former LA prosecutor who now practises law so he can fish more. Wisconsin's John Galligan is a college writing teacher who developed a series (*The Nail Knot, The Blood Knot, The Clinch Knot, The Wind Knot*) featuring a peripatetic fly fisherman named Dog who goes in search of fish and finds murder. Wyoming's David Riley Bertsch's Jake Trent series includes *Death Canyon* and *River of No Return*. California-based, outdoor and fiction writer Jim Tenuto's *Blood Atonement* features Montana fly fishing guide Dahlgren Wallace.

Michigan's Joseph Heywood has written a dozen novels in the Woods Cop series, including *Ice Hunter, Blue Wolf in Green Fire, Chasing a Blond Moon, Running Dark, Dark Roe* and *Strike Dog* in addition to the fly fishing fantasy novel *The Snowfly*. Ronald Weber, professor emeritus of American studies at the University of Notre Dame, has written a trio of mysteries set in Northern Michigan and featuring a male newspaperman and female natural resources officer: *Aluminum Hatch, Catch and Keep* and *Riverwatcher*.

Fly angling mystery writers are not limited to men. Wisconsin's Victoria Houston is one of the most prolific and popular. Her Loon Lake mystery series features retired dentist and fly angler Paul Osborne who is routinely deputized by police chief and fly angler

Lewellyn Ferris. Fishing, live-bait and hard-lure as well as fur and feather, punctuates the murders that Osborne and Ferris solve.

There are many more fly fishing mystery novels. These are simply the ones I have collected, read and enjoyed. For anglers eager to dip the toes of their wading boots into fly fishing mystery I suggest *Hook, Line & Sinister*. The collection of short fiction is edited by T. Jefferson Parker and features stories by such prominent mystery writers as Michael Connelly, C. J. Box, Houston and Tapply.

Although not primarily a fly fishing mystery writer, James Lee Burke is one of America's most accomplished crime novelists. He is also a fly angler who writes brilliantly about the recreational sport. I devour any novel that has the slightest taste of fly angling, whether it involves Louisiana sheriff's detective Dave Robicheaux or former Texas Ranger Billy Bob Holland.

I enjoy authors who are not specifically fly fishing mystery writers but set their crime novels in wilderness areas and feature protagonists who are forest rangers, conservation officers or game wardens. Box's Joe Pickett series is set in Wyoming and features an occasional fly fishing cameo. He devotes a story to the sport in his story collection *Shots Fired*. Paul Doiron's Mike Bowditch series, which is set in Maine, is equally accomplished. Both writers should appeal to mystery buffs with a nose for foul play in the great outdoors.

William Kent Krueger's Cork O'Connor series features an ex-sheriff of Tamarack County, nestled in the Boundary Waters of the Quetico-Superior Wilderness with its two-million acres of dense forest, white-water rapids and uncharted islands on the Canadian-American border.

* * *

Before introducing the fly angling mystery writer I most admire, I would like to mention a couple of literary authors who incorporate fly fishing into mysteries. *The Trout*, by Irish novelist Peter Cunningham, is a story about the dark stain the Roman Catholic Church casts across Ireland. The novel—which begins in Ontario's Muskoka before shifting to Ireland, with a detour to Michigan—is punctuated with lovely passages about fly fishing for trout.

Peter Heller's *The Painter* is an accomplished novel built on a foundation of the mystery genre featuring Jim Stegner (a nod to

Wallace Stegner?), a man who cannot avoid trouble. It is also a meditation on love and loss, authenticity and celebrity, obsession and inspiration, passion and violence, not to mention the redemptive power of art and fly fishing. Jim is not inherently bad. After all, he is a successful, self-taught artist—the darling of critics because of the blue-collar, outsider status. He is also an avid fly angler. Fly fishing for wild trout runs through *The Painter* like a Montana river, where much of the action takes place.

Jim is big and burly, with a thick, grey beard. The locals call him Hemingway because he looks so much like the famous writer. He is popular with attractive women. He is comfortable with kids. He is a good friend to good men. However, he can be violent, capable of shooting a sexual predator point-blank and killing two brothers—soulless professional poachers both—in cold blood.

A reformed alcoholic and gambler, and two-time loser at marriage, Jim controls his incendiary temper through painting and fishing. He is attuned to the melody of trout rivers, through which he communes with his dead daughter.

The Painter—Heller's sophomore novel following his critically acclaimed *The Dog Wars* (which also incorporates fly fishing)—adapts the conventions of the hard-boiled crime novel, but is pure literary fiction. He writes about fly fishing and rivers with lyrical elegance. Even for non–fly anglers, *The Painter* has a powerful allure.

Equally seductive is Heller's subsequent mystery *The River*, a canoeing misadventure set on a legendary river with a sinister history that feeds into Hudson Bay in northwestern Ontario. Two college pals, one from Vermont and one from Colorado, learn a great deal about themselves, and one another, when they paddle into white water murder fuelled by wildfire—literally.

Raymond Carver remains a giant among American short story writers. He was also an avid fly fisherman who wrote excellent poems about rivers and angling. He also has fun playing with the angling mystery genre in his short story 'So Much Water So Close to Home'.

The satirical tale tells of a group of buddies who go fishing for a few days, discover the corpse of a murdered woman and decide not to report the grisly finding to police until the conclusion of their wilderness rip. Their tardiness causes all kinds of grief for the narrator who comes into the crosshairs of his astonished and disbelieving wife.

I suspect that Richard Dokey, a philosophy professor and avid fly angler based in California, had Carver in mind when he wrote some of the stories collected in *Fly Fishing the River Styx*.

* * *

My favourite fly fishing mystery writer is Keith McCafferty. Since the publication of *The Royal Wulff Murders* in 2012, he has hooked the lip of my imagination. *Cold Hearted River*, his sixth Sean Stranahan mystery in as many years, is in my opinion his best. The novel is a fictional murder mystery wrapped around a real-life literary mystery. Its title will tip off most readers because it is a pun on 'Big Two-Hearted River'. Yes, the literary mystery involves none other than Ernest Hemingway, the writer who transformed fishing into an art form.

McCafferty shares some commonalities with the author which, at least for me, increase the novel's interest quotient. Both writers are connected to Northern Michigan. Hemingway spent the summers of his youth there. The region provides the setting for some Nick Adams stories, including 'Big Two-Hearted River', as well as his first novel *Torrents of Spring*.

McCafferty also spent the summers of his youth there, vacationing from Ohio with his family. Like Hemingway, it is where he learned to fly fish. He recalls one memorable summer in a *Field & Stream* article—'Wishing Tree: Fly Fishing Michigan's Au Sable River'—a reminiscence of the state's Holy Water. Some of McCafferty's personal story, which took place when he was twenty and worked on stream restoration, is given fictional shape in *Cold Hearted River*.

The connection between McCafferty and Hemingway, however, runs deeper. McCafferty knew the famous writer's oldest son, Jack, for more than three decades when they were contributing editors for *Field & Stream*. McCafferty remained as the magazine's survival and outdoor skills editor after Hemingway left.

In his preface to *Cold Hearted River*, McCafferty tells of a 'blustery November day' when the two were steelheading on a section of British Columbia's Thompson River known as the Graveyard. His colleague recounted the story of his famous father's steamer trunk being lost or stolen in 1940, en route from Key West, Florida, to Ketchum, Idaho. The trunk was reputed to contain all of the author's fly fishing gear, including bamboo rods and reels from England's House of Hardy—

and maybe, just maybe—an unpublished manuscript. (Hemingway's only surviving fly rod, a Hardy 'Fairy' model, is on permanent display at the American Museum of Fly Fishing.)

McCafferty had no intention of doing anything with the tale of the missing trunk until his wife persuaded him to set a novel in northwestern Wyoming, where Hemingway spent five summers and autumns fishing, hunting and writing. This backstory sets up a compelling fictional mystery built on the foundation of a literary mystery. A reader can never be sure where fact ends and fiction begins.

His assessment of Hemingway, which he expresses through a character in the novel—a retired English professor who bears an uncanny resemblance to 'Papa'—is perspicacious. I agree with his estimation of Hemingway as among the most misunderstood and disparaged, yet most celebrated, writers of the twentieth century—with the exception perhaps of Ted Hughes.

McCafferty puts his finger on the paradox that was very much the man: the dichotomy at the heart of Hemingway's public persona. He sketches a portrait of a complicated man who was a complex artist (these are not the same, nor are they interchangeable). Hemingway was certainly a poster boy for American masculinity. Although reviled as a misogynist, he was drawn to strong women. I believe a pathogically shy inner man hid behind the braggadocio exterior.

Depicted as a bully and a bore, close friends—who found in Hemingway a stimulating companion—stood by his side until the very end. His intelligence, emotional depth and passions were abundantly evident in his best writing.

McCafferty questions the simplistic explanation of Hemingway's mood swings as bipolar disorder. He suggests—rightly, I believe—that the paranoia and delusions of grandeur that dogged the writer at the end of his life were symptoms of schizophrenia, and that the brain trauma he suffered in an airplane crash in Africa caused psychological damage that led to diminished creativity.

McCafferty lives in Montana, which he has turned into a major character in his mysteries, along with the recreational sport itself. In his first mystery, *The Royal Wulff Murders*, we learn Sean is an ex-private eye who moved to Montana from New England to purchase a new lease on life. He unwittingly becomes involved in murder after a good ol' boy fishing guide reels in a corpse on the Madison, a legendary trout river. As events unfold Our Man in Montana crosses paths with Velvet LaFayette, a Southern belle who pays the bills as a nightclub singer, and Martha Ettinger who emits a slow, amorous burn beneath her sheriff's badge. McCafferty proves himself an accomplished writer. The setting is well-defined and his characters are not only fleshed out, they demonstrate potential for growth, like a good investment portfolio. Sean has sufficient emotional depth and intellectual breadth to carry a series. *The Royal Wulff Murders* brims with enough suspense and fly fishing lore to lure anglers and mystery fans alike—which he maintains throughout the series.

By his sophomore release, *The Gray Ghost Murders*, McCafferty had become my go-to fly fishing mystery writer—the literary equivalent of a Pheasant Tail Nymph or Woolly Bugger. The novel is held together by a pair of mystery threads that are as artfully tied as fur and feather. McCafferty never backs away from controversy, which should be of interest to fly anglers specifically and to outdoor enthusiasts generally. In *The Royal Wulff Murders* he introduces readers to the urgent danger of invasive species to trout streams throughout the West—which, by the way, extends to game fisheries across North America. In *Dead Man's Fancy*, he examines the politics of reintroducing wolves in the West. He sets *A Death in Paradise*, his seventh installment in the series, in Montana's Smith River Canyon. Referred to as 'America's Sistine Chapel' because of its grandeur and beauty, environmental groups have listed it as the country's fourth most endangered watershed due to threats from copper mining.

With mysteries such as these to keep me on the edge of my chair, is it any wonder I have no desire to while away the hours sitting at a tying vise during the season of reading?

Commedia dell'angling

Paul Quarrington lived large. We shared many passions encompassing writing, music, sports, partying hearty, Cuban cigars and fly fishing. He wrote hilarious accounts of his piscatorial exploits in two memoirs—*Fishing with My Old Guy* and *From the Far Side of the River*. He also wrote *King Leary*, in my estimation one of the best hockey novels ever written. Maybe the best!

I first read *From the Far Side of the River* when it was published in 2003. I had just returned to fishing after an absence of more than three decades. It was a couple of years before I would attempt my first clumsy cast with a fly rod. And it was before the celebrated Toronto-based, creative Renaissance man bravely announced publicly that he was dying from a particularly ferocious form of cancer and had only a few months to live.

I met Quarrington some time after *From the Far Side of the River* was released, when he visited Waterloo to perform with his bluesy, alt-country, rock band *The Pork Belly Futures*. It was a good band with a book of unapologetically literary songs including 'Hemingway', a tribute to a writer Quarrington admired. He also wrote or co-wrote a couple of angling ditties including the delightfully ribald 'Big Ol' Bass' and the wry romantic ballad 'Deep, Deep Blue'. After the show I complimented him on his books and songs; he complimented me on my shirt—a yellow Columbia short-sleeve sporting blue marlin.

When I reviewed *From the Far Side of the River* I had just returned from a fishing trip in the Kawarthas with my university pals. I had not seen most of them in more than a decade. As important as it was to reclaim friendships, it was just as important to acknowledge how much I had missed fishing.

The nineteenth-century English essayist William Hazlitt believed the associations we make with nature originate and are nurtured in childhood. When I was young, nature was so important to me that I thought of becoming a forest ranger or conservation officer. I camped, I fished and later I hunted. Priorities changed at university. Although most of my closest friends fished and hunted, I thought it was time to retire the pastimes of youth. Yet I remained an ardent armchair angler, casting my imagination into the streams, rivers and lakes of fly fishing literature.

The adventure with my university pals reignited my passion for fishing. So when I got home I eagerly dipped into *From the Far Side of the River* and got reacquainted with an angling soulmate, even though I had yet to hold a fly rod. I had greatly enjoyed Quarrington's earlier memoir *Fishing with My Old Guy*, an account of his friendship with Gord Deval, an international casting champion, rod-builder and fly tier. My signed copy is one of my most prized literary possessions. Quarrington contributed an 'Intelligent Commentary' to Deval's memoir *Fishing for Brookies, Browns & Bows.*

In his sophomore angling memoir, Quarrington refers to writers drawn to fishing and compares aspects of these complementary artistic activities, including what can best be described as creative deception, or lying, in the service of art—whether narrative, story or tall tale—rather than conceding to verifiable truth. I think this is why so many literary writers, both poets and fiction authors, are attracted to fly fishing.

He distinguishes between hunting and fishing, a moral conundrum that dogs anglers like a hound tonguing a scent. More than a few fly anglers get defensive when critics, dripping with contempt and condemnation, link hunting and fishing together as two sides of the same blood-sport coin. This cannot be dismissed as extremism under the guise of political correctness. It is a controversial topic a couple of other Canadian writers discuss in their fly angling memoirs: David Adams Richards in *Lines on the Water* and Mark Kingwell in *Catch & Release.* Quarrington's take is one with which I concur.

When people ask him why he fishes, he replies that it connects him to a life force, which in Freudian theory is known as Eros or the life instinct. Jungian thinkers associate this life force with the Anima. In contrast, he associates hunting with Thanatos or the death instinct. Quarrington also links fishing to literature because both appeal to, and engage with, emotions, feelings and such sensibilities as mercy and grief, joy and sorrow.

In *The Compleat Angler* Walton famously decrees fishing a

contemplative pursuit. Quarrington agrees that fishing is not only meditative, but a comfort for the soul. This is an element of fly angling that is losing ground among young people who take up the activity. This new 'gonzo' attitude is reflected in the numerous film festivals devoted to fly angling that is all the rage as the sport wades into the uncertain waters of a new millennia.

In his introduction, Quarrington places angling in a philosophical context—which he continues throughout the memoir. I take his words to heart; they embody my experience. When life is good, fly fishing is a celebration. When life turns turbulent, fly fishing offers respite. When things are utterly miserable, fly fishing approximates ceremony and ritual.

Life went from turbulent to miserable on the Bow River, in downtown Calgary, when Quarrington sought solace from an incomprehensible world on 11 September 2001—the year his father died and his marriage dissolved against a backdrop of terrorism in the skies. It would compromise the power of this intellectually engaging and emotionally resonant chapter to quote anything less than the entire 'Fishing Through Disaster'. Even those who have never cast a fly rod will be moved by this thoughtful and deeply felt meditation.

From what I have said so far, readers might get the impression the memoir is heavy slogging. On the contrary. In contrast to many contemporary angling writers, Quarrington does not spill much ink on such topics as nature, ecology or conservation. Although he writes eloquently about moments of solitude and reflection, fishing for him is a social act, a communal pastime.

He writes about his Old Guy (Deval); his fishing buddy and fellow author Jake MacDonald, otherwise known as Muskie Man; a fishing guide who moonlights as a mall Santa Claus; another guide nicknamed Bonefish Dundee (after Crocodile Dundee); and Wray McQuay, a conservation officer who is so tough because he loves nature so much. (It is intriguing seeing Quarrington through the eyes of MacDonald in his raucous essay collection *With the Boys*.)

Of course it would not be a Quarrington book without healthy doses of humour, as when he is caught poaching—really closer to trespassing—or when he impersonates a freelance photographer to gain entry into a lavish fishing lodge which is really a cover for an international drug operation. He delights in the role of fishing bumbler; however, I have reason to believe that he is more competent than literary licence dictates.

As a Father's Day gift a couple of weeks after I had reunited with my university pals, Lydia, Dylan and Robertson gave me a spin-casting reel and rod, my first since my teens. We spent a delightful afternoon fishing on the Grand River. Although highway traffic was within earshot, myriad insects and birdsong performed a pastoral symphony.

But more pleasing than the music of nature was Robertson, who was seven at the time, sitting on a rock in the river, singing sweetly while casting on peaceful waters. When I asked how he was doing, he replied: 'Dad, this is the life.' Such a remark might seem a mundane platitude, but for a high-functioning autistic boy who was not talking much, it was sentiment spoken from the heart.

Now that I have been fly fishing for more than a decade, literature devoted to the recreational sport is even more significant. I return to *Fishing with My Old Guy* and *From the Far Side of the River* with deeper satisfaction knowing that Paul Quarrington is casting a jocular line from the far side of Paradise—especially now that his Old Guy has joined him.

Reluctant Master of Fur & Feather

I joined KW Flyfishers in 2008, a year after I picked up a fly rod for the first time. Like the great Groucho Marx who famously quipped, 'I don't want to belong to any club that will accept me as a member,' I am neither by nature nor temperament a joiner of clubs. Still I support this organization, having served as a director, vice-president and secretary. I recommend that all beginners seek out such clubs as a component of their fly fishing apprenticeship. Not only have I learned a great deal, I have made some lasting angling friendships. One of the most charming members I met early on was Joan Kirkham, a master fly tier as well as an angler.

The long history of fly fishing does acknowledge a few notable female fly anglers, tiers and writers, from Dame Juliana Berners to Joan Salvato Wulff. Still it remains a predominantly male activity. Fly fishing clubs therefore tend to be men-only bastions. All of which makes Joan—a founder and honorary lifetime member of KW Flyfishers—an inspiring exception to the piscatorial rule.

Shortly after joining the club, I talked to Joan for a newspaper story. In all my years of journalism I interviewed few subjects more disarmingly modest than Joan. She avoided attention as if it were a cloud of black flies hovering over a hallowed trout stream.

Joan started fly fishing after she immigrated to Canada from England in 1953. Her husband, Dave, was a die-hard golfer, so when their eleven-year-old son Steven wanted to buy a fly rod, Mom answered the call. She had no idea about fly fishing, Joan confided from her home in Cambridge, Ontario, located within an easy walk from the Grand River. 'My idea of a fly was something you swatted,' she said with a hearty laugh.

Nonetheless she bought her son 'a rinky dinky' fly rod and took him fishing. Determined to join in on the fun, she bought a spinning outfit. Mom and son were fishing one day when they saw a fly angler in action. She tried a couple of casts with her son's rod. After 'thrashing the water into a foam', she eventually became a skillful caster. It was not long before Steven said he needed his own flies. Mom sprang into action by buying a rudimentary fly tying set. Steven soon grew frustrated with the shoddy material, so she tried her hand at the delicate art of imitating aquatic insects and critters with feather and fur, yarn and thread.

Initially she had no more success than her son, but patience triumphed, and she was soon tying flies. A few months later Joan was in a tackle shop when she overheard an angler complain about being unable to get good flies. 'I brazenly said I was a fly tier,' she confessed. Within three months she could not keep up with the demand.

* * *

A few select women have gained distinction in the fly angling 'fraternity' by tying flies that transcend craft to become art. I am sure Joan would allow me a brief digression. Think of it as prospecting a spring creek that flows into a river, a spot fish of all kinds favour.

Maine's Carrie Stevens's celebrated patterns include the famous Grey Ghost among others. There are also the legendary Catskill husband-and-wife couples of Elsie and Harry Darbee (whom angling scribe Sparse Grey Hackle called 'the world's best fly tiers') and Winnie and Walt Dette and their daughter Mary. (I have purchased flies from Mary's grandson, Joe Fox, on a couple of trips to Roscoe, New York.)

Legendary English-born fly tier Megan Boyd made flies for royalty and was celebrated around the world from the seclusion of her tiny cottage in Kintradwell, near Brora, Scotland. Best known for her Atlantic salmon patterns, she was awarded the British Empire Medal

in 1971. Filmmaker Eric Steel produced and directed a magical animated documentary on Boyd titled *Kiss the Water*. In the film, *Country Life* fishing editor David Profumo, who apprenticed with Boyd for a summer during his youth, praises his sessional teacher for her elaborate and delicate flies.

Canadian author Helen Humphreys has written a charming book ostensibly about Boyd. *Machine Without Horses* (which refers to a Highland country dance) is much more than the 'novel' referenced on the front cover. It is a genre-bending fusion of biography, memoir, confessional, elegy and natural history. As a literary hybrid the novel shares qualities with Humphreys's earlier book *The River*. Equal parts natural history, botany, geology, anthropology, geography, history, archeology, meteorology and historical fiction, the literary miscellany is a blend of fiction and non-fiction, poetry, archival photographs and illustrations, paintings, drawings, maps, lists and found objects.

Machine has a narrative frame of two complementary parts. In the first part an unnamed Canadian writer, who resembles Humphreys, becomes interested in Boyd after reading an obituary of the famous salmon fly dresser. So happens Humphreys shares many things in common with Boyd—both were born in Surrey, England, before moving away, both ride motorcycles and love dogs, both live somewhat solitary lives, both pursue perfection in the service of art. Moreover, both might share the same sexual orientation.

The writer becomes fascinated by the notion of an ordinary person blossoming into an extraordinary artist. Readers follow the writer as she contemplates the internal life of the fly tier while tracing the contour of the fly tier's external life. The writer even learns to tie a salmon fly (quite badly as it turns out) from a local tier as part of her research. In order to get inside the mind and emotions of the famous fly tier, the writer decides she must create a fictional character based on the actual woman. In the second part of the novel, the fictional fly tier is given a different name and is placed at the centre of a tender love story. Humphreys pays homage to Boyd and the fictional character she inspires equally.

Machine Without Horses is a literary fly pattern of exotic feathers. It is a meditation on the grief that follows loss, the complexity of love and the relationship between art and nature. All the while Humphreys bends, twists and blends fact and fiction. What I enjoy most is Boyd sitting in front of her fly-tying vise in her rustic cottage in the Scottish Highlands and creating *magic* with fur and feather.

Machine Without Horses is not the first accomplished work in Canadian literature featuring a fly tier heroine. There is Ethel Wilson's *Swamp Angel*. Born in South Africa and a resident of England before immigrating to the West Coast as a child, Wilson was the wife of a prominent physician and lived in an upscale neighbourhood in Vancouver much of her life. In addition to being an established mid-century author, she was 'an expert flyfisherwomen', according to authors George Bowering and Margaret Atwood, both of whom wrote critical appraisals of Wilson's most celebrated novel.

In his classic memoir *Going Fishing*, Negley Farson—an American journalist who always carried fishing gear with him whenever and wherever he travelled—recalls living in British Columbia in the early 1920s and purchasing flies 'invented by an English lady down on the coast'. I would bet my Sweetgrass bamboo rod that the lady in question was none other than Ethel Wilson. Her novel, *Swamp Angel*, follows Maggie Lloyd as she escapes a dead-end marriage by tying flies for a local sporting store. She learned the craft from her father, who in turn learned it from England's venerable House of Hardy. We meet Maggie as she is negotiating payment after winning praise for her work.

Maggie lights out for a fishing lodge forty kilometres from Kamloops. Whatever allegorical role the British Columbian interior plays in the novel, Wilson clearly loves its rich verdant splendour. En route to the lodge, Maggie spends an afternoon fishing the Similkameen River. Wilson's description of fly fishing is both evocative and attentive to detail.

For Maggie fly fishing in the wilderness symbolizes soul-singing freedom from a stifling urban existence and a suffocating marriage. Still Wilson grounds her protagonist in the here and now by encapsulating the essence of catching a trout on the fly. Refreshed after spending an afternoon of concentrated joy, during which she forgets her existential problems, Maggie gathers up her gear and resumes her journey into the future. Believe me, all fly anglers recognize this sense of momentary escape.

* * *

Following in the tradition of Boyd and Stevens and the Catskill fly-tying matriarchs, Joan proved highly accomplished at tying flies. Her objective is elegant in its simplicity: 'I want the fly to look as good to my eye as it looks to a fish's eye.' When asked about the pleasure she gets from tying, she drew a domestic comparison. 'It's the satisfaction of doing something as well as you can, like baking a terrific pie or cake.' And her skills have not been lost on fly tying's elite. The late Ian Colin James, one of Canada's most prominent instructors, tiers and guides, acknowledges Joan in his entertaining memoir *Fumbling with a Flyrod* as one of the country's best tiers. When I spent a delightful day with James on the Grand River he confided that meeting Joan 'was like meeting Wayne Gretzky'. Ruth Zinck, a Fly Fishers International award recipient, adapted a fly pattern in her friend's honour. A crayfish pattern based on Joan's original design, appropriately called *Joan's Cray*, was acknowledged in the 1990 *Patterns of the Masters*, in which Ruth described her friend as 'one of the best and most creative tiers I know'. The fly was subsequently praised in May 2002 on the *International Federation of Fly Fishers* website.

In the 1970s Joan got together with a half dozen fellow fly anglers. When the group dispersed, Joan and Ruth (before she moved West) were determined to continue meeting. They rented a room at a local community centre and soon a new fly fishing club was formed, eventually becoming KW Flyfishers.

Ironically a club owing so much to two women became dominated by men. Despite the disproportionate numbers, the club's male members—she refers to them as 'gentlemen'—always treated Joan with collegial respect, even admiration. She received a hearty ovation in 2008 when she joined the ranks of 'a very select group' by being inducted as a lifetime member.

Joan conceded that being a woman in a man's sport poses some challenges. 'At first fly fishermen would look at you slightly askance,' she said, adding she always believed that women 'had to be a little bit better than average to be accepted.' She need not have worried; she passed with flying fur and feather.

Joan has always believed that fly fishing offers a great deal to women who are temperamentally predisposed to doing it well. (Many male angling instructors concur with Joan's opinion.) 'Fly fishing requires patience and women are patient. They don't need the immediate gratification men do.' When I contacted Joan in 2016 I was pleased to learn that she was still tying masterful flies. Two years later her son contacted KW Flyfishers to donate some tying materials and to enquire whether any members would be interested in two pairs of women's waders and a waterproof Kede jacket, made in England—all in pristine condition. As with all the best things in life, fly fishing leads inevitably to a final cast.

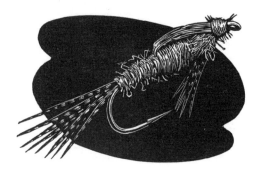

The Poetry of Fly Angling

The Compleat Angler brims with verse as well as song. In his celebrated discourse on angling Izaak Walton compares fishing to poetry. Good anglers 'not only bring an inquiring, searching, observing wit, [they] must bring a large measure of hope and patience, and a love and a propensity to the art itself.' Many poets before Sir Izaak, and many who followed, have given eloquent expression to the sentiments of the writer who, more than any other, is identified with the Contemplative Man's Recreation.

Angling poetry extends back thousands of years to China's Tang Dynasty, through Homer and Shakespeare, Donne and Goethe, Dylan Thomas and Yeats, to a range of contemporary poets including Federico Garcia Lorca, Derek Walcott and Margaret Atwood.

Those who have not been bitten by the mayfly bug might be surprised by the many prominent poets of the last century who have written about rivers, fish and angling, not to mention the thoughts and emotions, feelings and reflections they encompass. Some of my favourite American poets include: Ron Rash, Ted Kooser, Linda Hogan, Richard Hugo, Elizabeth Bishop, James Dickey, Robert Lowell, James Wright, William Stafford, Mary Oliver, W. S. Merwin, Sherman Alexie, Richard Wilbur, James Merrill, Robert Hass, Jim Dodge, Dan Gerber, Michael Delp and James Galvin. I am sure there are others, but I think I have made my point.

Walton's pithy observation applies to the fly angling poets—which is to say, the poets who sometimes write about fly angling—I cherish most: Raymond Carver, Ted Hughes, Jim Harrison and John Engels. These four writers do not merely write poetry about fly fishing, they embody and enact fly fishing in and through their poetry. Fly fishing is made manifest in, and emanates from, their poetry. In their distinct ways, they snatch sacramental language from the jaws of formal religion. They cast their poetic lines at sacred fish in holy water. They seek atonement and redemption through nature rather than within stone, marble and stained glass. Fly fishing, and the poetry it inspires, remain their covenant and testament.

Carver was celebrated as one of America's best short story writers before his death from lung cancer at the age of fifty in 1988. He was also an accomplished poet who published eight volumes in his lifetime. During the last five years of his post-alcoholic career, he oversaw publication of two major collections—*Where Water Comes Together with Other Water* and *Ultramarine*. A third collection, *New Path to the Waterfall*, was completed in the last weeks of his life and was published posthumously. His more than three hundred poems, including a handful of unpublished ones, are collected in *All of Us*.

Born in Oregon on the banks of the Columbia River and raised in Washington State, Carver spent much of his life in close proximity to the steelhead and salmon waters of the American Northwest Coast. He was an avid outdoorsman—both hunter and fisherman, including fly angler. He often hunted and fished with other notable writers who were also close friends, including Richard Ford.

In his lyric poetry Carver eschews the opaqueness and metaphorical obscurity that defines post-Pound and post-Eliot modernism. His spare and direct anecdotal poetry follows a tradition represented by Wilfred Owen and such Edwardian pastoralists as Edward Thomas, who before being killed in the trenches of Europe in 1917 was a close friend of Robert Frost.

Carver's poetry about rivers, fish and angling links him to English poet Ted Hughes. Not only did Hughes share the American writer's passion for fly fishing, but he also established a strong affinity with the salmon and steelhead waters of Canada's West Coast. He travelled widely in pursuit of trout and salmon including Ireland and Scotland, Iceland and Alaska, in addition to British Columbia. A passionate angler since childhood, Hughes wrote poems about fishing throughout his career. Some are among the best angling poems ever written. He wrote from inside fly angling with affection, respect and devotion, animated with a shudder of metaphysical terror and exultation.

Hughes acknowledged the importance of fishing to his identity, his life and his art in an interview with Thomas R. Pero conducted in British Columbia in 1995 and published in *Wild Steelhead and Salmon* in 1999. The poet describes fly fishing as a vital part of his existence, which connects him to elemental nature.

Had William Blake been a fly angler he would have written poems very much like Ted Hughes. Casting in the mystical tradition of Blake, Hughes saw fishing as a holy communion between tiger and lamb, as a sacrament between innocence and experience, as a marriage of heaven and hell. Hughes's love of fishing was part of his love of nature in all its raw, ferocious, predatory purity.

Hughes's great volume of river poems, simply titled *River*, not only accounts for rivers in all their manifold splendour, but the life rivers nurture and support, including eel, otter, bear, fox, mink, kingfisher, owl, crow, wren, skylark, heron and cormorant in addition to various species of fish, including bream, salmon and trout. The life cycle of salmon reflects the cycle of water from river to cloud to rain back to river. In *River* the currents of autobiography, hydrology and ecology merge with the currents of ritual, ceremony and myth to serve the river of poetry.

Hughes's love of fly fishing for salmon and steelhead in British Columbia—he dreamed of living in BC when he was a youngster reading the exploits of Roderick Haig-Brown—is chronicled in *Savage Gods, Silver Ghosts: In the Wild with Ted Hughes*, written by Ehor Boyanowsky, a professor at Simon Fraser University. Boyanowsky, who at the time of meeting Hughes was president of the Steelhead Society of British Columbia, offers a charming memoir that traces his relationship with 'my dear and great friend'.

The volume paints a portrait of the poet as 'a good, kind man', which contradicts the caricature painted in the popular media after his first wife, Sylvia Plath, committed suicide. With the exception of Ezra Pound, no poet in the last century was more vilified than Hughes. That he continued to write poetry, children's books, verse translations and literary criticism is a testament to his fierce devotion to literature, which was recognized in 1984 when he was appointed England's poet laureate.

Savage Gods, Silver Ghosts serves a full plate of talk about the joy of fly fishing for salmon and steelhead. Hughes was captivated by British Columbia and its rivers, especially the Dean, one of the world's great steelhead fisheries. Boyanowsky describes his friend as an unexceptional angler who was, nonetheless, a fish hawk.

Hughes was one of the twentieth century's supreme poets of nature who pierced the savage human heart. Just read his poem 'Pike' for confirmation. Boyanowsky depicts his friend as a committed conservationist, a man who defended the natural world with an eloquence befitting a poet of stature.

Like Hughes, Jim Harrison was a poet of wildness as much as wilderness. Writing poetry and fishing were synonymous because they penetrate the surface of consciousness to the dark primitive depths of the unconscious, both personal and collective.

Harrison wrote about water, fish and angling in many of his forty-two volumes of poetry, fiction (including novels, novellas and a children's book) and non-fiction (including a memoir and two essay collections), not to mention poetry broadsides and chapbooks, screenplays and hundreds of magazine and journal pieces from 1965 through 2017.

His two most significant river poems—the twenty-four-page title poem of *The Theory & Practice of Rivers* and the lyric suite 'River I' through 'River VII' in *Songs of Unreason*—comprise the heart of his writing. For Harrison rivers were not only metaphors or even symbols of life, but *life* itself. Writing and fly fishing were contractual bonds: the river of life and the river of art.

In a *Paris Review* interview with Jim Fergus, collected in *Conversations with Jim Harrison*, edited by Harrison's friend and fellow fly angler Robert DeMott, Harrison insisted that life becomes a river when lived properly. He made a similar point to Eleanor Wachtel in an interview on her syndicated CBC Radio show *Writers & Company*, saying that, humans, like any other creature, are an integral part of nature. He wrote about trees, bears, crows, ravens, wolves, coyotes, dogs and fish as if they were brothers and sisters of the same species—biologically as well as metaphysically or spiritually. In interviews he often observed that humans are linked genetically to trees, that he felt religious feelings towards bears and that humankind was connected mythically to animals.

The shared identification between humanity and nature, most notably water, fish, birds and animals, recurs throughout Harrison's poetry, especially his last four collections: *Saving Daylight, In Search of Small Gods, Songs of Unreason* and *Dead Man's Float*.

In 'Water', the opening poem in *Saving Daylight*, the poet asserts he was water before he was born and fish after he was born, which themselves become water. In 'Waves' the poet observes that water and humans are kin telling the same story. He adds that bodies are full of creeks and rivers. In 'The Fish in My Life' he refers to fish as brother and sister.

In Search of Small Gods abounds in shared identifications between humanity and nature. In 'Calendars' the poet says he *is* moving water; however, he resumes human shape so as not to scare his children, grandchildren, dogs and friends. In 'Spring' a spring creek is described as a liquid mouth that keeps the secrets of all local inhabitants. In 'Burning the Ditches' the poet imagines a distant land where life is a free-flowing river. In 'A Strange Poem' humans are depicted with fins bequeathed by gods who bestow life.

In 'Midnight Blues Planet' humans are categorized as marine organisms living at the bottom of the ocean of air. In 'Goat Boy' the poet declares humans are nature, *too*, adding that not all do well in our invented world. In 'Time' humans are compared to dogs that love morning walks. In 'Father' clouds are portrayed as cousins of the old man who is the poem's subject. Finally, in 'Eleven Dawns with Su Tung-p'o' the poet anticipates the glorious kingdom he will share with dogs, birds and fish.

In 'The River', near the end of *Dead Man's Float*, the poet imagines the beautiful river that flows by the throne of God, where He invented all the fish and birds that grace our Good Earth.

In an interview with Jerry Dennis, a fellow writer and fly angler

from Michigan's Upper Peninsula, Harrison recalls trout fishing with his father when he was a boy. When he asked his dad whether there was any difference between animals and humanity, his dad replied an emphatic *no*, adding that animals live out of doors, humankind lives indoors. Through his writing Harrison bridged the imaginal or spiritual gap between animal and human. In 'Herring', a late poem in his last collection, *Dead Man's Float*, he identifies with an unnamed bird more closely related to dinosaurs than to people. Similarly he sees himself in a bear as he sees the bear in himself. Like Hughes, Harrison acknowledges the primacy, potency and significance of nature not only through empathy and sympathy but through imaginative identification. For Harrison there was no schizophrenic split between self and nature, wilderness and culture, spirit and matter, subject and object, either and or, us and them, I and Thou. The tyranny of ego never factored into his love of, and devotion to, nature in its purest form. His stance toward the natural world—in which he lived and wrote all of his life, first in northern Michigan and then in Montana and Arizona—was one of deep humility and profound gratitude.

Reflecting Harrison's worldview as expressed though his poetry and prose, fly fishing is more than a practice of male macho pursuit (as it is often misunderstood), but a human pursuit in its own element— Nature. Harrison was a student of Zen for many years. In an interview with Lindsay Ahl, he suggests that fishing a river is akin to a Taoist practice because it is an aesthetic experience enclosed in mortality.

There is growing evidence that fly fishing, like music, is therapeutic, that it is healing. I am not going to pretend to be a doctor. Yet the motion involved in fly fishing—standing in, and amidst the sound of, moving water and engaged in the repetitive rhythm of casting—releases beneficial endorphins. Add to this physical element the mental element of erasing bad thoughts and it becomes even easier to affirm fly angling's holistic potential.

Harrison is one of a number of angling writers who have connected the art of fly fishing to Zen or Taoism.

John Engels's *Big Water* is the first volume of poems devoted solely to fishing and rivers to be published in America. His collected works, *Recounting the Season*, contains many others, including the superb 'An Angler's *vade mecum*' and the 'Fishing the Source' sequence from *Sinking Creek*. His longtime teaching companion and fly fishing buddy David Huddle wrote an afterward for *Big Water*. His words apply equally to Carver, Harrison and Hughes. Reading the poetry of these writers involves a return to the beginning of things, to the source, to the origins of existence. Their poetry poses elemental questions that do not offer answers, but encourages readers to be still and quiet in deep reverence. Ultimately, this is what fly fishing is about: to be enveloped in the golden light of Mystery.

Huddle puts his finger on why fly fishing appeals to so many poets, even those who do not fish. Poetry and fly fishing are compatible habits of imagination. The ability of poetry to distill vast distances of time and space and express complex ideas in evocative metaphors and symbols are just two applications of imagination that connect poetry with fly fishing.

Sounding like Blake, Huddle goes on to observe that returning to this elemental world—the visionary world of poetry—opens the shutters of purified, sophisticated perception. This is cleansing of the senses through the power of the imagination. What he is referring to here is the lost and essential world of childhood vision, of radical innocence that most adults forsake somewhere along the way—except those who possess poetic imaginations. And fly anglers.

Like Samuel Taylor Coleridge's poems of friendship (commonly known as 'conversation poems'), Raymond Carver's angling poems use casual, everyday language to examine the shared place of nature and humanity in the cosmos. Both intimate and personal, with a sense of the extraordinary underlying and informing the commonplace, the poems are about more than angling with their themes of mutability and mortality, love and death, joy and sorrow, rebirth and redemption. Following Coleridge's example, Carver's poems rise out of a particular set of circumstances (fishing) at particular places (rivers). They introduce sympathetic readers to the significant people in the poet's life including father, spouses, children and angling companions. The poems describe feelings and emotions occasioned by fishing in the present, while evoking memories of the past. They are by turns candid, vulnerable, tender, open and self-deprecating.

Carver's blue-collar poetic voice is clear and concise. He uses the contract between angler and fish or angler and water as symbols of deeper relationships: past and present, human (society) and non-human (nature), father and son, husband and spouse. He is a keen and attentive observer of nature, bringing to mind fellow West Coast poets Robinson Jeffers, Theodore Roethke and Gary Snyder. The natural world is both character and mood-setter, the atmospheric background to the poet's thoughts and anxieties—a momentary stay against uncertainty. At bottom Carver is a meditative poet. His poems are sombre reflections framed by the immediate environment.

* * *

Following are impressionistic reflections on some of Carver's angling poems. I believe that during his troubled life, fishing provided respite from the demons that lay in wait, ready to pounce from dark pools at the edge of his prose and verse. Although strikingly particular in their description of fly angling, they transcend subject, theme and setting.

'**Near Klamath**' captures and celebrates the male camaraderie that has always been a component of fishing (and hunting), not to mention fishing (and hunting) camps. This sense of brotherhood or fraternity is often dismissed and ridiculed as male-bonding. I know men who hunt and fish, not only to catch fish or kill animals, but to share fellowship in communion with nature. Such thoughts would embarrass these men who know nothing of Robert Bly's *Iron John*. The poem is an expression of a male communal experience. It is a primeval impulse of the clan, a remnant of a time when men ventured out together to hunt and fish to feed women and children, the elderly and the sick. It was a rite of passage from childhood to manhood, when the ability to bring home the meat (including fish) was celebrated and revered. It was a mark of honour. And it remains a form of masculine love.

'**Poem for Hemingway & W.C. Williams**' is an account of the perennial angling debate of 'catch & eat' vs. 'catch & release', the latter a conservation ethic developed after the Second World War. It also pays homage to two very different men and very different writers, both of whom bridge the two streams of Carver's art—short story and poetry. Carver knows well the 'ex-heavyweight' Ernest Hemingway's stories, especially the Nick Adams stories, including 'Big Two-Hearted River'. Similarly he recognizes the influence of the physician/poet in his poetry. Slyly Carver sends the two writers off upstream without resolving the debate on which the poem is built.

'**Bobber**' might well be titled 'Fathers and Sons'. In a few lines Carver reveals what all men know: there are blood fathers and chosen fathers, the latter of whom are teachers, mentors—and fishing companions. The poem is a work-in-progress toward a definition of masculinity, of manhood. It is also one of Carver's many memory poems, extending back to his troubled childhood, with his difficult father and the spectre of alcohol that would usurp Carver's life for many years and shape much of his writing. It is futile, but readers cannot help wondering what kind of writer Carver would have been had alcohol not dominated so much of his life. It is useless to speculate about whether he would have been more prolific or even more accomplished. Would he have ever written a novel, not that it matters. Or was alcohol essential to the writer and his art—even if ultimately destructive?

'**The Current**' asserts that all true anglers are dreamers. David Adams Richards opens *Lines on the Water* by recalling a dream he had in childhood of fishing before he ever went fishing, of fishing before he ever caught anything and knowing fishermen before he became one. I often enter a dream-state while fly fishing, casting to my inner river as much as to the river in which I am wading. I lose track of time, I cast from muscle memory. I am jolted 'awake' when a fish suddenly strikes.

Conversely, all anglers must be realists. Dreaming does not put food on the table. That requires the example of fish holding against the current, who survive by eating more calories than they burn getting food. Dream or not, this poem conveys a sense of nature up close and personal. It is based on careful, attentive observation, the result of a heightened awareness of the behaviour of fish, viewed sympathetically and compassionately. I cannot help thinking of Thoreau looking into the depths of Walden Pond, only to find his Self peering back.

'**Deschutes River**' begins with a scene of violent nature reminiscent of Tennyson's 'red in tooth and claw'. It is survival of the fiercest, beginning in nature and ending in domestic discord.

The poem is a reflection on the winter of the heart, a meditation on despair made bearable by the sacramental act of fishing. It is devastating, starting mundanely but crawling inextricably to its train-wreck final two lines. The poem is a reminder that solitude, so necessary to writing, is one of fly angling's great gifts.

I know of what Carver speaks. I was once wearing a comparable pair of waders, fishing alone on a river on my birthday, eight months after my wife and I separated. She was in the arms of another man and, because my two sons were 'far away' figuratively rather than literally, I feared losing them more than anything I had ever feared. Fly fishing helped me survive that time of abject failure, aching loss and regret verging on clinical despair.

'Where Water Comes Together with Other Water' wades into the current of such memorable birthday poems as Dylan Thomas's 'Poem on His Birthday' and Engels's 'Poem for Your Birthday.' It is also a hymn of love, a bardic ode not only to rivers but to what rivers symbolize—the continuum of life from source to mouth. With the exception of his love poems to Tess Gallagher, Carver never wrote a poem more joyous because he surrenders to the sacred places of rivers. These are tears of joy set to the music of rivers.

'The Catch' is another devastating poem that creeps up on a reader until the last two lines deliver a punch to the solar plexus. The angler's sense of loneliness is not only profound but final—the lid closing on a coffin. Observing the difference between a raindrop and a brook trout is Carver at his poetic best. It initially seems prosaic, but upon contemplation becomes quietly visionary, reminiscent of William Blake when he writes:

> To see a World in a Grain of Sand
> And a Heaven in a Wild Flower
> Hold Infinity in the palm of your hand
> And Eternity in an hour.

'The Debate' poses the question: to work or play, that is the question. There is a little bit of Tom Sawyer in all anglers. There is a little Huck Finn in all fly anglers. Like all sport, fly angling is play—men playing a boys' game.

In a lecture given at Montana State University examining whether fishing has meaning, Thomas McGuane referenced twentieth-century Dutch philosopher Johan Huizinga when he considered fly fishing in terms of fun. He affirmed that the recreational sport is neither inane nor shallow, but is an aesthetic activity. Fun and play allow us to expel feelings of monotony. The first characteristic of fun is freedom which satisfies a hunger for beauty. Casting a fly line is casting to Beauty.

I would like to turn to my two favourite Carver poems before ending with a consideration of the poem that is likely to leave most non-angling readers perplexed.

'**For Tess**' unites Carver's two great loves: Tess Gallagher and rivers. It is a poignant poem, more complex than it initially appears, celebrating a fleeting moment of unconditional happiness. It begins by stating a fact that is obvious to those who fly fish—catching fish is wonderful but simply being out on the water is its own reward. The gratitude regarding fishing is in a minor key; the gratitude regarding Tess is in a major key. The poem of thanksgiving is too tough to be maudlin and too honest to be bathetic.

'**The Trestle**' is as beautiful as it is tender; equal parts dream poem, memory poem and love poem. It also pays homage to the creative imagination. The poet recalls fishing as a youngster with his 'sweet' father. Cold pure water flows into memory as cold pure memory flows into water. He remembers the love his father had for his deceased wife and for the place where he lived in the West. His father died in his sleep and the poet wishes his own life and death were as simple. *If only....*

It might seem questionable judgment to end the chapter on a menacing note. However this is the Carver poem that is likely most difficult for readers, including some fly anglers, to wrap their imaginations around. Although the poem describes a common enough occurrence on the water, it might require something of a suspension of disbelief fully understand. *Unless you have experienced it yourself.*

'**The River**' records a momentary encounter with an actively malevolent nature. One evening an angler wades into the dark water with the current swirling around his legs. He feels the angry eyes of the salmon watching him. It makes his skin crawl. But there is something else, unidentified and unspecified, that brushes against his wading boot, causing the hair on the back of his neck to rise. The whole riverscape becomes ominous. He is scared, but continues casting, praying that nothing strikes. For me Carver's poem strikes a sympathetic chord with Ted Hughes's anthropological imagination which is roused by menacing currents. In 'Last Night', a poem collected in *River*, Hughes writes about the *evil* mood that results from casting to *evil* fish in an *evil* river.

The experience Carver (and Hughes) writes about might be difficult for some readers to grasp. However, I recognize the encounter with hostile nature as an experience that permeates the Canadian literary imagination. Those who feel lost in this sinister forest can get their bearings by reading Margaret Atwood's *Strange Things*, a collection of lectures about the Malevolent North in Canadian Literature.

Art history provides another guide by way of an aesthetic system of classification drawn from nature developed in the eighteenth century involving notions of the Sublime, the Beautiful and the Picturesque. This might seem wide of the piscatorial mark, but stay with me as I apply this system of analysis to fly angling literature which, in turn, describes existential experiences on the water.

As I have done frequently in *Casting into Mystery* I turn to Thoreau. As a meditation on living *Walden* is an example of the Picturesque. As a literary and philosophical travelogue *A Week on the Concord and Merrimack Rivers* is an example of the Beautiful. *The Maine Woods*, specifically when Thoreau ascends Mount Katahdin, is an example of the Sublime. In his intellectual study *Henry Thoreau*, Robert D. Richardson describes the top of Mount Katahdin as cold and primitive. In *Natural Life*, David M. Robinson identifies the ascent as spiritual along the path to enlightenment. Finally in *Thoreau*, Laura Dassow Walls characterizes the episode as a parody of the pastoral. Thoreau himself describes confronting 'Titanic inhuman nature'.

Now to apply this aesthetic model to an imaginary portrait of fly fishing. A solitary angler dressed in tweed casting dry flies upstream to rising trout on an English chalk stream on a warm summer day is an image of the Picturesque. The scene is familiar rather than wild, in which the angler fits in comfortably with his surroundings. Add mountains in the background and rolling clouds and the picture of tranquility becomes an image of the Beautiful.

But fly fishing runs deeper and darker. A fly angler sometimes casts toward the Sublime, at least momentarily, with its intimation of awe and terror. This is when solitude becomes overwhelming, inciting a sense of fear. I am not talking Stephen King horror story here, but a shiver of the sinister. Following are examples from angling literature, specifically prose, that describe a comparable experience to what Carver describes in his poem.

Fly anglers who fish off the grid—in dense forest or isolated mountain streams or in the darkness of night—have at one time or another been spooked by 'the indistinct edgings' of 'something too wild to trust', as Kevin Brennan observes in his novel *Parts Unknown*. This is an apprehension of momentary dread—complete with psychological and metaphysical anxiety.

Most fly anglers agree that the darkness of night is the spookiest time to be on a river, casting to unknown depths at unseen fish engaged in an audible ritual of voracious cannibalism. Anglers cannot employ light sources because to do so would be unsporting, if not outright illegal. Consequently they are engulfed in suffocating darkness.

In his essay 'Night Fishing', collected in *Fishless Days, Angling Nights*, Sparse Grey Hackle writes evocatively about a thick and claustrophobic darkness that conceals both menace and terror.

In *Holy Water* Jerry Kustich recalls fishing into the night:

I pass by the defunct power pole where on another occasion the bone-chilling banshee shriek of a great-horned owl rudely awoke me from the somnolent trance only fishing in blackness can induce. I am never comfortable in this world, a state of constant goose bumps, a realm best suited for creatures that are not human. The night holds many mysteries.

But there is more than darkness lying in wait, ready to pounce on the sensibilities of unsuspecting fly anglers. In *Blood Knots: A Memoir of Fathers, Friendship and Fishing* English writer Luke Jennings writes about landing a Northern pike and glimpsing the face of creation in all its cruel, fearless, exaltation.

Scots-bred writer Ian Niall is more nuanced in *Trout from the Hills*, but he too expresses a sense of something unsettling beyond sensory apprehension, quietly lurking in the shadows. He writes about a fly fisherman on a remote lake, deep in the hills of Wales. Alone and far from the warmth, comfort and companionship of the hearth, the angler is shrouded in an unsettling enchantment as he perceives the spirits of men, long dead, whispering from the deep shadows.

In his angling memoir *A Man May Fish* Irish writer T.C. Kingsmill Moore opens the door of perception onto another dimension when he recalls fishing alone at night and hearing the voices of the dead calling from the river, as time and place dissolve into darkness.

It is interesting that one of the great works of fiction that involves fly angling describes an encounter with malevolent nature: Ernest Hemingway's 'Big Two-Hearted River'. Considering that so many fly anglers have felt this uncanny apprehension of unspecified dread, is it any wonder Hemingway recognized its presence? I believe he knew this feeling intimately—perhaps it was the last thing he felt on 2 July 1962, in Ketchum, Idaho, when he placed his double-barrelled, twelve-gauge Boss shotgun in his mouth.

Conjecture aside, he gives expression to the sensation when Nick Adams comes across the swamp at the end of the story. I have often wondered what Hemingway means by 'tragic' in regard to fishing. Might he be getting at that which Norman Maclean refers to as shadow-casting? One thing I know, his conclusion to 'The Big Two-Hearted River' is both eerie and haunting:

Ahead the river narrowed and went into a swamp. The river became smooth and deep and the swamp looked solid with cedar trees, their trunks close together, their branches solid. It would not be possible to walk through a swamp like that.... In the swamp the banks were bare, the big cedars came together overhead, the sun did not come through, except in patches; in the fast, deep water, in the half light, the fishing would be tragic. In the swamp fishing was a tragic adventure.

The poems of fish, rivers and angling are many and diverse, spanning thousands of years and encompassing the globe. They span literary traditions, genres and styles. In imagery and metaphor, theme and form, function and practice, they transcend their ostensible subjects. It is unlikely that William Blake ever held a fishing pole, let alone a fly rod. Had he followed in the waders of John Donne, he might have declared that every fish that swims is 'an immense world of delight'. Regardless, I am grateful for Raymond Carver, Jim Harrison, John Engels and Ted Hughes—fly anglers who cast into the mystery with lines of visionary poetry.

Rivers of Song

I am a fly angler with big ears, which is to say I love music—all genres and all styles. I learned to play guitar in my teens and continued fingerpicking my way through the same couple of dozen songs for half a century. At one time I knew every chord and every word of every song on Gordon Lightfoot's first half dozen records.

I first wrote about acoustic music while an undergraduate at Trent University. I wrote about music professionally for close to four decades. After taking up fly fishing I became interested in music about rivers, fish and angling, which complemented my interest in literature, film and visual art devoted to the same subjects.

As my personal library of books and my art collection grew in response to my passion for fly fishing, so did my music library. Some of the music predates becoming a fly angler. Most I would have collected because of my interest in music. However, I acquired some in response to fly angling specifically.

I most often cast my ear on contemporary acoustic roots music, whether folk, country, bluegrass, country blues or vintage jazz. Although I am not a big fan of country pop, some of its biggest stars have written and/or recorded songs related to fishing including Nitty Gritty Dirt Band ('Fishing in the Dark'), Brad Paisley ('I'm Going to Miss Her'), Kenny Chesney ('Save It for a Rainy Day'), Trace Adkins ('Just Fishing') and Tim McGraw ('Don't Take the Girl').

Anglers who enjoy acoustic music and prefer one-stop shopping can do no better than *Fishing Music* and *Fishing Music II*. The companion volumes were co-produced by Ben Winship and David Thompson, close friends, fellow musicians and keen fly fishermen who were living in the shadow of Yellowstone Park in 2002 when they first started discussing the project. Each album features sixteen instrumentals and songs bridging a variety of genres.

Encompassing adaptations, covers and original compositions, the material is performed by accomplished acoustic musicians including

Tim and Molly O'Brien, Mike Dowling, David Grier, Matt Flinner, Karine Polwart, Rob Ickes and Jeffrey Foucault.

The pair of discs cover such familiar musical water as Django Reinhardt's 'Pêche à la Mouche' ('Fly Fishing'), Duke Ellington's 'I'm Gonna Go Fishin'', Hoagy Carmichael's 'Lazy Fishing' (the composer is the father of master bamboo fly rod builder Hoagy Carmichael Jr.) and A. P. Carter's 'The Winding Stream', in addition to arrangements of Doc Watson's 'Deep River Blues' and Taj Mahal's 'Fishing Blues'. 'The Fishin' Hole' was the theme song for *The Andy Griffith Show*, a television sitcom from the 1960s. Remember the town of Mayberry, Aunt Bee, bumbling Barney Fife and Opie (a young Ron Howard)?

While many songs depict water and fishing literally, others express fishing and water as metaphors for life, including desire and romance, love and heartbreak, family and companionship, community and the outdoors. A few songs are specifically about fly fishing including Tim Bays's 'The Importance of Fishing', Foucault's 'Mayfly', Thompson's 'Upstream and Old Bamboo', Winship's 'Waiting on the Evening Rise' and Winship and Thompson's 'Madison Brown'.

These are the CDs I most often slip into the car audio system when heading out for a day's fishing. Playing them loud with the windows down, I traverse southwestern Ontario farm country, passing Mennonite horse and buggy en route to rising trout or hungry bass. Although few Canadian songwriters have written specifically about fish or fishing, the Canadian wilderness, not to mention lakes and rivers, are abundant leitmotifs.

No songwriter has expressed the beauty of the Canadian wilderness, and used nature to represent human emotion, more eloquently than Gordon Lightfoot. From 'Long River' on his major label debut, through the serene ballad 'Peaceful Waters' to 'River of Light', a more recent song, rivers have inspired Canada's great balladeer who was also an enthusiastic canoeist. He mentions rainbow trout in a song of that title. However, it is one of his weaker efforts, a light ditty with forgettable melody and hackneyed lyrics unworthy of the species.

Joni Mitchell's 'River' from her masterwork album *Blue* is one of the loveliest, most plaintive songs I know of. For decades I have listened to this national dream-song deep into the long lost hours of lonely nights. At some time or another we all yearn for a frozen river on which to skate away.

Blue Rodeo—a country-rock band I have followed since their early days as darlings of Toronto's Queen Street West indie music scene—has recorded songs inspired by rivers, including 'Mystic River'. Co-songwriter Jim Cuddy associates rivers with hope in the heart-aching romantic ballad 'Pull Me Through'.

Eileen McGann is a visual artist in addition to a songwriter, interpreter of traditional folk song and composer. Spanning genre and form, recurring themes inform her art, including nature, ecology, spirituality, social justice and gender identity. In 'Rushing River' she acknowledges salmon as symbols of wisdom (following the Celtic tradition) whose life cycle is emblematic of perseverance and sacrifice.

> Rushing river, sparkling water
> You share your joy with me
> Dancing downward to the ocean
> Bringing new life to the sea ...
>
> And meantime like the salmon, I
> keep struggling 'gainst the flow
> Maybe someday I will learn to turn
> And tumbling dancing down I'll go.

Before disbanding after a quarter century, Tamarack—the Guelph, Ontario–based folk trio consisting at the time of founding member James Gordon with Alex Sinclair and Gwen Swick—recorded a concept album *On the Grand*, a collection of thirteen historically inspired songs celebrating the Heritage River. The album consists entirely of original material, augmented by Gordon's musical setting of Mohawk poet Pauline Johnson's nineteenth-century poem 'The Song My Paddle Sings'.

Over the years Tamarack recorded many songs in praise of the Canadian landscape and wilderness experience from various perspectives including aesthetic (natural beauty of the land), historical and political. Gordon, the group's primary songwriter, continued to write about these subjects after going solo, including 'Riverboy Blue', 'The Silence of the Snow' and the title track from *Coyote's Calling*.

Rivers become a primary subject in Gordon's concept album, *This Canoe Runs on Water*, which celebrates the Trent-Severn Waterway system. The title track pays tribute to Peterborough's canoe-building tradition, spanning history, manufacturing and curatorship thanks to the Canadian Canoe Museum.

Like his earlier song, 'Our White Man's Word' from *On the Grand*, Gordon expresses his deep respect to First Nations people. This time he honours the indigenous stewards of the Narrows, a traditional waterway meeting place between Lake Simcoe and Lake Couchiching. In 'Pretty Channel' Gordon evokes the spirit of Tom Thomson. The artist is so inextricably linked to the landscape that he has become a figure of speech:

> The ochred rocks the jack pine
> trees, looking so Tom
> Thomsony
> Striking poses against the
> purple Severn Sky....

Gordon is one of many Canadian acoustic artists, groups and ensembles who have written songs and/or musical portraits of Thomson and the Group of Seven, including Mae Moore ('Tom Thomson's Mandolin'), The Tragically Hip ('Three Pistols'), Rheostatics (*Music Inspired by the Group of 7*), Tony Quarrington (*Group of Seven Suite*), Kurt Swinghammer (*Turpentine Wind*) and Algonquin Ensemble (*Sonic Palette*).

The pastoralism that informs 'River Country' applies equally to the rivers and lakes I routinely fish. Gordon endows a section of the Trent River in Eastern Ontario with the peace and tranquility that I find through a fly rod.

> Nestled in the Seven Hills, you
> will find a peaceful place,
> Where the rat race slows to a
> gentle flow ...
> You'll find that life is but stream ...
> Where the fishermen gather ...

The album concludes on a cautionary note in which desecrating rivers is described as communal emotional abuse. Environmental destruction is the single most significant and urgent threat to the survival of fly angling.

Ian Tamblyn is unique in terms of music devoted to the landscape. While he has not written songs devoted specifically to fish or fishing, no Canadian songwriter or composer has been inspired more by wilderness than Tamblyn, whether North of Superior, Algoma, the Laurentians, Far North or Antarctica. No contemporary musician better embodies and reflects the enduring spirit of Thomson and the Group of Seven. Tamblyn casts his lyric line on Thomson and the Group with *Walking in the Footprints: Celebrating the Group of Seven*. Produced in partnership with the Art Gallery of Sudbury, the concept album features fifteen original tracks. 'My Heart Belongs to the Northland in Spring' tells of Thomson returning to Algonquin Park after a winter of painting in his Toronto studio, which he did for five consecutive years until his death in 1917:

> Back to Algonquin springtime is coming
> Ice on the lake the geese on the wing
> Shadows still long, snowflakes white blinding
> My heart belongs to the Northland this spring....

Of all the music devoted to Canada's most famous collective of artists, *Walking in the Footsteps* is my favourite. The songwriter has intimate experience of the Canadian Shield which inspired the painters. He not only researched his subjects but developed his own perspective. Listeners familiar with the artists can identify them through the lyrics, which capture their personalities and creative temperaments. Conversely, listeners discovering Thomson and the Group for the first time are well served by such a knowledgeable and generous introduction.

A playwright, composer and writer who has travelled the globe, bridging the Arctic Circle and Antarctica under the auspices of scientific and artistic adventure, Tamblyn has spent a lifetime immersed in the natural world. His relationship to nature defines his art and provides the soundtrack of his life.

'Woodsmoke and Oranges' is an earlier song which Tamblyn describes in liner notes as 'at the heart of the Superior Quest'. Long before *Walking in the Footsteps*, the song is reminiscent of Group of

Seven paintings inspired by the north shore of Superior in the decade following the First World War.

> By woodsmoke and oranges, path of old canoe,
> I would course the inland ocean to be back to you.
> No matter where I go to, it's always home again
> To the rugged northern shore, and the days of sun and wind ...

I know of no artist in any discipline who views himself as such an integral part of nature, which therefore shapes the contours of his art.

> In the land of the silver birch, cry of the loon
> There's something 'bout this country, it's a part of me and you.

Tamblyn is painting a picture with words—sorry for the cliché but I am being literal. The words arise out of the songwriter's direct and immediate experience of nature. He and nature are one sentient organism. Rivers continue to pull on the guitar strings of Tamblyn's heart, soul and imagination. His most recent recording, *Let It Go*, released in 2018, opens with 'Where the Wild River Flows':

> Where the wild river flows I will follow
> Northbound with the geese on high
> I will follow the sound of their calling....

The song reminds me of two poems set in rural Kentucky I greatly admire. Wendell Berry's short poem 'Listen!' recounts the pleasure of hearing wild geese crying above the river. Robert Penn Warren's 'Tell Me a Story' is a memory poem in which the sound of geese flying northward is equated with storytelling as anodyne to the erosion of Time. I have stopped casting many times, taking deep delight in Canada geese laying claim to a stretch of river.

Chris Hadfield is Canada's celebrity guitar-wielding, crooning astronaut. While less famous, brother Dave Hadfield is a talented songwriter whose songs are devoted to the Canadian North. A pilot, canoeist, sailor and wilderness tripper as well as a musician, the lesser-known Hadfield conveys a deep respect for the spirit of the land through albums such as *Northern Breeze* and *Wilderness Waltz*.

Clawhammer five-string banjo virtuoso Chris Coole is well known to Canadian fans of old-time country, bluegrass and folk music. He has fished all his life. In the liner notes to *The Road to the River*, which follows his earlier release *The Tumbling River and Other Stories*, he writes that the collection of fourteen tunes and songs was 'inspired by the fishing passion'. He adds that he comes from a family with 'a fishing tradition' that grew out of a cottage in rural Ontario. It was only a matter of time before he became a fly angler.

He acknowledges that fishing influences his music as much as music influences his fishing. Both are forms of artistry. 'For me, the artist's highest challenge is to create something that somehow attempts to reflect nature's perfect, simple, beauty, while acknowledging his or her place within it.' The fly anglers I know agree with this sentiment. Coole recognizes many parallels between the tradition and practice of fly fishing and music-making, including 'rhythm, timing and touch'. Not surprisingly he shares my enjoyment of listening to fishing tunes in the car en route to a river. With such titles as 'Rainbows on the Moormons', 'Lost River', 'Copper Run', 'The Tumbling River', 'Elk River Blues' and 'Cutthroat', Coole not only keeps me company but inspires me to take my chances with fur and feather.

When I contacted and informed the musician I wanted to include him in *Casting into Mystery*, my timing could not have been better. He replied that he was preparing for a trip to the Catskills.

'I just walked upstairs from my tying vise to discover your email,' he wrote. 'I'm heading down to the Delaware and I am tying up some streamers as the river is bound to be high. I'm going with my friend Joe, who is a mandolin maker and player who guided on the Delaware for something like thirty years. The other friend we are meeting up with is a banjo maker/fiddle and banjo picker named Glen Carson. They are both excellent fishermen who probably get in a hundred days a year down there. There is definitely something to the music and fishing connection.'

Our exchange confirms that, while you can take the musician out of fly fishing, you cannot take fly fishing out of the musician.

The fly fishing songs closest to my heart involve a trio of longtime friends, two American, one Canadian: fly angling and sometime creative companions Greg Brown and the late Bill Morrissey, as well as Garnet Rogers.

Morrissey was an avid bamboo fly angler. He published all his original songs on Dry Fly Music. A photo on the back of his sophomore album, *North*, shows Morrissey landing a trout in what is most assuredly a river in his native New England. The artwork on *The Essential Collection* is a graphic of a broadly smiling artist waist deep in a river, waving a fly rod. *North* contains a pair of angling songs including 'Ice Fishing' and the superb closing track, 'Fishin' a Stream I Once Fished as a Kid'.

'Ice Fishing' is an account of that most elemental form of fishing. There is nothing more basic than drilling a hole into a frozen lake, sitting on a bait bucket and dropping down a wiggly creature on the end of a hook. Nothing is further from casting an artificial fly at rising trout. Yet, like any true fisherman, Morrissey finds redemption in the act. The song conveys a sense of wonderment. Its lyrics express the important things in life: love, family, home and creative gifts, which have to be cared for through attentiveness and devotion.

'Fishin' a Stream I Once Fished as a Kid' is a memory song about the journey of life that refutes Thomas Wolfe's notion of never going home again. Morrissey contends you never really leave—at least if you are a fly angler. He prefers trout, but will fish for bass in the alternative. He prefers whiskey but will not turn down a frosty beer. When standing in a trout stream, he casts to the still point of the Eternal Now, where past and future merge with the present.

This is a song of yearning, nostalgia and dream—feelings fly anglers recognize inherently. I cannot listen to the song without my eyes welling. It is prophetic, sadly the reference to whiskey is revealing because it was the demon that drew the gifted songwriter to a premature grave. *Greg Brown & Bill Morrissey: Friend of Mine* features a dozen duets of traditional ballads, covers (including Ferron's 'Ain't Life a Brook') and original songs, including Brown's heartfelt 'Fishing with Bill'. The two longtime friends reunite after a winter of undisclosed sorrow.

There is growing medical evidence that fly fishing can help heal those who are broken, estranged or lost. Veterans returning from harm's way, survivors of diseases that ravage mind, body and spirit and first responders who suffer the pain and grief they witness find solace in fly fishing. The angling companions cast their souls on the river, acknowledging that fly fishing is restorative, by turns ritualistic, metaphysical and spiritual. They are not only fishing buddies, but pilgrims in waders on the path of life, symbolized by the river.

Brown uses his knowledge of fly fishing to sketch a detailed picture. He begins by drawing a distinction between the delicacy of fishing for fussy brook trout in New England and the coarseness of tossing gaudy flies at proletarian crappie and chub in the midwest.

He affirms that fly angling is about both friendship (a communal act) and imagination (a solitary act). It is a creative partnership with nature, as he acknowledges through his reference to Roderick Haig-Brown, one of the great writers in the history of fly fishing who lived most of his life on Canada's West Coast. The songwriter acknowledges that fly fishing for trout is neither sport nor pastime—something inconsequential to while away the hours—but part of a noble tradition extending back centuries.

Brown views fly fishing as quiet respite from the vagaries and vicissitudes of living before engaging in improvised banter with his dear friend, creative collaborator, drinking buddy and angling companion. This is about as close as fly fishing gets to a fellowship. Two troubadours in hip waders casting forward the tradition represented by Walton and Cotton, they exchange barbs about choice of fly and where to cast to entice wily trout. Then they debate the merits of catch-and-release versus catch-and-eat.

Rogers met Morrissey and Brown long before he pursued a solo career following the death of his brother Stan on 2 June, 1983. He is not a fly angler but he conveys the essence of the recreational sport in 'Shadows on the Water', his deeply felt and moving tribute to Morrissey. In one of my many chats with Garnet over the years he asked whether he got the fly fishing right. I replied that he got it as right as an upstream cast with a dry fly to rising trout.

Rogers begins by listing the fly angling gear his friend can expect to find in Paradise, including:

> … a split cane rod, with two-pound test
> there's an old felt hat you like the best.
> And there's a book of flies
> in a canvas vest
> in the hallway by the door.

And there's a river, deep and cool
lots of shade, and sheltered pools.

Rogers has the stage demeanour of a standup comedian. His irreverent banter often contrasts with the emotional sensitivity of his songs. His sense of humour comes across, when he observes:

Those damned trout
still make you look a fool
there's just so much even God can do.…

In the penultimate verse Rogers associates fly fishing with other creative acts: music, books and poetry. And there are 'lots of friends for you to see.' For me, this succinctly sums up the essentials of a fulfilling life. He ends by acknowledging that he has 'lost track of all the souls who've passed/Like shadows on the water …'.

As much as I admire 'Fishin' a Stream I Once Fished as a Kid', 'Fishing with Bill' and 'Shadows on the Water', great songs by any standard, my favourite fly fishing song is Brown's 'Eugene', the heart of *The Evening Call*. In my estimation it is the single *best* angling song ever written. I think of it as Thoreau's *Walden* set to music—as high a level of praise as I can offer.

The interrelated themes of rivers, fish and fishing recur throughout Brown's music, including 'If I Had Known' from *Down in There*, 'In the Water' from *In the Dark with You*, 'The Poet Game' from *The Poet Game* and 'Spring Wind' and 'Laughing River' from *Dream Cafe*. 'Eugene' is greater than the sum of all the earlier songs.

Following in the tradition of *Walden*, 'Eugene' demonstrates how readers and listeners can open their arms to the earth's embrace. Book and song are philosophical in espousing an ethic as well as an aesthetic. They are religious in the sense of being awake and alive to the holiness of nature. Both are handbooks on how to live the good life, a life of honesty, integrity and dignity along the path less travelled.

Brown never mentions Thoreau, but the New England Transcendentalist casts a long shadow across 'Eugene'. Consequently I view the narrative song as a spiritual brother of Edward Abbey's essay 'Down the River with Henry Thoreau' which opens his collection *Down the River*.

In his pastoral ballad Brown evokes the spirit of Thoreau to 'simplify, simplify, simplify'. Talking in a walking blues rhythm rather than actually singing, the songwriter's rich bass-baritone reaches a deep spot, like Kentucky bourbon sipped from a tin cup in front of a campfire under a blanket of stars. Solace for a restless mind, a searching heart, an aching soul.

Brown starts off on his soul journey deceptively prosaically. He thinks he will drive his pickup and 'slide-in camper' to Eugene, Oregon. The destination might seem casual, but it is chosen with care. Eugene is located at the southern end of the Willamette Valley, near the confluence the McKenzie and Willamette rivers, about eighty kilometres east of the Oregon coast. These are legendary fly fishing waters with a rich tradition of salmon, wild trout and native steelhead. Do not be fooled; Brown is not your average trout bum. Eugene is a cultural centre, home to two universities, including the state university and a community college. The blend of verdant natural beauty, recreational opportunities tied to the outdoors, and range of arts is critical to Brown, a most literate songwriter.

Like Thoreau, Brown is interested in the nature of life as much as the life of nature. He begins by framing fly fishing, with its custom-built bamboo rod and 'book of flies from a Missoula pawn shop', in a tradition of master craftsmanship he equates with vintage music instruments—in this case the classic Gibson JF45 'made by women

during World War II'. I agree wholeheartedly with the correlation between guitars and fly rods. Both instruments of rhythm are extensions of the human body. Thus he connects fly fishing with music, two of his great passions.

He then catalogues the practical essentials—'coffee stained stack of maps', propane stove, quilts, can opener, cans of kippers and smoked oysters, 'gun powder tea, a copper teapot and a good sharp knife'. I would bet money Brown has in mind the American-made Buck knife, originally made from steel files and farm tools. The list reminds me of the 'Economy' chapter in *Walden*.

Thoreau accompanies Brown as he rises to the New England mystic's challenge to 'front only the essential facts of life, and see if [he] could not learn what it had to teach, and not, when [he] came to die, discover that [he] had not lived'. Like Thoreau, Brown is 'a sojourner in nature', albeit with a bamboo fly rod in one hand and a guitar in the other. The song is his response to Thoreau's declaration: 'However mean your life is, meet it and live it.'

> Sometimes you have to go—look for your life.
> I'll park by some rivers, cook up some rice and beans, read
> Ferlinghetti out loud, talk to the moon, tell her all my
> life tales, she's heard them many times…

Again like Thoreau, Brown is interested not so much in fly fishing, but in how to live. Fly fishing is a metaphor for living with open heart and attentive mind—in other words, consciously aware of one's surroundings and one's self. This is an integration of inner and outer in which the disparate elements of existence coalesce into one harmonious whole.

Unfolding like a meandering river, the song is Brown's reply to Thoreau's philosophy of living 'deliberately' in opposition to those who 'lead lives of quiet desperation.' Echoing Thoreau's accusatory voice, not to mention the scolding tone of Abbey, the songwriter repudiates 'the blandification of the whole situation'.

After casting his line in the Northwest, Brown plans to head southeast, through 'the moonscapes of Utah', to the White and Kern rivers of the Ozarks—another angling haven, not of trout, but of bass. Brown's distinction between the two species is both charming and accurate. I smile every time I hear him meander through this passage in his bottom-of-the-barrel voice. Using a cultural metaphor he succinctly acknowledges a historical debate among fly anglers about the status of species deemed 'worthy' of the fly.

> Those smallmouth are great on a fly rod. And
> they're not all finicky like trout. Trout are English and
> bass are Polish. And if I wasn't born in Central Europe I
> should have been. Maybe it's not too late. Sometimes you
> have to dream deep to find your real life at all.

Brown invites listeners to bite off, chew and digest the last couple of lines. Dream deep, dream deep, dream deep. The songwriter's advice recalls Thoreau asserting: 'If one advances confidently in the direction of his dreams, and endeavours to live the life he has imagined, he will meet with a success unexpected in common hours.' Like all fly anglers, he knows with certainty that hours spent on a trout river are never wasted.

Brown then traverses Tennessee into North Carolina. Although born in the midwest, where he has lived all his life, the Blue Ridge Mountains become a sanctuary at the sacred heart of his journey around America. For Brown the area—which was home to abundant wild brook trout before the devastation of acid rain and other industrial practices—is the equivalent of Walden Pond. Consequently he honours brook trout as holy creatures.

Brown's description of brook trout as 'God's reminder that creation is a good idea' reminds me of 'River VII', a late poem by Jim Harrison in which he describes trout as so lovely it makes his heart flutter. Brown and Harrison read from the same Book of Nature. Both have held these precious jewels—the essence of ferocious, primal life—in the palm of wet hands and looked into their red spots with dark halos glowing luminous like the setting sun at eventide.

Like Blake, Brown sees eternity and infinity in the materiality of 'old Mother Earth'. Is it any wonder he set the English visionary's *Songs of Innocence and Experience* to music? I cannot picture him darkening the doorways of churches. However, it is clear from 'Eugene' that he is a pilgrim who—like all fly anglers, past, present and future—casts his imagination to the riseform of grace.

Spring Redux

Balm for a Winter's Sorrow

For five years I shared my life with a good woman in a home surrounded by trees. Wherever I sat in her red-brick townhouse—whether reading or writing, chatting over freshly ground coffee in the morning or a dram of single malt at bedtime—I could see trees out of a window. The view offered a sense of deep contentment, a welcome refuge from a manic world.

After Lois Hayward—who first edited the blog postings that evolved into this book—and I went our separate ways, and before moving to the Neighbourhood of Poets, I lived on the ninth floor in a midtown apartment building. From my desk above the treetops I would look out on the city. I enjoyed the nights best when city lights twinkled beneath a carpet of dark rooftop silhouettes. For some reason it reminded me of Charles Dickens's London.

The winter prior to moving into the apartment above the treetops had been fraught with change and transition circumscribed by sadness. Separation almost always travels in the company of sorrow and regret. Loss is an ache with long fingers that dig deep beneath tender skin. But with endings come beginnings—or so the fly angler in me insists. After all, being an optimist is mandatory in order to love fly fishing. For at bottom it is an act of faith. However unsuccessful a day on the water might seem, there is always the next pool, next bend, next hatch, next outing, next season. Hope is the precise, delicate cast to rising, upstream trout. This symmetry of expectation and execution gives fly fishing its grace.

Known by fly anglers as 'The Sweet of the Year'—with a nod to a classic memoir in praise of angling in the Catskills by Ray Palmer Baker Jr.—spring is the season of new beginnings. It doesn't matter that the hardy among us fish for mighty steelhead through the pewter-bleak days of fall and winter. Or that many spend long nights of anticipation at the fly tying vise. I pass wintertide in a Mission-style chair, with an angling book in hand and a dram within reach.

The secret of fly fishing is that waving a rod, tying a fly pattern or reading a book all involve casting lines of imagination. This makes fly fishing above all else a creative act in partnership with nature.

For this reason I have always been grateful that the season for inland trout opens around the Celtic celebration of Beltane, a festival of new beginnings on the first of May which falls about halfway between the spring equinox and the summer solstice. Like Samhain, Beltane is a liminal time when the boundary between the mortal world and the spirit world is thinnest, allowing the *Aos Sì* (nature spirits) to cross over so they can mingle with humans.

It is a time of gathering and feasting, when ceremonial bonfires are lit, providing protection and purification. It is a ritual of optimism and fertility associated with the waxing of the life-giving sun. Sacred wells are visited, prayers are made requesting good health and offerings are left. The first water drawn from the holy wells is considered especially potent. Consequently Beltane is a festival fly anglers are predisposed to celebrate.

There are insects that hatch on open water year-round—tiny midges and blue winged olives hatch throughout winter. And there are hatches of mythic proportion to excite fly anglers' imaginations, like

Michigan's Hexgenia or Montana's Salmonflies. Yet nothing stirs the heart like the magical Beltane hatches that accompany the explosion of green that is spring.

Like most fly anglers in southwestern Ontario, I was eager to get on the water to mark the opening of trout season. Persistent rains had delayed our collective gratification. When the rainfall subsided and river levels dropped, Dan Kennaley and I decided to check out Whiteman's Creek, a tributary of the Grand River close to where Dan grew up outside of Paris, Ontario.

Known for its rainbows and browns, Whiteman's was a tad high, a tad fast and a tad muddy when we arrived. This made for tough fishing. Still Dan landed a handful of small rainbows. I landed one so tiny I mistook it for a chub. At least I was not skunked.

In response to occasional Hendrickson bugs fluttering about against a backdrop of late afternoon sun, we used cinnamon Bivisibles—an attractor dry fly dating back to the 1920s that, if not invented by Edward Ringwood Hewitt, was popularized by the Catskills legend in his 1926 book *Telling on the Trout.*

As the descending sun kissed the tree tops it cooled down quite rapidly. I confessed to Dan that one of the satisfactions of gaining experience on the water is dressing properly. When snooty trout reject carefully crafted flies it is no small compensation to be cozy in wool and fleece. If I bow to age here, so be it.

We were the only anglers on the river, save for a few startled ducks, a perturbed blue heron, a couple of darting kingfishers and a trio of dipsy doodling swifts performing their aerial acrobatics over the river. We saw lots of deer and raccoon tracks in the muddy bankside, so we were not alone. Anglers are sometimes solitary but never lonely on the water. After a hearty supper and a couple of pints, we headed home.

Two days later I met up with a new angling friend, a physician who learned fly fishing from his father. He came with an Orvis Trident passed down from his dad. I recognized the rod by its handsome cranberry tube with brass label at one end because I too own a Trident. One of the things I learned while wading with Mark Brown was that we share the same hometown of London, Ontario. In fact he grew up on the same street as an aunt and uncle of mine. Fly fishing is sometimes a small world of wonder.

We had prearranged that Mark would take me to a couple of

favoured spots on the Conestogo River, in the heart of Mennonite country north of Waterloo. I had agreed to return the courtesy on the Grand River tailwater. I did not tell Mark—I *couldn't* tell him—that the place he took us to was the very place where Lois and I had gone on our first fly fishing date. We enjoyed a few piscatorial outings during our time together, but the first, which did not work out well, cut the deepest impression.

We arrived late after I drove too fast to get there. She was not impressed. The spring grasses were shoulder high and she was suffering from allergies before we hit the water. Things disintegrated from there. A perfectionist since childhood, Lois grew frustrated because her casting belied her exacting standards.

Maybe it was bad timing. Or it might have been premonition, prediction or foreboding. Whatever it was, our inaugural fishing adventure together marked the beginning of the end. It is a memory that burns like a wasp sting on the back of my neck.

As it turned out, Mark and I were both skunked, despite casting to places that looked fishy, felt fishy, smelled fishy, sounded fishy and even tasted fishy. I failed with an Isopod (sometimes called a Scud) which is usually productive on the Conestogo. I also tried a Bivisible and an otherwise dependable Parachute Adams. Mark experimented with numerous patterns, including one that usually works on the river. He led me to a couple of pools I had never fished before that are sure to call me back.

On the way home I showed him a good stretch of river in gratitude for a pleasant day of angling punctuated with spirited conversation. Despite promising bug activity and inviting rises for the first time that day, we reluctantly turned away so Mark could fulfill Mother's Day commitments. A couple of days later in an email, he rhapsodized: 'It made my heart sing watching the river start to bubble with duns.'

Did I mention Mark keeps bees so he can make mead, a drink of fermented honey and water that dates as far back as 6500–7000 BC? In the Old English epic poem *Beowulf,* warriors guzzle the spirit to loosen tongues recalling tales of adventure told around the great stone hearth. It was the drink of heroic poetry in ancient Celtic and Germanic cultures. As if mead were not enough, Mark and a couple of friends are planting crab apple trees so they can make cider. Talk about an angler after my own heart, even if my spirit of choice remains malt whisky.

I returned to the pool of promise three nights later. Fishing solo, I found myself casting a good news–bad news story on the river. I landed a dozen fish with a Bivisible within a couple of hours—some of which were rising. But nary a trout. Instead, there were tiny white suckers—which I nicknamed Mennonite walleye because they catch them for the pan. Fun, but, like so much in life, not what I was hoping for. But no matter.

Stepping into a river in the season of new life, with its promise of rebirth and renewal, is balm for a winter's sorrow. It brings sun and warmth to the dark cold winter of the heart. It turns a cry of loss into a hymn of forgiveness, like a songbird in the clear pure air.

Standing waist deep in the baptismal flow is a ritual of redemption—at least potentially, provisionally, symbolically. Waving a long, tapered stick in a graceful arc gives me pause to reflect on the continuum of life: what was, what might have been and what lies ahead. For all I can do is cast as straight and as true as I can into the beckoning future—however uncertain and unsure it appears. And therein lies the mystery.

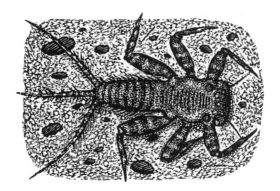

Permissions

I am grateful to James Stewart Reaney, a friend and hockey linemate I met at Trent University nearly fifty years ago, for granting permission from the Estate of James Crerar (Jamie) Reaney to quote passages from 'To the Avon River, Above Stratford, Canada'.

I thank Bernadette Rule and Seraphim Editions for giving me permission to quote 'Canoeing the Rapids'.

I am indebted to the songwriters, some of whom I have known professionally for more than three decades, for granting permission to quote passages from their songs or liner notes. Thank you Ian Tamblyn, James Gordon, Eileen McGann, Garnet Rogers, Greg Brown, Chris Coole and Kathryn Briggs and Terry Tufts.

I thank Ken Collins and Steve May for the genersoity with which they have passed along their knowledge and experience to an eager angling student.

Words cannot express my gratitude to Jerry Kustich who gave me permission to quote passages from his quartet of fly angling memoirs (*At the River's Edge, A Wisp in the Wind, Around the Next Bend, Holy Water*), which remain constant sources of inspiration as I continue my own literary ramblings dedicated to the contemplative recreation.

Portions of this book draw on material previously published in a different form in *Grand Magazine, Rex Magazine* and the *Waterloo Region Record*.

Acknowledgements

My first reader, Judith Miller, set me on the right path with respect to these wandering, untamed essays. This was not the first time she offered a guiding hand. When she was an English professor at Renison University, affiliated with the University of Waterloo, Judith invited me to be the first non-fiction writer-in-residence. Together we developed an exciting arts initiative that bridged the university and the community. I am delighted my writing evoked memories of her childhood in Montreal. She recalled 'winter evenings in the kitchen near the wood stove, helping [her] father make his bamboo fishing rods and tie flies' and 'a lively exchange when he cut a piece out of [her] mother's fur coat because it was just the shade of brown he wanted.'

I have known Dave Amor for more than three decades. I worked with him for many years at the *Waterloo Region Record*. I regard him as one of the best editors I met over four decades of journalism at a half dozen newspapers across Ontario.

I did not know until after he agreed to read my manuscript that a distant ancestor was married in a small town in Wiltshire, England, by Izaak Walton's only surviving son, Isaac, who served as a rector in a number of the county's parishes from 1679 onwards.

I met Chad Wriglesworth, associate professor at St. Jerome's University, at a screening of *Look & See*, an impressionistic biopic on American agrarian writer Wendell Berry. Chad had just edited *Distant Neighbors*, the letters of Wendell Berry and Gary Snyder. Over a pint a couple of months later we discovered a shared passion for many of the same American writers, including Wallace Stegner and Raymond Carver. Chad was born and raised in Oregon. He spent quite a few years as a fly angler, particularly when he 'lived in Brightwood, Oregon, at the base of Mt. Hood.' At the time, he was a high school English teacher and recalls racing 'home from work to hit the Salmon River or get into his float tube out on Trillium Lake.' He was also advisor to a student who wrote his master's thesis on fly fishing and literature.

My angling companion Dan Kennaley also read my manuscript and, as usual, offered his knowledge and experience with generosity, grace and humour.

Finally I would like to express my deepest appreciation to Stephanie Small at the Porcupine's Quill for the contribution she made to my modest discourse on what Sir Izaak celebrated as 'the excellent art of angling'.

ROBERT REID is a writer, journalist and avid angler whose career in journalism spanned forty years. Reid got his start writing for newspapers in Strathroy, St. Thomas, Timmins and Simcoe before he landed a position covering the arts at the *Brantford Expositor*, and later, the *Waterloo Region Record*. Since his retirement, Reid has continued to write about his passions—art and culture, malt whisky, dining and travel, and especially fly fishing—on his website: reidbetweenthe-lines.ca

WESLEY W. BATES was born in Whitehorse, Yukon Territory. One of Canada's best-known wood engravers, Bates has ventured into book illustration, film, commercial art, letterpress publishing and acoustic country—played, naturally, on a bouzouki. A retrospective of his engravings, *In Black and White*, was published by Bird & Bull in 2005, with a revised edition published by Gaspereau Press in 2008. He now maintains his studio, which is open to the public, in a nineteenth-century storefront on the main street of Clifford, Ontario.